THE HAPPINESS PROBLEM

THE HAPPINESS PROBLEM

Expecting Better in an Uncertain World

Sam Wren-Lewis

First published in Great Britain in 2019 by

Policy Press
University of Bristol
1-9 Old Park Hill
Bristol
BS2 8BB
UK
t: +44 (0)117 954 5940
pp-info@bristol.ac.uk
www.policypress.co.uk

North America office:
Policy Press
c/o The University of Chicago Press
1427 East 60th Street
Chicago, IL 60637, USA
t: +1 773 702 7700
f: +1 773 702 9756
sales@press.uchicago.edu
www.press.uchicago.edu

British Library Cataloguing in Publication Data
A catalogue record for this book is available from the British Library.

Library of Congress Cataloging-in-Publication Data
A catalog record for this book has been requested.

ISBN 978-1-4473-5355-3 paperback
ISBN 978-1-4473-5356-0 ePub
ISBN 978-1-4473-5357-7 ePdf

Cover design by Liron Gilenberg
Front cover image: Shutterstock
Printed and bound in Great Britain by TJ International, Padstow
Policy Press uses environmentally responsible print partners

Contents

About the author

Sam Wren-Lewis is an independent scholar with a PhD from the University of Leeds on the philosophy of happiness and the author of a number of published papers on the study of happiness and wellbeing. He is also a self-employed wellbeing consultant, and former Head of Research and Development at Happy City, where he carries out collaborative research and policy work with a wide range of wellbeing policy organisations. His website is www.happinessproblem.com.

Acknowledgements

This book is a product of a number of different stages of my life: my time in academia, in the world of wellbeing policy, and as an independent author. At each of these stages, I received invaluable support from colleagues, friends and loved ones, and had countless conversations with strangers on long train journeys and other people interested in what it means to be happy.

From academia, I'd like to thank Jamie Dow, Valerie Tiberius, Matthew Kieran, Anna Alexandrova, Dan Haybron, Dan Hausman, Kevin Macnish, Helen Morley and Andrew Stanners. From the world of wellbeing policy, I'm grateful to Liz Zeidler, Mike Zeidler, Ruth Townsley and Helen Brown. And from my time as an independent author, I'd like to acknowledge the people who have put up with me while I hid away in front of my laptop for weeks on end: Molly Brown, Oliver Kynaston, Harriet Parish, Rebecca Temple, Rosie Gilchrist, Robert Burgess, Badger Brown, Kate Fenhalls and Sophia Morgan-Swinhoe.

A special thanks to my family, who have supported me throughout each stage, and my good friend David Bowerman who has been an inspiration throughout.

Last, thanks to all the authors of the hundreds of books that resulted in the production of this one. I have been fortunate to spend years reading about a topic that covers so many areas of thought – from philosophy to cognitive science to anthropology. Thinking about happiness has become a fascination with how the mind works, what it means to be human, and the wider systems we live in. This journey of discovery has been a very happy one indeed.

INTRODUCTION

The happiness problem

The right and wrong way of thinking about happiness

I don't know you, but I know that you have a list inside your head.

On that list are a number of items that you think you need to be okay. Food, drink, shelter, being in good health – those kinds of things are probably on there. Work, love, home – they are most likely on there too. There may also be more specific things, particularly suited to you and your personality: dance music, feeling the sun on your face, watching football, drinking coffee, eating chocolate and so on. And there may be more serious things, which you probably think should be on everyone's list: doing no harm, being kind, paying taxes.

Most books about happiness are about this list. And so many books have been written about happiness because there is a lot to say about our lists. We currently live in a culture that encourages us to create lists that are as long and wide-ranging as possible – to pursue the perfect job, relationship, home, body and mind. We can have it all, so long as we work hard enough. And if something isn't possible yet, we can invent a new product or service that makes it so.

This strategy has taken us a long way. A lot of people now take many of the things on our lists for granted – the basic stuff, such as food, drink and shelter. But this is a very modern, and privileged, situation to be in. In fact, over the past 250 years, Western societies have been so successful at guaranteeing these things that the list itself has come to be of primary importance. People didn't always have lists in their heads. Or, at least, their lists were not so extravagant and readily achievable as our lists are today.

Our lists have come to dominate our lives. And the word we use to describe the achievement of their items is 'happiness'. More so than at any other point in history, we think we can have all the basic and inspiring and worthwhile things on our list. Happiness seems to be within our grasp.

Most books written about happiness take all this as a given, and dutifully promise to help you on your path to personal fulfilment. This is the realm of self-help. By reading a best-selling book, attending a life-changing course, getting down an efficient morning routine, or whatever, we can achieve all our goals and ambitions. We can be successful. We can find Mr or Mrs Right. Why settle for anything less?

An obvious problem with this approach is that life is hard. Failing to achieve all the items on our list doesn't necessarily mean we are a failure. We might have simply been unlucky. Or, more likely, the odds may have been stacked against us from the start. Cue the second kind of book written about happiness: the realm of 'spiritual wisdom'. In contrast to the more motivational kind of self-help, these books – or retreats or lifestyles – are not premised on the idea that any problem can be fixed, or that any obstacle can be overcome. Instead, they show us how we can let go of all the items on our list – how we can be at peace with the world without having to achieve all the things we think we need.

Although this is a potentially radical idea – to throw away the list entirely – most people who veer towards the spiritual wisdom shelf accept that they are not going to live quiet, contemplative lives. But they would very much like some of what those Buddhist monks seem to have. Spiritual wisdom is simply another flavour of self-help for those who have a sense of calm and peace of mind – or awe, wonder, beauty, gratitude, hope, trust and so on – on their list.

It is at this point that a third kind of book written about happiness seems appropriate. More recently, there have been a number of books – and social commentaries – that criticize the idea of happiness. These books often recognise that the eternal satisfaction or peace offered by the two different brands of self-help are not possible – or, at least, only possible for the lucky few. We would all be better off, according to these critiques, if we seriously revised the items on our lists. We should care less about having the perfect job, relationship, home and so on, and care more about other people. We should care less about having more stuff, and care more about doing the right thing. In fact, while we're at it, we should forget about happiness altogether, which is largely wrapped up in ideas of personal fulfilment. With a radically different kind of list in our heads, other words might be more fitting, such as 'contentment', 'meaning' or 'virtue'.

Although I agree with the spirit – and sometimes despair – of these cultural critiques, I do not think we should abandon the idea of happiness. The list in our heads is not going to go away, and it will always contain items that have to do with our own satisfaction, safety and wellbeing. Happiness is one of the primary values in modern society. We want our kids to be 'happy and healthy', we want to have a job or relationship that 'makes us happy', and, overall, we want to look back and say we've had a 'happy life'. We are better off working with happiness than either trying to pretend it's not there or bullying it out of existence.

How, then, does this book fit into these three categories of books-on-happiness? The simple answer is that it doesn't. But it does take inspiration from all three.

This book is about the right and wrong way of thinking about happiness. The wrong way is simply trying to achieve everything on our list. Although this is predominantly how people think about happiness in modern society, it is, unfortunately, a fantasy. No matter how many of the items on our list we achieve, we will be still be insecure – vulnerable to disappointment, loss and suffering. All the progress we make will merely be the tip of the iceberg.

This is what the spiritual wisdom books get right – we need to relate to the items on our list in a different way. However, we cannot let go of our list completely, nor would we want to. We have needs to meet, after all – for food, drink, shelter, health, connection and so on. And our other achievements are part of what makes life worthwhile. This is what the other flavour of self-help books gets right. The items on our list are there for a reason – we should do our best to achieve them.

We can neither ignore the list inside our heads nor can we simply try to achieve everything on it. The right way of thinking about happiness is about how to find this balance. What the critiques of happiness get right is that how we think about happiness matters – not just for ourselves, but also for society as a whole. We see reality through the lists we have inside our heads – the items on our list are the things we care about. How we think about happiness makes a difference to how we change our own lives, as well as how we change society and the world.

There is no secret to happiness

One of the reasons it made sense to start this book by talking about other books written on happiness is because I've read a lot of them. I began thinking about happiness over 12 years ago, fresh out of university and an already disillusioned activist. I had spent a lot of time campaigning for worthy causes such as trade justice and ending global poverty. I didn't understand why most people seemed to care little about these issues – why they were more concerned with their careers, status and material comforts. The conclusion I (somewhat naively) came to was that they had mistaken views about happiness. Although people wanted to be happy, they didn't know how to be – in their pursuit of happiness, everyone around me looked stressed and anxious. Why campaign for the end of global poverty if economic development didn't make people happier? Instead, I did what seemed to be the logical thing to do and studied for a PhD in happiness.

Now, happiness is not the normal subject of a PhD. But that all changed with what appeared to me to be the solution to all our problems: the new science of happiness. Since the 1970s, psychologists and economists had started to study people's happiness and had already come up with some interesting findings. They agreed that an excessive amount of money doesn't make people happier, but that relationships do. This was music to my ears. I thought I'd spend a brief amount of time in academia reading all this stuff and then tell everyone about it.

The outcome would be a book on what makes us happy, much like the many other self-help books written on the subject; only, this one would be true.

Of course, it didn't take long before I realised that things were more complicated. Much more complicated. When people find out that I study happiness for a living, the first question they often ask is: 'What's the secret of happiness, then?' I can now positively say that there isn't one.

Don't get me wrong — it's not that there aren't things we can do to be happier. The items on our list may well be worth achieving. But what I learned over many years of reading about happiness is that our list never ends. No matter how many items we tick off the list, we will always replace them with more. It may seem impossible to imagine, but even if we solved all our problems, protected ourselves from all our fears and achieved all our goals, we would still find plenty of problems to solve, things to be scared about and new goals to achieve.

The list inside our heads is endless because we are insecure. We are mortal beings, whose survival and wellbeing are entirely dependent on our relationships with others and our wider environment. Within this insecurity, none of our life plans and achievements can make us immune to disappointment, loss or suffering. We can of course do things to be more secure, and even happier. But many of the things that make our lives worthwhile have vulnerability at the heart of them. We cannot have love without loss, or success without failure.

The items on our list are an attempt to have more of the good things in life, and less of the bad things. This is a valiant battle to fight. The study of happiness can even show us how to win a few battles — what items should be on our list and how we can achieve them. But we must acknowledge that, ultimately, going to war with reality is not a fight we can win.

The question is not, 'What is the secret to happiness?' but instead, 'What is the secret to living well within insecurity?' It's not as sexy a question, and not one that promises a life of bliss. But that is what we have to work with. The answer to this question is what this book is about.

The happiness problem

The book has two main characters: control and understanding. When we fail to acknowledge our insecurity, we pursue happiness through the means of control. If only we get everything in our lives just right – the perfect job, relationship, home, body, mind and so on – then we'd be happy.

The problem with this way of thinking about happiness is not just that it is wrong. By focusing only on the things we can control, we also blind ourselves to the other things in life that matter. What we think will make us happy is only the tip of the iceberg. In simply trying to achieve everything on our list, we fail to see what really matters. This is the happiness problem.

This strategy of control has come to dominate modern society. If there is a problem, we can work out how to fix it. If something is difficult, we can innovate our way towards making it easier. If there is pain or suffering, we can eliminate it. All of these goals and aspirations are commendable. But we are beginning to see the negative consequences of this constant need for improvement.

On an individual level, despite people having a greater amount of freedom and opportunity than ever before in history, we are witnessing a 'mental health crisis' – with addiction and depressive and anxiety disorders all on the rise. The more productive we can be, the more we feel that we aren't good enough. The busier we can be, the more we can't sit still. Under the logic of control, our intrinsic worth as individuals is less important than what we can achieve.

We can also see the happiness problem on a societal and global level. We think that, if only we had more economic growth and technological innovation, then we'd all be better off. But the limits of this progress are becoming increasingly apparent. Two hundred and fifty years of burning fossil fuels and five thousand years of destroying the natural environment is rapidly catching up with us in the form of climate change. Our complex environmental and social problems cannot be so easily fixed.

The strategy of control focuses our attention on the wrong things. Instead of understanding what we really need, we focus on the next accomplishment. Instead of understanding the underlying causes of our social problems, we focus on simple narratives, temporary solutions and technological fixes. When we pursue happiness through the means of control, we cannot see beyond the items on our list. We are certain that, 'if only we had ___ then we'd be happy', or we'd all be better off. We fail to look beyond the items that fill in the blank.

In this book, we will see that there is an alternative way of thinking about happiness – one that switches our focus away from control and towards understanding. We have the psychological capacities to question the items on our list and pay more attention to the things that might be missing. This is the secret to living well within insecurity – to understand the limits of the list inside our head as much as achieving the items on it.

This journey from control to understanding will take us on a tour of how the mind works and what it means to be human. We will draw on a wide range of research from psychology and economics to philosophy and anthropology. This includes looking at a number of things that might not at first seem relevant to happiness, such as why we can't tickle ourselves, what the welfare state and trees have in common, and why psychedelic experiences are like a shot of elderhood. These things are relevant because happiness is a much more complex topic than we often give it credit for. The lists in our heads have been shaped by our culture and dictate how we see reality. We are not simply isolated beings thinking about what we most enjoy. Happiness is political. And it's about time that the political started paying attention to the workings of the human mind.

The book is in three parts. Part I is about the wrong way of thinking about happiness – control. Part II is about the right way of thinking about happiness – understanding. Part III applies this alternative strategy to our major societal and global problems. By the end of it, I cannot guarantee that you will be happier. In fact, there's a good chance that you'll be the opposite. But you will have a better understanding of what it means to be happy without being blind to what really matters.

Part I

ONE

Security

> The trouble with human happiness is that it is constantly beset by fear. It is not the lack of possessing but the safety of possession that is at stake.
> *Hannah Arendt*[1]

There is a right and a wrong way of thinking about happiness. We are currently thinking about it wrongly. We believe that happiness comes from *control*, that, if only we get everything in our lives just right – the perfect job, relationship, family, home, body, mind, and so on – then we'd be happy. In Part I of this book – Chapters One, Two and Three – we will see why this is not true.

In Part II – Chapters Four, Five and Six – we will look at a better way of thinking about happiness. Instead of control, we will see how happiness comes from an unlikely source: *understanding*. Through curiosity and compassion, we can discover what we most care about and are truly capable of. We may not get everything we want, but we will remain flexible to the challenges that life throws at us and have a deeper understanding of the things that really matter.

The difference between these two ways of thinking about happiness is not arbitrary – they reflect different ways of seeing the world. The control strategy begins by seeing what is wrong with the world, how we can change it and how we can be happy as a result. In contrast, the understanding strategy begins by trying to see the world more clearly and only then acting to change it, knowing that, whatever changes we make, we are unlikely to stay happy for long.

The control strategy is about *going to war with reality*. According to this strategy, we know what we need to be happy – it is only reality that stands in our way. In contrast, the understanding strategy is about *striving for peace with reality*. According to this strategy, the world is too complex to always know what to do – with a better understanding of reality, we can respond to it more flexibly.

These different ways of viewing the world can be broken down into three parts: the *outcome*, the *process*, and the *mindset*. The outcome is about what we want the world to be like: how can things be different? What do we need and care about? The process is about how we can get there: how can we change the world? How can we achieve the things we want? And the mindset is about what the world is like as it is: what things in our lives are currently good or bad? We tend to view things in this order – the desired outcome first, followed by an effective process and mindset. It is the outcomes that ultimately matter. We have needs and must act to fulfil them. We don't always have the time and resources to see the world more clearly. We think that we know what will make us happy.

In Part I, we will look at how the control strategy answers these questions.

- Its outcome is *security and stability*. Happiness is getting everything in our lives just right – the perfect job, relationship, home and so on. These stable circumstances will bring us a lasting sense of meaning and satisfaction.
- Its process is *control and achievement*. To achieve happiness, we need to control everything in our lives to our liking – solve all our problems, protect ourselves from our fears, and achieve all our goals and ambitions.
- Its mindset is *certainty and predictability*. We know what we need to be happy – what feels good or bad, who is right or wrong. Happiness is about sorting and changing our circumstances to have as many of the good things, and as few of the bad things, as possible.

In Part II, we will look an alternative way of viewing the world. The answers of the understanding strategy mirror those given by the control strategy.

- The outcome is *care and compassion*. Happiness is not getting everything in our lives just right – at some point, things will fall apart. Instead, we can learn how to live well within insecurity, with care and compassion.
- The process is *curiosity and exploration*. To live well within insecurity, we need to be curious towards our lives and explore our whole selves – discover what we most care about and are truly capable of.
- The mindset is *uncertainty and unpredictability*. We don't know what will make us happy – things are too complex to be seen as good or bad, right or wrong. According to the understanding strategy, happiness is about learning from everything in our lives, the good and the bad.

These two ways of thinking about happiness are very different, with significantly different outcomes. In the first three chapters of the book, I will show what is wrong with the control strategy – of thinking about happiness in terms of security, control and certainty. I do not think we should drop this way of thinking entirely, however. Going to war with reality has its place. The problem is that this has become the dominant way of thinking about happiness in modern society. We need to understand the merits of this strategy, including its potential harms, and use it only when necessary. My optimistic belief is that we can switch from a strategy of control to one of understanding more than we tend to think.

In this chapter, we will look at the merits of the outcome of the control strategy – happiness as *security*. We think that happiness is about having stable circumstances that will make us lastingly satisfied and fulfilled – the perfect job, relationship, home and so on. I will show that this is simply untrue. No matter what we have in our lives, and no matter what we achieve, it will never be enough. We will still be insecure – vulnerable to disappointment, loss and suffering. Of course, we can improve our lives, alleviate our suffering and make ourselves more secure. But we cannot eliminate our insecurity entirely.

This is the first problem with going to war with reality. We may win some battles, but will ultimately lose. We need to know what we are up against. By the end of this chapter, I hope to have convinced you that we need to learn how to live within insecurity, as well as fight against it.

We will begin this journey by looking at what the science has to say about happiness. The study of happiness is our first window into our insecurity.

Happiness: what have we learned?

Becoming happier

Over the past few decades, the study of happiness has sought to bring clarity and empirical legitimacy to a subject that has traditionally been the domain of philosophy, theology and self-help.

In the 1970s, with his seminal paper on the happiness of lottery winners and people with disabilities,[2] the psychologist Philip Brickman paved the way for what became known as the academic field of 'positive psychology' – the study of what makes people mentally healthy, beyond the absence of mental illness.[3]

Around the same time, the economist Richard Easterlin compared the gross domestic product (GDP) of nations with their average levels of happiness.[4] He showed that the latter does not necessarily follow from the former, which paved the way for the academic field of 'happiness economics' – the study of what makes people better off, beyond the accumulation of financial wealth.[5]

Together, positive psychology and happiness economics form the backbone of the 'study of subjective wellbeing', which is often referred to as the 'study of happiness'.[6] This burgeoning interdisciplinary field of academic study also includes research from sociology, anthropology, critical studies, politics, evolutionary biology, affective neuroscience and philosophy.

The study of happiness has also attracted the attention of policy makers around the world. In 2010, the UK launched its ground-breaking wellbeing programme, which aims to monitor national progress beyond measures of GDP, and assess and develop policy partly on the basis of its impacts on people's wellbeing. In 2011, the United Nations followed suit. The UN General Assembly adopted a Bhutan-sponsored resolution that called on member states to measure and promote national wellbeing. The UN now produces an annual *World Happiness Report*, which includes a global ranking of countries on happiness.

These global happiness rankings sum up the optimism shared by many happiness researchers and policy makers. Typically, Scandinavian countries top the list. These countries are prosperous, healthy and trusting. Corruption is low. Generosity is high, individuals feel empowered to make key life choices. The social welfare state limits the inequalities between wealth and poverty, and delivers public services to all citizens. This reflects the six conditions that explain most of the variety in life satisfaction scores between the most and least satisfied countries in the world. According to the *World Happiness Report*, average national happiness is determined by economic prosperity, physical and mental health, political freedoms, social support, generosity, and social trust.[7]

On the basis of such findings, proponents of happiness stress that although economic prosperity matters, other key conditions such as health and social capital matter too. Other findings from the subjective wellbeing literature support this view.[8] When it comes to people's level of happiness, close relationships are often cited as the most important factor. Marriage makes a lasting positive difference to people's happiness, whereas divorce has the opposite effect. Being religious also has a positive impact – a finding that tends to be put down to the benefits that come from being an integrated member of a community. Last, one of the most harmful factors for people's happiness is unemployment. Beyond the financial insecurity involved, unemployment can often be socially isolating.

The study of happiness highlights just how important non-material conditions can be in our lives. Relationships matter. Health matters. For instance, according to the UK national wellbeing programme, citizens who reported having bad health were 13.6 times more likely to report having the lowest combined levels of life satisfaction, happiness, anxiety and sense of worth.[9] This is a big factor – one that dwarfs the impact of other conditions, such as people's levels of income. Happiness research shows the importance of the things we may have sacrificed in our pursuit of financial and material wellbeing.

In general, the happiness literature has identified five major ingredients for happiness:[10]

- health and longevity
- close relationships
- community belonging
- purpose and achievement
- financial and material wealth.

It is hard to imagine being happy without these conditions in place. Nations are right to promote these things in their public policies, and individuals are right to try and achieve them in their own lives. The question is, even if these things make us happier, will they make us happy? Will they provide us with a lasting sense of meaning and satisfaction?

We are not built for lasting happiness

One of the most interesting things about the study of happiness is that it has not just identified the conditions that make people happier. It has also identified the conditions that *don't* make people happier in the long run. It turns out that increases in income, above a certain level, do not make people lastingly happier. Nor does educational attainment. In fact, the list of things that do not make people any happier in the long term is potentially far greater than the list of things that do.[11]

Happiness researchers initially explained these findings with reference to the ideas of 'hedonic adaptation' and 'set-point theory'. Hedonic adaptation is the idea that, once we have achieved a particular state of affairs – a new promotion, a fancy car, getting married and so on – we soon get used to it and move on to the next achievement. We do not wake up months after receiving our promotion still feeling the same amount of happiness we did when we initially got it. This is an instance of the more general process of psychological adaptation – the more times we are exposed to something, the more it fades into the background. When we walk, for example, we do not feel all the sensations going on in our feet. We have got used to these sensations – walking becomes something we do largely on autopilot. The same goes for the circumstances that make us happy. After a while, we cease to pay much notice to them.

The phenomenon of hedonic adaptation inspired set-point theory – the idea that people have fixed levels of happiness, which are determined more by their genes and their personality than by their circumstances. This goes back to Brickman's influential paper on lottery winners and people with disabilities. He found that, around six months after either winning the lottery or becoming severely disabled – which, not surprisingly, made the former happier and the latter unhappier – people's level of happiness went back to what it was beforehand. Although we think that these conditions would have a lifelong impact on our level of happiness, Brickman found that, in reality, the impact these events had on people's happiness was short-lived.[12] This study was followed by a number of other studies that found the same thing: no matter what happens to us, our level of happiness eventually goes back to normal.[13]

Set-point theory is no longer widely held by happiness researchers. More recently, a number of important exceptions have been found, showing that, even if we adapt to most conditions, we do not adapt to everything. Marriage, divorce and employment, for instance, all have a lasting impact on people's happiness. The five major ingredients of happiness listed above are all made up of conditions that people do not entirely adapt to.

But the influence of set-point theory lives on. It showed that happiness is not straightforwardly a result of our circumstances. Our psychology plays a big part in what makes us happy or unhappy in the long term. Many of the things we think will make us lastingly happier do not. And many of the things that do make us happy in the long run, do not make us as happy as we think they do. Happiness research has shown that nothing makes us live 'happily ever after'.

Psychological adaptation makes sense when achieving a stable state of affairs is impossible. Consider again, for example, that new promotion. It may be that our new promotion signifies the pinnacle of our career – there is nowhere else to go, we have achieved everything that we could possibly achieve. More likely, however, is the fact that our promotion is the next step in a long line of potential improvements. In fact, if we fail to work harder, we may even lose our newly achieved work status to someone who would like to be where we are. We must continue to improve our situation because improvements can always be made and staying still may not be an option. It makes sense, then, to quickly adapt and set our sights on how to do even better.

One way of making this point is that psychological adaptation reflects our *insecurity*. Our circumstances are never entirely safe or stable. We must continue to advance to make them as secure as we can. And we must continue to stay vigilant – to protect ourselves from any potential threats.

This explains why most conditions do not make us lastingly happier or unhappier, and why some do. When we achieve most things, it makes sense to quickly adapt to our new circumstances and move on. This is likely to be the case, for example, with increases in income above a certain level – where our basic needs have already been met. There is little to be gained from basking in our newly acquired wealth, and more to be gained from the next potential achievement. In contrast, there are some conditions that require our continued attention. Having a chronic health condition, for example, may require us to monitor how we're feeling on a daily basis to figure out how best to manage our symptoms. Maintaining a close relationship may require our continued care and affection.

The fact that we are insecure makes the pursuit of happiness much more complicated. We can no longer look towards the study of happiness for a list of ingredients that will make us happy. The five key ingredients listed above will not provide us with a lasting sense of meaning and satisfaction because they are not stable circumstances. We must constantly work on them – either by achieving more or by protecting ourselves – to maintain our level of happiness.

Our psychology is built for insecurity. Lasting happiness is impossible because there are no stable states of affairs. Our thoughts, feelings and behaviours respond to the *news* of our own lives, not to what we already know. How are things different today? What can we achieve? What pressures and demands do we face? What could go wrong? What should we *do*? These are the kinds of questions we must answer on a daily basis to cope with the fact that nothing in our lives can be taken for granted.

From the study of happiness, we have learned two very important things. First, we have learned about the key ingredients of happiness – the conditions that make people lastingly happier. Second, we have learned the limitations of these things. No matter what conditions we create in our lives, they will never be stable enough for us to have a lasting sense of meaning and satisfaction. In the remainder of the chapter, we will look at in more detail this insecurity and what it means for the pursuit of happiness.

Acknowledging our insecurity

Our insecurity runs deep

The study of happiness gives us a window into our insecurity and how our psychology is not built for lasting happiness. But we still tend to believe that, 'if only we had ___ then we'd be happy'. This phrase encapsulates a way of thinking about happiness that has come to dominate modern culture. We now have more control over what our lives look like than at any other point in history. We can imagine a better, happier world, and it seems to be within our reach.

We have already seen that this way of thinking about happiness is mistaken. Despite the fact that we now have an unprecedented amount of control over our lives, we still don't have control over many of the things that matter. We might find ways of being happier, but they will not necessarily make us happy.

The problem is that, no matter what we do and have in our lives, we will still be vulnerable to disappointment, loss and suffering. We will still be insecure.

Don't get me wrong – clearly there are things we can do to be more secure. On an individual level, we can improve our lives by achieving our goals and plans. On a societal level, the significant improvements in standard of living that have taken place over modernity – such as the huge decreases in infant mortality rates – have made all of our lives better.

If we can improve our circumstances, without significant costs to others or ourselves, then we should. We will probably be happier as a result.

However, even if we can increase our security and standard of living, this does not mean that we can do so sufficiently. The stable circumstances that can improve our lives – such as having a good job, relationship, home and so on – will never be stable enough to bring us a lasting sense of meaning and satisfaction.

This might all seem a bit over the top. Does it really matter that we are inherently insecure? If we can continue to improve our lives, on both an individual and societal level, then what's the problem? Okay, doing so may not bring us lasting happiness, but surely we can just learn to adjust our expectations and settle with being a bit happier instead?

We will look at the problem with seeing things this way in Chapter Two. For now, it is enough to say that, without acknowledging our insecurity, we think that happiness comes from controlling everything in our lives to our liking. We truly believe the phrase, 'if only I had ___ then I'd be happy' (or, alternatively: 'I need ___ to feel okay'). The worry behind this phrase is that, if we don't get whatever fills in the blank, something terrible will happen. The hope behind it is that, if we do get whatever fills in the blank, everything will be fine. Neither the hope nor the worry is true. The problem is that, by focusing only on what we think will make us happy, we miss out on the other things in life that matter.

In this chapter, my aim is to show that our insecurity runs deep. We can be more or less secure, but we cannot create the stable circumstances we so long for. The perfect job, relationship, home and so on – none of these things will be devoid of insecurity. No matter how good our lives are, we will still be vulnerable to disappointment, loss and suffering.

This is a very different story about what it means to be human than the one we typically get told in modern societies. As we will see in Chapter Two, over the past 250 years, from the Enlightenment onwards, the way we think about happiness has changed. We have gone from thinking of ourselves as small creatures at the whim of larger forces to autonomous beings in control of our individual and collective destinies.

The predominant story of modernity is one of control and manipulation, power and domination. We can view the history of human civilisation through this lens: how we have continued to find new ways of controlling each other and the natural environment.[14] We can view the history of an individual life in a similar way – each of us develops our skills and gains personal resources to have some sense of control over our circumstances.

There is something beautiful about this view of human nature. In the face of suffering, we do not give up, nor do we merely grin and bear it. Humans overcome their challenges with a vengeance. We do not simply wait for the next disaster to strike; we make plans to prevent disaster from happening again. We cooperate on a mass scale to achieve things that previous generations would never have dreamed of.[15]

There is also something terrifying about this picture. In Chapter Two, we will look at how individuals control others to cope with the insecurity of their relationships. Misguided attempts at control can result in people being distant, having affairs, causing arguments or being violent. On a societal level, we have invented new technologies with the power to control others and our environment on an unprecedented scale. We are now minutes away from a possible nuclear war. Over the next few decades, advances in artificial intelligence (AI) and big data may displace people's consumer and political choices. And, according to most environmental scientists, we are now increasingly affecting the earth's climate beyond its natural cycles of change.

In our scramble to solve all these problems, it is perhaps no surprise that we have largely forgotten how vulnerable we are. As social animals, we are still mortal, embodied creatures, almost entirely dependent on others for our survival and wellbeing. These vulnerabilities and dependencies make life hard. And, at least for the foreseeable future, they are here to stay.

Life doesn't go to plan

The depth of our insecurity is illustrated by the fact that, despite our well-intentioned life plans, the events that make up our lives rarely stick to the script. We form our life plans relatively early on in life, and largely unconsciously. They often reflect the familial expectations we have been exposed to and the cultural norms we are embedded in – the sort of life that seems possible within our circumstances, with enough luck and determination. For people in modern societies, with a reasonable amount of resources and opportunities, our life plan may look something like the following:

> We'll get educated, make friends along the way, have fun, explore hobbies that interest us, and maybe find love. Then we'll have a career, which will provide us with financial security, respect amongst our peers, meaningful projects, and opportunities to make a positive contribution to the world. We'll fall in love again, this time getting married and raising a family – not only will such companionship stave off loneliness, it will inspire us to be our better selves, see the formation of joint projects, be supportive, intimate and include an enjoyable sex life. Bringing up our children will be the most important thing in our lives, giving us a new sense of meaning and experiences of deep joy in their development and achievements. Last, thanks to modern medicine and the liberal democracies we live in, we will retire comfortably, with plenty of time to relax and explore some of the things in life we have always wanted to do. Hopefully, when the time comes, we will die with few regrets, our loved ones close at hand, and content in the knowledge that we've lived a good life.

Of course, this kind of life plan may not hold for all, or even most, people – someone might plan to have multiple careers and committed relationships in their lives; they may decide not to have children; they may choose to retire later and work much longer, and so on. The point is neither that the above is a typical life plan, nor that it is something we should aim at. The idea is that people often have images like this in their minds when thinking about what to do with their lives and what will make them happy. Feel free to change the above description in whatever way suits you and your own values, goals and ambitions.

No matter what the content of our life plans is, at some point things will not go to plan. It is a tragic likelihood that someone we care about, and depend upon, will get unexpectedly sick or die. Some of our romantic relationships will probably end in rejection or heartbreak. We may find ourselves unexpectedly unemployed through no fault of our own. From taking on challenging goals and projects, we are bound to make mistakes and witness a variety of other setbacks and failures. Our children and other loved ones will struggle in life – there will be nothing we can do about it and some of it will be our own fault. In our old age, we may find our family have moved too far away to regularly visit.

We don't tend to write these things into our life plan, but something along these lines will probably happen to us. Consider the following statistics: according to the World Health Organization, one in four people in the world will be affected by mental disorders at some point in their lives;[16] in the US, nearly one in two has at least one chronic medical condition;[17] and the lifelong probability of a marriage ending in divorce is 40–50 per cent.[18] It may be that further political and social freedoms, or technological and medical advances, can reduce the likelihood of these things happening to us. However, in the meantime, there is little we can do to protect ourselves from at least some forms of adversity.

It is tempting to think that we can simply learn how to do things better – to avoid as many of these forms of adversity as possible. This is especially the case within modern societies, where so much responsibility is put on the individual to make their own success in life. When times are tough, we have multi-billion dollar industries of self-help, therapy and pharmaceuticals to help get us through.[19]

But this way of thinking underestimates the problem. The insecurities we will look at in this chapter are not the kind we can make go away. One of the reasons this is so hard to see is that we can so readily see success all around us. In his book *Success and Luck*, the economist Robert Frank shows how the success of people like Bill Gates was partly down to a series of fortunate long shots and coincidences.[20] According to Frank, where the success in question is great, and where the context in which it is achieved is competitive, it is luck that separates only a handful of people from a large amount of equally skilful and resourced others. And yet our culture often celebrates the winners and downplays the losers, emphasising how success is available to all.

In the remainder of this chapter we will look at how the things we care about in life have insecurity built into them. We cannot have life without death, love without loss, and success without failure. We could, perhaps, lower our expectations in order to save ourselves experiencing as much disappointment as possible. However, by doing so, we will make less progress in life. We will fail to commit to what we most care about and find out what we are truly capable of.

This runs contrary to the rhetoric of happiness, which is often one of sorting: having as many of the good things in life as possible, and avoiding as many of the bad things as we can. Modern society does a great job at telling us how we can achieve all these things, as long as we work hard enough or have enough stuff. But, ultimately, we have to recognise that, whereas our images of happiness and success are neat and tidy, our actual lives are likely to be much more messy and complex in comparison. We don't know how our choices will affect the other things in our lives. We don't know what opportunities our commitments will shut down or open up. All we can do is our best.

We will look at five of our deep insecurities – starting with our individual bodies and making our way up to the wider environments we are a part of. For each of these insecurities, we can make ourselves more secure. But we cannot eliminate the insecurity entirely. For instance, when it comes to our bodies, we can live longer, healthier and more comfortable lives – and we already do in comparison to our ancestors. But we will still experience discomfort, sickness and death. These experiences are a necessary part of being embodied, mortal creatures. We can say a similar thing about the insecurities involved in our close relationships, the communities we are a part of, the challenges we take on, and the human and natural environments we live in.

Health and longevity

In this section, we will see that we cannot have life without death, and we cannot function well in our bodies without experiencing physical discomfort. We are unlikely to eliminate these things from our lives in the foreseeable future, and even if we could, we wouldn't necessarily want to.

We have bodies

As much as we try to separate ourselves from other animals, we clearly are one. We have biological needs for nutrition, water, shelter and body warmth, touch and connection, and physical safety. Our body unconsciously and automatically regulates the satisfaction of our needs through a number of ongoing homeostatic processes: feedback loops that track our internal levels of energy, hydration, temperature and so on, and motivate us to change those levels accordingly.[21]

We feel the outcome of these processes in our bodies. More specifically, we feel them in the form of bodily imperatives – physical sensations that are either pleasant or unpleasant, that effectively scream 'more!' or 'less!' at us. For example, the feeling of a beating heart can feel pleasurable when directed at a new love ('more of this!'). Alternatively, it can feel uncomfortable when directed at something scary ('less of this!'). We are always trying to keep hold of the pleasurable sensations and get rid of the painful and uncomfortable ones.[22]

And yet we cannot escape our bodies, nor would we want to. The point of biological needs is that they are non-negotiable – our survival depends on us meeting them. The point of homeostatic processes is that they are ongoing – they are constantly at work behind the scenes, guiding our behaviour in ways that help us meet our needs. We only need to introspect on our bodily feelings for a brief period of time to realise there is a cacophony of action going on under the blanket of our conscious awareness. As the neuroscientist Antonio Damasio notes in his book *The Strange Order of Things*, at the core of our being is 'a deceptively continuous and endless feeling state, a more or less intense mental choir underscoring everything else mental'.[23]

This chorus is fine when everything is working harmoniously and our needs are being effectively met. But this state of well-functioning cannot be guaranteed. In fact, the opposite is likely to the case – at various points in our lives, our circumstances are bound to make our bodies uncomfortable places to inhabit. I do not mean just feeling cold, hungry or tired. Our bodies also respond to our personal concerns for safety, connection and self-worth.[24] It is rare to see someone who is comfortable in their own skin. The majority of us go throughout our days holding tension in our bodies, which we try our best to ignore.

This is most obvious in cases of individual trauma. For traumatised individuals, the body can be a frightening place. As the psychiatrist Bessel van der Kolk notes in his book *The Body Keeps the Score*, for people with traumatic histories 'the past is alive in the form of gnawing interior discomfort'.[25] Their bodies and minds are constantly bombarded by visceral warning signs, and, in an attempt to control these processes, they often become experts at ignoring their gut feelings and in numbing awareness of what is played out inside.

The problem with numbing our bodily responses is that we need them in order to function well in the world. The Enlightenment philosopher René Descartes is well known for his statement 'I think, therefore I am,' which effectively separates the mind from the body. According to Descartes, what makes us human is our ability to think, not to feel. However, more recent research from biological neuroscience shows that our bodies and minds are in fact inseparable.[26] How we feel influences how we think, and vice versa. People who suffer from neurological conditions in which the flow of information between their bodies and minds is disrupted have been shown to function worse as a result.[27] By ignoring our bodies, we may cease to be able to respond fully and flexibly to life's demands. Physical discomfort is part of being fully alive.

We are going to die

We are stuck, then, in our painful and uncomfortable bodies. Of course, we can find better or worse ways of coping with our bodily sensations, such as meditation and healthy distractions or medication and drugs like alcohol. But many bodily sensations are persistently difficult to experience. This is most clearly the case with chronic physical pain, which can be unbearable. Pain can turn our body from a transparent medium with which we explore the world into an object in that world – we are no longer 'at home in our body'.[28] This is also true for intense negative emotional episodes, such as loneliness and heartbreak (which is called that for a reason).

Our bodily sensations feel painful and uncomfortable so that we change our situation – either by removing the thing that is causing us damage or by stopping whatever we are doing so that the body can heal itself. In the case of illness and disease, however, healing can either take a long time or may not even be possible. Illness and disease can happen to all of us, no matter how healthy a lifestyle we lead. As noted above, according to the World Health Organization, in the US nearly one in two has at least one chronic medical condition.[29]

Modern medicine may have successfully eradicated and produced effective treatments for a number of diseases, but we are still fragile beings. In our attempts to achieve more in life, we often go against the wisdom of our bodies: we spend most of our working lives sitting down, we eat diets rich in processed foods, and we fail to get adequate amounts of sleep, natural light, physical activity, human contact and touch. When our bodies are functioning well, we may pay them little attention. However, when something goes wrong, it is hard to focus on anything else beyond our physical struggle and discomfort.[30]

This will happen to all of us who are lucky enough to live to until old age. The physical process of ageing is a steady decline in bodily well-functioning. And, of course, at some point we will get so sick that we will die.

Death is something we think surprisingly little about, given that it is one of the few certainties in our lives. Many philosophers have argued that while death is typically seen as a bad thing – perhaps the worst thing that could happen to us – it provides us with a finitude that makes our lives meaningful.[31] Knowing that our life is not going to last is what spurs us on to make something out of it.

The problem is that we only have one chance at doing so, and there's a strong chance we'll screw it up. We will never know whether we would have been better off doing things differently. If we chose to have children, we will never know how our career would've progressed if we had chosen otherwise. If we chose to get married, we will never know what it would've been like to have romantic relationships with other lovers, or to develop deeper friendships. If we chose to be a doctor, we will never know what our life would've been like as a musician. We can always doubt whether we have made good use of our life.

In an attempt to remove this doubt, we can focus our efforts on things that will last beyond our death, such as our relationships with others or our 'personal legacy'. However, this does not remove the problem – it merely moves it along a step. We still need to ask whether we have had a positive impact on others or whether our personal legacy is a good one – questions we cannot answer with any kind of certainty. Again, we can only do our best. And for many, looking back at their lives, they may not feel that their best was good enough.

Close relationships

So far, we have looked at the inherent insecurities involved in being embodied – having a physical body with an expiry date. Humans are more than just moving parts, however. We are uniquely social animals. We do not just depend on our bodies for our survival. We also depend on others. We rely on close relationships, friends and a wider community for acknowledgement and support, and a sense of safety and security.

In this section, we will see how our close relationships make our lives meaningful on the one hand, and expose us to rejection, loss and heartbreak on the other. No matter how good our relationships are, or how much work we put into them, we cannot have love without loss.

We are social animals

We like to think of ourselves as self-contained individuals – rational, autonomous and self-sufficient. However, meeting our biological needs is so entwined with meeting our needs for connection that, for most purposes, there is no reason to even distinguish them. Without touch, for instance, infants can die from their bodies' growth and immune systems shutting down.[32]

For humans, social contact is like food – without it, we cannot survive. (It is also why short-term solitary confinement is such an effective means of torture.) We experience the world, and meet our needs, through our connections with others.

Humans have particularly long periods of infancy because of our big heads. We are born with undeveloped minds, as any further brain development in the womb would make our heads too big to safely fit through the birth canal. Whereas other mammals are up and running not long after being born, human infants rely on their primary caregivers for much longer. Instead of coming into this world with a complete set of survival skills and instincts, we learn most of what we need through a process of constant interaction with our caregivers – a complex dance of facial mimicry, physical touch and emotional contagion.[33] The psychologist Alison Gopnik calls this the 'research and development stage' of human development.[34] We learn, through our attachment relationships, what we need to know to get on in the world.

Our carefully attuned attachment systems make us highly sensitive to vocal cues, facial mimicry, physical proximity and touch.[35] When infants receive these things from responsive primary caregivers, they feel a sense of safety and security, warmth and trust. It is from this secure platform of love and attachment that children can begin to be curious and safely explore their environment.[36]

However, things do not always go this way. In the absence of responsive parenting, we can instead learn that the world is a very dangerous place. These kinds of early traumas are more common than we'd like to think. For instance, research in the US by the Centers for Disease Control and Prevention has shown that one in five was sexually molested as a child; one in four was beaten by a parent to the point of a mark being left on their body; and one in three couples engages in physical violence. A quarter grew up with alcoholic relatives, and one out of eight witnessed their mother being beaten or hit.[37]

For those fortunate enough to not experience abuse or neglect, their early attachment relationships may still have been traumatic. The existence of traumas that parents pass down to their children is one of the major insights of psychotherapy. In his *Outline of Psychoanalysis*, Sigmund Freud defines childhood trauma as 'an inability to deal with early emotional challenges that a person could endure with utmost ease later on.'[38] Psychotherapy is built round the idea that every childhood involves an inevitable degree of emotional wounding, even if nothing obviously sinister occurred to cause it.

To love and be loved

The insecure nature of our close relationships is supported by research into child and adult attachment styles. In the 1950s and 1960s, the psychologists John Bowlby and Mary Ainsworth showed that, in the absence of responsive caregiving, children are prone to developing 'insecure attachment styles': relationship coping strategies that are either 'anxiously insecure' or an 'avoidantly insecure'.[39]

'Anxiously attached' children are more likely to feel distress upon being absent from their caregiver and are harder to console upon being reunited. In contrast, 'avoidantly attached' children display less distress upon being absent from their caregiver and ignore their caregiver upon return. Despite appearances, later studies showed that avoidantly attached children still feel separation distress on a physiological level, but learn to internalise outward displays of that distress, such as pained facial expressions and erratic behavioural tendencies.[40] Insecure attachments are distressing (and potentially traumatising) no matter what coping mechanisms children develop to navigate them.

The attachment style we develop in infancy often continues well into our adult lives. As the immunologist Esther Sternberg puts it, in her book *The Balance Within: The Science Connecting Health and Emotions*:

> Somewhere in our brains we carry a map of our relationships. It is our mother's lap, our best friend's holding hand, our lover's embrace – all these we carry

within ourselves when we are alone. Just knowing that these are there to hold us if we fall gives us a sense of peace ... social psychologists call this sense embeddedness. The opposite is perhaps a more familiar term — we call it loneliness.[41]

Our early attachment relationships shape how we relate to our romantic partners and other loved ones, as well as our lives in general.

Of course, there are ways in which we change our attachment style – it is not an immutable part of our personality. We can become more trusting and secure within our close relationships. And more responsive parenting styles can help raise more securely attached children. In fact, about half the population (both children and adults) tend to be 'securely attached.'[42]

However, the difference between secure and insecure attachment styles is a matter of degree. Even if we can work at developing a more secure attachment style, our relationships still require us to trust and depend on our loved ones. This level of trust can easily be abused, or simply fail to be met.

This is made worse by the romantic ideal held up in modern society, where we are expected to rely on our partners to meet all our needs and make us live happily ever after.[43] With these high expectations, it is no wonder that people find it difficult to either enter into committed relationships or stick at them. In the US, the lifelong probability of a marriage ending in divorce is 40–50 per cent.[44] Clearly even our most committed relationships are not secure.

Could we not rely on our partners less, or expect less of them? This would probably make our close relationships more secure, but it would also be missing the point. Much of what makes intimate relationships valuable comes from being vulnerable – from exposing our whole selves in front of another person, and receiving acknowledgement and support in return.[45]

To remove this level of vulnerability and reliance would make our close relationships more like friendships. Friends tend to be less dependent on each other – less vulnerable and less intimate. This makes our friendships more secure, but also less likely to meet our needs for deeper connection. As Andrew Sullivan notes, 'friendships do not solve loneliness, yet they mitigate it.'[46]

There is no way out of this predicament. We crave the acknowledgement and support, and sense of safety and security, that our close relationships provide. But that means such relationships are inherently insecure – they require trust, vulnerability and intimacy. We must expose ourselves to our loved ones – including our weaknesses and the seemingly unacceptable parts of ourselves – and trust that they will continue to see us with love and affection.

These are the insecurities that come from being loved. Loving someone else also brings new sources of insecurity. We cannot avoid at least some amount of suffering in our lives, and this is sometimes worse when the suffering belongs to someone we care about. Of course, we can help our loved ones to feel better. But, to some extent, their internal experience of pain or discomfort is out of our control. Sometimes our loved ones may even require us to simply acknowledge how they are feeling rather than try to change or fix their situation. Similarly, being a good parent sometimes requires letting children overcome their own challenges rather than creating a risk-free existence for them to grow up in.

And sometimes there are forms of suffering that cannot be fixed. We often cannot help our loved ones in the face of chronic illness or at the end of their lives. Having loving relationships makes us vulnerable to loss and grief. Until we grieve, we may not realise just how much our lives revolved around our close relationships – how we would talk through our ideas with our loved ones, how much we needed their reassurance and support, how refreshing we found their perspective on life, how much helping them out gave us a sense of meaning, and so on. Grieving can be a slow and agonizing process of developing a new sense of self and identity in a context outside of our close relationship. For some, this transformation may not be one they want to go through. Life without their loved one may not seem worth living.

My point is not to endorse these sentiments, but just to illustrate how painful our close relationships can be. Our close relationships may be the most meaningful things in our lives. But that does not mean that they will always make us happy.

We would do better to acknowledge the fact that we can't have love without loss – that grief and sorrow are as much a part of being human as love and joy.

Community belonging

In this section, we will look beyond our close relationships towards the other people we rely on in our lives – our wider set of family, friends and acquaintances that make up our community. Having a wider community that we are a part of creates the potential to be of *worth* – to have a life's purpose that makes a positive contribution to the lives of others. We want to belong to, and care about, something larger than ourselves. However, our need for belonging also makes us vulnerable to shame and rejection.

We are tribal animals

We are only just beginning to get a scientific understanding of how social human beings are, and, in particular, our tribal nature.[47] For instance, the psychologist Susan Pinker, in her book *The Village Effect*, shows that the two most significant predictors of longevity are having at least one close relationship (three is even better) and being *socially integrated* – having daily interactions with our wider set of family, friends and acquaintances.[48]

Pinker shows that loneliness and social isolation kills – it is worse for our health than smoking and obesity. Disconnection is also bad for our mental health, with links to depression, anxiety, addiction and suicide.[49] We need to feel we belong. We need to feel valued as an individual. We need to feel secure about our future. When we don't have these things, our physical and mental health suffers.

Belonging to a wider community gives us a sense of security and self-worth. For the majority of our evolutionary history, humans lived in small groups where group membership was a matter of life or death. If an individual were to be ostracised by the group, it would have been personally disastrous. Although these group pressures are not as acute in modern society, we are still dependent on our wider communities. For instance, we are beginning to understand that our casual friendships and acquaintances – our so-called 'weak ties' – are not just nice things to have. The support we receive from our wider community can take a number of different forms, including: a) recognising the worth of our traits, b) encouraging the development of our skills, c) collaborating with us on various projects, d) accompanying us throughout difficult activities and hard times, e) connecting us with others, f) energising us and having fun, g) opening our minds, and f), guiding us and providing us with mentorship.[50]

It is no surprise, then, that we are extremely sensitive in our day-to-day interactions with others. We're incredibly attuned to even the subtlest emotional shifts in those around us. Even if we're not always aware of these intuitive reactions, we can read another person's friendliness or hostility from imperceptible cues such as brow tension, lip curvature and body angles.[51]

Feeling generally safe around other people may be one of the most important aspects of our mental health, and having meaningful and satisfying lives. We can see this on a bodily, emotional level. When we feel attuned to those around us, we tend to feel full of energy and vitality to do what we most want in life. However, when we feel unsafe, we tend to feel energetically drained or a pervasive sense of dullness, conserving our limited resources for staying 'on guard' and dealing with the threats and demands of our social environment.

The psychologist Matthew Liebermann, in his book *Social*, shows how our minds are equipped with a 'sociometer' which we use to continuously measure which side of this line we are on – whether we belong and are secure or whether we are an outsider and under threat.[52] We test our social status in almost all of our social interactions, not just in our close relationships. For instance, one study that made people feel ostracised while playing a ball-tossing game with a computer showed that participants not only reported significantly lower feelings of belongingness, self-esteem, control, and meaningful existence, but also became more sensitive to future rejections.[53]

The philosopher Lorraine Besser-Jones, in her review of this psychological literature, concludes that we cannot simply choose to get by without interacting well with those around us. When people are cold and impersonal, or fail to include us, our need for connection is frustrated. This negatively affects our emotional and cognitive capacities and makes us more sensitive to further potential experiences of social exclusion. The upshot, according to Besser-Jones, is that 'the person who believes she can fulfill her need for relatedness solely by developing a narrow circle of friends and family is misguided.'[54]

Being useful

We need community. But does our community need us? In modern society, this is something we must negotiate for ourselves. We can no longer rely on a village rites of passage initiation ceremony to determine and solidify our role in the community. We must prove our worth to our wider community of family, friends and acquaintances in other ways. If we fail to 'fit in', we risk being rejected by others and no longer receiving the acknowledgement and support, and safety and security, that being part of a wider community provides.

This is what makes community belonging an insecure process. Faking membership to a wider community can only get us so far. We cannot have a stable sense of self-worth by acting in ways that are deemed acceptable: following social norms, being polite, helpful, cool, productive and so on. This may buy us approval and recognition in the short term, but is also likely to instill a pervasive sense of shame and backfire in the long run.

Placing our self-esteem and sense of worth entirely in the hands of others makes us more sensitive to what other people think about us than what we need to do to act well. Just think of the difference between someone who is desperately trying to fit in and someone who is acting on their own interests and enjoyments. The latter is more likely to do well at those activities, whereas the former is only doing them to look good. The tragic irony of the situation is that the person pursuing their own path is more likely to succeed and receive the recognition of others than the person who wants that recognition the most.

Psychologists refer to this difference as contingent versus genuine self-esteem. We receive contingent self-esteem from the approval of others. In contrast, genuine self-esteem comes from achieving the goals and projects we think are valuable independently of what others think about us. Genuine self-esteem is more stable in nature – it is a by-product of doing what we most care about, rather than trying to gain the approval of others in whatever way we can.[55]

The ways in which we try to 'fit in' with the groups and communities we want to belong to are not too dissimilar to the ways in which we try and gain a sense of security within our attachment relationships. We have already seen above that our close relationships are inherently insecure – we must rely on the ongoing affections, acknowledgement and support of our loved ones, which is ultimately out of our control. We can say a similar thing about the relationships we have with our wider community. We must rely on the approval and recognition of others, which is, ultimately, out of control. We can deliberately try to fit in – to follow group norms and practices, and styles and fashions – but, much like insecure attachment styles, this can actually make things worse in the long term. Trying to be 'normal', or acceptable, may seem like a safe bet. But it also prevents us from having a genuine sense of purpose and belonging.

Purpose and achievement

Our sense of worth and purpose, as well as our ongoing attempts to meet our own needs and the needs of those we care about, create a number of challenges. In this section, we will see how the nature of the challenges we take on exposes us to both success and failure. The challenges we face may give our lives a sense of purpose and achievement, but they also make us insecure.

Difficult yet achievable goals

Humans are active creatures. We develop a large range of skills and competencies, and form goals and projects that stretch far into the future. Achieving our goals and ambitions doesn't just help us better meet our needs, it also gives us a sense of self-worth that comes from doing something meaningful. It is the challenges we take on that give our lives a sense of purpose.[56]

The problem is that, by definition, challenges are difficult. In trying to overcome the challenges we face in life, we are likely to make countless mistakes and witness numerous setbacks and failures.[57] We cannot expect to take on challenges without experiencing failure along the way. Ideally, we will eventually learn from our mistakes and experience success too.[58] But we must accept that, due to the challenging nature of our goals and activities, we cannot have one without the other: failure and success are two sides of the same coin.

This way of thinking runs contrary to the optimism of self-help authors and motivational speakers who enthusiastically tell us that we can achieve all our goals and dreams without too much suffering. Much of this guidance is about the content of our goals: are we being realistic in our expectations? We may want to be an astronaut, but how likely is that if we are unfit and lack a science degree? We could either create less demanding goals or simply focus on the next achievable step: go to the gym or take a beginner's physics course. Slowly but surely, we can make more and more progress until we have achieved substantial success.

What is wrong with this way of thinking? It reminds me of a so-called 'happiness formula' which states that: 'Happiness = Reality / Expectations'.[59] The idea is that, if we aim high, we are likely to be disappointed by reality, whereas if we lower our expectations then we have more chance of being content with how things actually are. The problem with putting this idea into a formula (and ultimately into practice) is that it assumes our expectations are under our control. But the opposite is more often the case. Our expectations are largely automatic and unconscious.[60] We use our implicit expectations to navigate the world: from interpreting the meaning of someone's facial expression to how much energy we need to get us through the day.[61]

Of course, we can consciously lower our expectations and set small, achievable goals. This can, to a certain extent, make us happier, or perhaps more content. But trying to apply this strategy in a more general sense ignores the function that our goals and expectations have been set up to perform.

We are motivated to achieve goals that are neither *too difficult* nor *too easy*.[62] Too difficult – like learning how to fly or living on the Moon – and we are destined for failure. Too easy – like eating and sleeping – and we could've set our sights higher. When having to eke out as many resources from our environment as possible, or when in competition with others trying to do the same, finding this sweet spot between achievability and difficulty is essential.

In many of the circumstances and challenges we face in our lives, either we want to develop our capacities and push ourselves as much as we can or we have little choice over the matter. Often, life demands the best of us. We face challenges in life because the things we care about are insecure. We cannot always afford to lower our standards and settle with what we have. Instead, we must find out what we are truly capable of by putting our most ambitious expectations into practice and hope they are not too far off the mark.

Knowing and changing ourselves

We are motivated, and often required, to challenge ourselves – to develop our capacities and achieve goals that are neither too difficult nor too easy. But how do we know what we are capable of? As noted above, we often only know what challenges we can overcome in practice. Sometimes we will be pleasantly surprised and find out that we are more capable than we had thought. At other times, we will make mistakes and be disappointed. Is there any way in which we can have more of the former experiences and fewer of the latter?

To know what we are capable of, we need to know ourselves. Without having a good idea of our mental and physical abilities, we cannot set ourselves appropriate goals. This requires knowing our specific habits, emotional dispositions and general personality traits. If we are introverted, we might not want to find a career that involves a lot of public speaking. If we are a 'social smoker', we might not want to hang around others who smoke regularly. This kind of self-knowledge can help us go with the grain of our habitual, automatic ways of thinking, feeling and behaving.

Not only does going with the grain of our personality make things easier, it may also be essential in dealing with many of the challenges we face. The more we can rely on our habitual responses, the more we free up our cognitive resources for when we need them most. This combination of reliability and flexibility is often crucial, especially when performing novel or complex tasks.[63]

We can look towards our specific habits, emotional dispositions and personality traits to get a fairly good idea of what we can do.[64] But we can also *change* – develop new skills and habits. In fact, the psychologist Brian Little talks about how many of us possess 'free traits' – traits we have learned in order to deal with the specific challenges we face that nonetheless go against the grain of our personality. For example, Little talks about having learned how to be proficient in public speaking, despite being a staunch introvert.[65] When push comes to shove, we may find that we are much more capable than we think.

We cannot know in advance, however, how much we can push ourselves. We are now in the realm of self-help authors and motivational speakers who enthusiastically tell us that we can achieve all our goals and dreams through sheer positive thinking and endurance – 'no pain, no gain'. However, some challenges can require us to go against the grain of our personalities too much – beyond what we have the cognitive resources to do. This is especially the case in stressful circumstances, where the demands and pressures of our situation can take up the majority of our energy and attention. It is like telling someone to give up smoking while they are going through a major life crisis.

To find out what we are truly capable of can be nothing short of heroic. It requires, in the words of the philosopher Friedrich Nietzsche, 'to face simultaneously one's greatest suffering and one's highest hope.'[66] Exploring our interests and enjoyments risks making mistakes and witnessing failure, and experiencing shame and rejection. And committing to the things we most care about risks loss and heartbreak.

The challenges we take on require us to take these leaps of faith. We can never know the sequence of events that will lead to either success or failure once we've committed to a particular challenge or project. Instead, we have to go beyond ourselves – our identity, our beliefs and our comfort zone – to find out.

Financial and material wealth

In the final section of this chapter, we will see how our human and natural environments, beyond our close relationships and community, also make our lives insecure. We are, to a large extent, victims of our circumstances. We can succeed at the challenges we set ourselves, but sometimes the odds can be stacked against us. Ultimately, how well our lives go is a matter of luck – determined by systemic forces well outside our control.

Connected disadvantages

Conditions of poverty make people's lives considerably insecure. The impact of this insecurity is significant. For instance, the average life expectancy gap between rich and poor in the US is 12 years. People in conditions of affluence can expect to live to age 82, whereas people in conditions of poverty can expect to die by age 70.[67] This is similar to the difference in average life expectancy between people in the world's most and least developed countries.

There are a number of reasons why poverty is so harmful. First, poor people are multiply disadvantaged – people in deprived neighbourhoods have less access to decent jobs, affordable housing, quality schools, public services, and have to live with high crime rates. In contrast, people in more prosperous communities grow up in less toxic environments, with less crime, decent schools, ample doctors and hospitals, better food and nutrition, and superior social services. They also tend to have two financially stable parents, and the ability to secure good jobs that provide decent salaries and other career opportunities.

Second, these disadvantages are chronically stressful, which has an additional negative impact on people's health. Scraping to come up with routine living expenses – food, shelter, medical care, transportation – can cause chronic insomnia and anxiety, which boosts levels of cortisol, the stress hormone in the blood.[68] This already makes poor people more vulnerable to a cascade of debilitating, life-threatening ills, from diabetes to high blood pressure and heart disease.[69]

Third, in order to cope with this ongoing stress, people in poverty are more likely to take up drinking, smoking and other addictive behaviours, which escalate these health risks. Making the right choices and adopting healthy lifestyles within chronically stressful conditions is easier said than done. When you only have 48 hours of food left, it is hard – or even dangerous – to plan for the future. Financial insecurity comes with a 'massive cognitive load': research shows that the stress of living in poverty is akin to losing 13 IQ points.[70]

Together, these three reasons add up to create the most important factor in why poverty has such a grip on people's lives: all of these disadvantages are *connected*. With fewer resources and opportunities, poor people have fewer buffers to protect them against loss. As the neuroscientist Christian Cooper notes, 'being poor is a high-risk gamble'.[71] It is harder to hold down a stable job when chronic illnesses and unexpected trips to hospital are more likely. It is harder to remain healthy when living in temporary, unsafe accommodation. Deprived conditions are full of risk because each part of your life is dependent on each of the other parts holding together. As Cooper goes on to say, 'The reality is that when you're poor, if you make one mistake, you're done.'[72]

This is what the philosophers Jonathan Wolff and Avner de-Shalit define as the hallmark of disadvantage – it's 'clustering' nature.[73] It is not simply that people in poverty face multiple disadvantages. It is that that these disadvantages are connected to each other. Losing our health can mean losing our job, which can put strain on our relationships. Without the support of others, we are less likely to recover from illness and find employment again. Which puts even more strain on our family lives. And so on. It is in this way that a vicious cycle of seemingly bad luck and deprivation can perpetuate itself.

Status anxieties

The conditions of poverty are striking in comparison to conditions of relative affluence. However, it is important to realise that the difference between rich and poor is a matter of degree. One of the most significant findings to have come out of public health research is that the health impacts of inequality affect everyone, not just the poor. The lower down the ladder of socioeconomic status (SES) you are, the unhealthier you are likely to be.[74] Of course, this is worse for those who are poor, who are at the very bottom of the ladder. But none of us is immune from the negative impacts caused by each step down on the SES hierarchy.

Why might this be the case? One possible cause is the negative impact that stress has on our health. With each step down the SES ladder, we have fewer resources and opportunities, which in turn gives us less control over our lives. We are less able to protect ourselves against adversity. This lack of control is stressful. In contrast, with each step up the ladder, we can create more and more buffers against things spiralling out of control. For example, we can buffer ourselves against the negative impacts of temporary unemployment by living in a cohesive community, where we can find opportunities for short-term work or the social support we need to help get us back on our feet.

In societies where we are in competition with others for resources and opportunities, having control over our lives requires that we get ahead and stay ahead of everyone else. Our position on the SES hierarchy is always under threat. As the sociologists Richard Wilkinson and Kate Pickett point out in their book *The Inner Level*, within situations of inequality, everyone is prone to a heightened sense of status anxiety.[75] If we don't secure a particular resource or opportunity, someone else will get it instead. We have to continue striving to keep the same level of control we currently have over our lives.

As an example of this process at work, consider our increasing standards of educational attainment. Although education is valuable in its own right, it can also be a 'positional good': a limited resource that is available to some people, and not others.[76] The best jobs tend to go to people with the best educations. By getting a better education than others, we're more likely to get a good job.

Even when education is available to everyone, people's level of education attainment is still largely determined by the amount of resources and opportunities they have. For instance, the political scientist David Reeves, in his book *Dream Hoarders*, shows how upper-middle-class families tend to give their children more educational opportunities in a number of ways: they move to, or already live in, neighbourhoods with access to better schools and other public goods (parks, libraries and so on); they give their children private tutoring; they read to them at an early age; they have higher educational aspirations, such as expecting their children to enter higher education, and so on.[77]

The dynamics of inequality means that the control we have over our lives is always insecure. With fewer resources and opportunities, people are less likely to get a good education, which means they are less likely to get a good job, and so on. We must continue to accumulate greater resources and opportunities so that we don't spiral down the social ladder, which, as we have already seen, brings with it increasing levels of disadvantage.

Shocks and disasters

Both poverty and inequality create insecurities that exist within a stable society. The idea that society is stable, however, is not necessarily something we should take for granted. The financial crisis in 2008 is just one example of how shocks and disasters can negatively impact people's lives across the planet.

According to the optimistic modern day 'neo-Enlightenment' view, these kinds of shocks are merely blips on an upward trajectory of progress. In general, modern liberal nations can protect themselves from disaster and conflict through a combination of democratic political institutions and stable economic growth.[78] I cannot go into detail about the merits of this view here. However, there is one obvious worry that is relevant to the stability of societies: the more powerful we get, the more vulnerable we are to abuses of that power.

Here are some potential examples: at any given time, we are minutes away from a potential nuclear war; as income inequalities increase, people at the top gain increasing political power, which can further harm people at the bottom; AI may cause mass technological employment and greater inequality; and decision-making algorithms could render democratic political institutions redundant.[79]

The most important threat to the neo-Enlightenment view comes from the fact that we are rapidly destroying the natural environment and causing potentially catastrophic climate change.[80] The changes humans are making to the Earth's climate and natural habitats are extremely complex. They may end up causing negative impacts on the world's food and water supply that cannot be fixed by pre-existing and new technologies. There are limits to what Earth can put up with, and we are vulnerable to exceeding them.[81]

The human ecosystems we have built have an inertia to them that may be in conflict with the natural ecosystems they rely on. Societies will continue to grow until they step dangerously over planetary limits, potentially not realising until it's too late. It is this dissonance between human and natural ecosystems that makes us all vulnerable in the long term. It is these kinds of conflicts that make civilizations vulnerable to collapse despite being so powerful.[82]

Looking forward

In this chapter, we have seen that there are things we can do to be happier and more secure. But the idea of being lastingly happy and secure is a fantasy. We have looked at five key ingredients of happiness – health and longevity, close relationships, community belonging, purpose and achievement, and financial and material wealth. None of these circumstances are stable or guaranteed. Each of them comes with their own unique set of vulnerabilities and insecurities.

To some, this may all seem a bit depressing. We don't like the idea of being inherently insecure. It is often met with one of two different kinds of response.

The first is to think of ways in which we can eliminate our insecurity. Perhaps we could find a way, after all, to live longer, pain-free lives thanks to modern medicine; or to depend on people without being so vulnerable; or to build more stable and just societies in harmony with the natural ecosystems, and so on. I have tried to show that, although we should definitely work to improve things, and alleviate some of our insecurities, we cannot eliminate them altogether. This mistaken response is at the heart of the happiness problem.

The second response is simply to ignore our insecurity. In our lives so far we might have been lucky. We might have avoided anything going drastically wrong – a loved one getting ill, a major failure, rejection and so on. Perhaps it is worth carrying on living in ignorance of our insecurities, at least until something tragic actually does happen? This may work for some people, but it is unlikely to help the majority of us. Moreover, it may work on an individual level, but it ignores the tragedies that do happen for people across society and the planet. Not only can we acknowledge the potential for things to go wrong in our own lives, we can also acknowledge the fact that things will continue to go wrong for others.

I want to suggest an alternative response, which we will develop throughout this book. It is to remain hopeful *within* our insecurity – not by the prospect of eliminating all our insecurities, but instead by our efforts to improve our lives while acknowledging we will continue to be insecure.

Consider, for example, the fact that we will die. In response, we could try and ignore this fact (something that is surprisingly easy to do) or desperately find ways of living longer. Alternatively, we can acknowledge our mortality and learn how to live well in light of it. For some, this may mean living life 'to the full' knowing that we won't be alive forever – stepping outside our practical concerns and appreciating each day, taking a few more risks, expressing how we feel and so on. For others, it might mean prioritising the things that will outlive us, such as caring well for our loved ones or making a positive contribution to society. Neither of these approaches aims to either ignore or 'beat' death. Despite the suffering that our mortality causes, we can still acknowledge that it is a part of our lives and that part of life is about finding a meaningful relationship with it.

I think we can say a similar thing about the risks and insecurities involved in our relationships, community, challenges and wider environments. Instead of either ignoring or trying to eliminate these vulnerabilities, we can face up to them and understand them better. We can then work out how to best deal with them, knowing that we will never be completely rid of them. In future chapters, I will show how this approach can help us better understand the problems we face, on both an individual and societal level.

This should perhaps come as no surprise. Our insecurity is a deep truth about human nature. Of course, we can ignore this. Or we can try and change the world and create a different truth. But, at least for the foreseeable future, we will continue to be insecure in the ways we have seen in this chapter. Acknowledging our insecurity will help us better deal with it because we will be acting on the basis of what is true. I am optimistic that we can handle the truth.

TWO

Control

In Chapter One, we looked at the desired outcome of the control strategy – happiness as *security*. We think that, by going to war with reality, we can achieve a stable set circumstances – the perfect job, relationship, home and so on – which will give us a lasting sense of meaning and satisfaction. The problem with this idea is that our lives are inherently insecure. There are things we can do to be happier and more secure, but we can never eliminate insecurity from our lives entirely.

Okay, so we can't live happily ever after. But does that mean we should stop trying to control our lives to our liking? After all, there are circumstances that make us happier, even if they do not make us happy. We may eventually lose our war with reality, but the strategy of control might still be worth it for the few battles we win along the way.

In this chapter, we will see why this process of control is problematic. By trying to control everything in our lives to our liking – solving all our problems, protecting ourselves from our fears and achieving all our goals – we might well make ourselves a bit happier. But, in the process, we are likely to miss out on many of the things in life that matter.

Happiness and control

What really matters

Let us begin by considering the past few days. Most likely, you've spent a large amount of time in your own *problem-solving bubble* – made up of all the things in your life you feel you can control to your liking. You may have woken up with a to-do list already in your head – a list of pressures and demands on your time, some threats or anxious thoughts on your mind, or a number of small achievable goals to tick off throughout the day. Between work and necessities, like sleep and feeding yourself, you may have organised to meet up with some friends, do some physical or cultural activities or spend time with loved ones. In general, you may have been successful at all these things – protecting yourself from anything going too wrong, but also finding time to do some of the things you enjoy and care about. If only there were more hours in the day, you could have been even more successful.

Well, the good news is that, even if there aren't more hours in the day, there are more days. Tomorrow, you can continue to do all the things you feel you need to do. So, naturally, the to-do list in your head rolls over to the next day ... and the next, and the next. In fact, your past few days may have been much like your past few weeks, months or even years: waking up with problems already in your head and setting about the day doing your best to solve them all. There is always stuff to do – always circumstances under our control that we can change.

The bad news is not that this process never ends – the fact that we are surrounded by immediate and potential problems is the nature of life. As the poet Emily Dickinson noted, 'Low at my problem bending, / Another problem comes /'.[1] This endless problem solving is, in part, what makes life meaningful – we can always find ways of improving our own lives and the lives of others.

No, the bad news is that we can become so consumed by our internal to-do list and problem-solving chatter that, after the days and years have rolled by, we may realise that we haven't spent them as we really wanted to – we haven't done the things that really matter to us. We can improve our lives in countless ways. But we only have one lifetime in which to do so. What matters is that we improve our lives in the ways that we most care about.

In thinking, 'if only we had ___ then we'd be happy' we can end up *overdoing* things. We may fill in the blank with 'money', 'status', 'relationships', 'growth', or whatever. But no matter how successful we are at achieving these things, it will never be *enough*. We will either want to achieve more of them, or quickly fill in the blank with something else. The more we focus on whatever we fill in the blank with, the less we focus on everything else in our lives that matters too.

This is most obvious when it comes to our long-term goals and ambitions. We can devote the majority of our time to careers and projects that we aren't really that interested in or don't find enjoyable. In doing so, many of the small pleasures that make life meaningful – like observing the passing weather or watching our children play – can pass us by.

But the same goes for what we pay attention to on a moment-to-moment basis. Whereas some people may recognise the view out of the window, others may see the dirty windowsill. Neither perspective is incorrect – their value depends on how we want to spend our time. Sometimes it is useful living in our problem-solving bubble. At other times, it can be better to step outside it.

Over time, how we allocate our attention in the short and the long terms adds up. Improving our lives in the ways we most care about is easier said than done. There's no guarantee that we will get it right. A poignant illustration of this predicament is the 'regrets of the dying'. During her career as a palliative care nurse, Bonnie Ware recorded what she found to be the most common regrets people have towards the end of their lives.[2] The top five were:

1. I wish I'd had the courage to live a life true to myself, not the life others expected of me.
2. I wish I hadn't worked so hard.
3. I wish I'd had the courage to express my feelings.
4. I wish I had stayed in touch with my friends.
5. I wish that I had let myself be happier.

Reading this list, you may already resonate with some of the things on it. You may also recognise that doing these things, despite sounding relatively simple, can actually be really hard. Each comes with its own set of risks, from disappointment to financial insecurity. For instance, going against other people's expectations is hard because we don't know what negative consequences we might have to face from doing so – all the potential failures and rejections. There may be very good reasons why people can get to the end of their lives having not prioritised these things during their lifetimes. It is easier to focus on the things we know we can get right, even if that means neglecting the things we most care about.

The 'regrets of the dying' illustrate the extent to which we can continuously overdo things at the expense of what really matters – not just over the past few days, but potentially for the majority of our lives. We spend the majority of our time in our problem-solving bubbles, but what if the problems we are constantly trying to solve aren't the things that are most important to us? What if being continuously successful at solving them will never be enough?

In the remainder of this chapter, I will show just how prevalent this problem is. It is what underlies a wide range of problems, from the seemingly trivial, such as the 'fear of missing out' (FOMO) to more serious issues such as addiction.

There is, however, hope. By getting to know the opportunity costs associated with living in our problem-solving bubbles, we can begin to see the value of doing things differently. As well as trying to control ourselves, others and our environment, we have the psychological capacities to better *understand* all these things. From Chapter Four onwards, we will see how these capacities can open up a profoundly different way of thinking about happiness – one that focuses less on control and more on understanding.

The story of progress

Before looking at the harmful consequences that our problem-solving bubbles can have on our lives (and the lives of others) it is worth taking a step back and looking at how we got here. Happiness has not always been about getting everything right. The idea that 'if only we had ___ then we'd be happy' is a relatively recent one in human history.

According to the historian Darrin McMahon, there have been three major turning points, or 'revolutions' in thinking about happiness through recorded history.[3] The first was the agricultural revolution, which began around ten thousand years ago, taking us out of our hunter-gathering lifestyles and into more 'civilized' forms of living. The second was what McMahon calls the 'Axial Age', which began around two thousand five hundred years ago, and where our brief story will begin.

This was a time in which illness and strife were common. Life was considered to be so predestined and out of people's control that any kind of happiness must be fleeting by default. Lasting happiness was thought of as something in the hands of the gods, and therefore in the realm of good fortune.

In fact, the word happiness comes from the old German word *happ*, which translates as 'luck'. In Spanish and Italian, the words *felicidad* and *felicite* translate as 'fortune'; similarly, the French word *bonheur* translates as 'good fortune'. And the ancient Greek word for happiness, *eudaimonia*, translates as having a good daemon. Any kind of lasting happiness was generally considered to be the result of some divine influence – a god or daemon on someone's side, rather than anything down to that person's own actions.

This is well illustrated by the following quote from the philosopher Herodotus, in the 6th century BCE:

> Short as [the human life] is, there is not a man in the world, either here or elsewhere, who is happy enough not to wish – not once only but again and again – to be dead rather than alive. Troubles come, diseases afflict us, and this makes life, despite its brevity, seem all too long.[4]

The picture Herodotus paints is grim, reflecting a view of the world as at once hostile and unpredictable, governed by forces beyond people's control.

McMahon shows how the major religions of the Axial Age tried to make sense of the pursuit of happiness within these conditions. According to most religious teachings, happiness was not a matter of getting all the things we want in life, including basic conditions such as food, shelter, good health and safety from violence. Instead, people were encouraged to think of 'true happiness' as something only available to them beyond the material world.

Although true happiness was something that people could only attain in the afterlife, most religious teachings emphasised how they could nonetheless prepare for it, and catch glimpses of it, throughout their lives. With a focus on moral virtue – doing the right thing at the right time, in harmony with the natural order – people could be at peace with their circumstances, even if they seem extremely barren from an external perspective.

For instance, according to Daoism, 'genuine happiness' required devotion to the Dao or Way, the true order and harmony of the universe that transcended the self. Similarly, Confucius taught that living well went far beyond ordinary pleasures and comforts. It was from being well aligned – between the individual and the transcendent, between right conduct and right order – that true harmony, peace and joy could be found.

This all changed with the advent of the Enlightenment and the Industrial Revolution – the third major turning point in happiness, which McMahon calls the 'Revolution in Human Expectations'. With the opportunities created by modern capitalism, happiness suddenly became something under our control.

By 1776, happiness was enshrined in the United States Declaration of Independence, with US citizens entitled to 'life, liberty, and the pursuit of happiness'. Happiness was no longer something that required either good fortune or virtuous activity. Instead, most individuals could now pursue happiness by satisfying their desires and achieving their goals – something that we largely take for granted in our definitions of happiness today.

With these opportunities for individual achievement came the idea that happiness was about maximising satisfaction and pleasure. The Enlightenment philosopher, jurist and social reformer Jeremy Bentham created the 'hedonic calculus' as a way of measuring how pleasurable people's lives were – the more pleasure, the better.[5] The philosophy of utilitarianism was created, with the explicit aim of producing the 'most happiness for the greatest number'.

This was a big shift in the way people started to see their lives and what they could make of them. From the first time in human history, the kind of happiness we now pursue – which includes fulfilling our values, getting the things we want, and achieving our life plans – became a widespread goal. From the Enlightenment to the modern day, this way of thinking about happiness has continued and been built upon. We now hold happiness as one of our primary values, reflected in common phrases such as, 'I want a career that makes me happy', 'I want a happy relationship' or 'I just want my children to be happy'.

This way of thinking has not just changed how individuals pursue happiness. As a society, we also cherish and promote institutions that help us avoid as much suffering as possible. Modern medicine has helped to prevent and avoid various diseases and illnesses, including delaying death as long as is currently possible. Modern technologies have helped to solve many of the inconveniences involved in social life, such as slow communications and transport, as well as more personal inconveniences such as cooking and cleaning.

Social and technological progress has resulted in almost every part of our lives becoming under individual control. We can now arrange our lives to our liking. We can achieve success in our financial and material lives, our relational and social lives, and in our physical and mental lives. As individuals, we are encouraged to do what we are passionate about and follow our dreams – to be our most 'authentic selves'. This is the logical implication of modern liberalism – the 'revolution in human expectations' – where individuals have gained multiple opportunities to maximise their happiness and minimise their suffering. All our problems can be fixed. Everything is possible.

Controlling our lives

The costs of opportunity

The question is: have all these freedoms and opportunities to make our lives better made us lastingly happier? It would seem foolish to suggest otherwise (remember Herodotus?). However, it's not obvious that having greater control over our lives always creates greater happiness.

For instance, according to the well-known 'Easterlin Paradox' from the study of happiness literature, average national happiness levels have stayed relatively constant over the second half of the 20th century, despite huge increases in GDP (which increased threefold in the UK and US since 1950).[6] More recently, happiness researchers have found that people's subjective wellbeing has been decreasing since 2010, despite continued economic growth.[7]

Of course, money isn't everything. In fact, further happiness research has also found that, above a certain point, increases in income do not tend to make people happier. For instance, in the US, increases in annual income above $75,000 do not tend to make a lasting difference to people's happiness.[8] The general story associated with these findings is that having a sufficient amount of money is necessary to help us meet our basic needs, but, above this amount, money doesn't necessarily make us happy.[9]

There is no denying the benefits that economic growth and modern technologies have brought us. For instance, at the beginning of the 19th century, it's estimated that 43 per cent of the world's children died by the age of five. On average, families had five children, of which only two were likely to survive into adulthood.[10] It is only over the past few generations that this has significantly decreased. Due to improvements in health, education and political freedom, and tackling violence and poverty, average global child mortality is now 4 per cent (1-in-25 children). In the world's richest nations (such as in the EU) it is 0.4 per cent (1-in-250).[11]

However, converting these dramatic improvements into happiness is not as straightforward as we often think it is. A good example is the role of digital media technologies in the lives of adolescents. In her book *iGen*, psychologist Jean Twenge documents how depression, suicidal ideation and self-harm have increased sharply among adolescents in the US and UK since 2010, particularly among girls and young women.[12] She describes how these alarming changes may be largely down to the overuse of digital media, such as gaming, social media, texting and time spent online.

At first glance, the fact that, after 2012, the majority of the US population owned a smartphone is a good thing. With digital media technologies, people can be connected to each other and to libraries of information and other useful services, wherever they are, within a moment's notice. There are, after all, good reasons why so many people choose to spend their money on such devices. However, the more time we spend using digital media, the less time we spend doing other things that matter. Every way we choose to improve our lives comes with a hidden cost attached.

Twenge shows that the more time adolescents engage in digital media activities (such as the internet, social media and texting), the less time they spend doing other activities that make them happy. For instance, in 2017, the average 17- to 18-year-old in the US spent more than six hours a day of leisure time engaged in digital media activities. As a result, they spend less time interacting with each other in person, including getting together with friends, socialising and going to parties. Twenge shows that iGen adolescents spend an hour less a day on face-to-face interaction than adolescents did in the late 1980s. In-person social interaction (and sleep!) has taken the hit for the increase in digital media use among adolescents over the past decade.

Twenge concludes that 'digital media may have an indirect effect on happiness as it displaces time that could be otherwise spent on more beneficial activities'.[13] This is the logic of opportunity costs that we described above. There are countless ways we can improve our lives – and an increasingly large number of products and services that promise to help us do so. What matters, however, is that we improve our lives in the ways that we most care about. For modern day adolescents, this would mean shifting the balance between online activities and face-to-face interaction. In general, it means shifting away from the things we can readily control towards the other things that matter in our lives.

The temptations of control

That last sentence makes it seem simple. Perhaps happiness research can tell us all about the things that make us happy, and then we can prioritise those things. No doubt, these are the well-meaning intentions behind much of the research on happiness, as well as a plethora of self-help books on the subject.

However, as illustrated by the 'regrets of the dying' described above, this way of thinking underestimates the problem. There is a reason why adolescents spend more time texting people on their phones than they do meeting up with them in person. It is the same reason that people can get to the end of their lives and regret that they have worked too hard instead of having spent more time with the people they loved.

The reason is that texting and overworking are examples of activities that, for most of us, are readily under our control. Both activities offer relatively guaranteed ways of improving our lives. As the computer scientist Cal Newport notes, in his book *Digital Minimalism*, this is the same logic behind the idea of 'FOMO' ('fear of missing out').[14] We are enthusiastically told that we 'don't know what we're missing' when it comes to the latest TV series or electronic gadget. The more connected we are (on social media, that is) the more we can find out about countless other things that will probably make our lives better. The problem is not that we lack information. It is that we are acutely aware of what we could be doing, with each minute or hour of our day, to improve our lives. It is no wonder that, in response, we fill up as much of our time as possible trying to consume all the products and have all the experiences we have been duly recommended.

To not give into these temptations would require more than just an intellectual knowledge of what makes people happy. We must, like the person who smokes 40 a day and is trying to give up the habit, gain a deeper understanding of what is good for us. As Newport notes, people don't experience 'fear of missing out' when they know, on a deeper level, that the activities they are doing provide them with meaning and satisfaction:

> They're the calm, happy people who can hold long conversations without furtive glances at their phones. They can get lost in a good book, a woodworking project, or a leisurely morning run. They can have fun with friends and family without the obsessive urge to document the experience.[15]

The references to habit and addiction are deliberate. Our habitual ways of thinking, feeling and acting are largely unconscious and automatic. They are tried and tested ways in which we have received rewarding outcomes in the past.[16] When they work in our favour, they seem effortless and we barely notice them (just think about how you automatically open the fridge door when you're hungry). However, when they consistently make us act against our better judgement – such as opting for the chocolate bar over the piece of fruit, or watching television instead of doing some exercise – they can make us feel 'stuck', a slave to our unconscious selves.

The problem with our habitual behaviours is they are relatively fixed and narrow. They are ways in which we have been able to reliably control a repeated feature of our environment. But when the context is different or more complex, they are less useful. In response to new challenges, we need to be flexible and open to new ways of doing things. Instead of being stuck in our habitual patterns of control, we need to be more creative and spontaneous.

When our habitual behaviours have a significant negative impact on our lives, we enter into the realm of addiction. One definition of addiction is a) the pursuit of a short-term reward, which b) alleviates a particular craving, despite c) the risks and negative long-term consequences associated with its pursuit.[17] This accounts for someone who alleviates their stress by smoking a cigarette, despite the financial costs and long-term health risks involved. But it may also account for way in which 43 per cent of adolescents in the US are online 'almost constantly',[18] or the way in which 10 per cent of the US adult population report to be addicted to working (what is known by researchers as 'workaholism').[19]

According to a recent study, it is estimated that around half of the US population suffers from one or more addictions at any one time.[20] This includes drugs, tobacco, alcohol, food addiction, gambling, the internet, exercise, workaholism, shopping addiction, and love and sex addiction. Addictions can be viewed as desperate coping mechanisms – things that once made life a little more bearable that have since become necessary, no matter what the costs. They are often harmful in themselves, such as the health risks caused by smoking. But they are largely harmful due to the opportunity costs involved. Addictions have the power to make everything else in our lives fall apart.

One notable feature of addiction is that it can create a vicious cycle of immediate rewards with harmful consequences. The more people pursue their object of addiction, the more their lives fall apart, which makes them more likely to continue their addictive behaviour, which makes things even worse, and so on. However, this process is not exclusive to addiction. It can happen whenever the opportunity costs of a given behaviour are high, but the alternative opportunities still seem too difficult or impossible.

For instance, the psychologist Tim Kasser, in his book *The High Price of Materialism,* shows that the pursuit of materialistic goals can create such vicious cycles.[21] Kasser shows that the more that people prioritise materialistic goals – attaining money and having many possessions – relative to other aims in life, the lower they score on outcomes such as life satisfaction, happiness, vitality and self-actualisation, and the higher they scored on outcomes such as depression, anxiety, behaviour disorders and a host of other types of psychopathology.

If materialism is so bad for us, why does it persist? In addition to its glorification in advertising and the media, Kasser's research suggests that we continue to pursue materialistic goals because we feel insecure. Psychological threats – such as imagining our own mortality, underemployment during a recession, or being with someone who doesn't accept us for who we are – orient people towards goals such as financial success, popularity and image, and away from goals such as personal growth, affiliation and community contribution. Status, image and sufficient resources may all guarantee rewards in the short term, even if they are less valuable than non-materialistic goals in the long run.

This is how the vicious cycle begins: the more insecure we are, the more short-term rewards we pursue, and the more insecure we become in the long term; this, in turn, makes us pursue even more short-term rewards, making us even more insecure, and so on. Materialistic goals can end up 'crowding out' social relationships, making us feel disconnected and lonely. In turn, loneliness can make us more insecure and materialistic if we don't have social forms of meeting our needs for connection.[22] Material substitutes and compensations – such as status goods, comfort eating and television – are often readily available, immediately rewarding, and less anxiety provoking than attempts to reconnect.

Materialism may not have the extreme negative impacts of addiction, but it does follow a similar, vicious structure. In fact, any goal or behaviour that prevents us from focusing on what really matters has the potential to be 'addictive' in this way. The question is whether we notice the opportunity costs involved, and change our behaviour and priorities accordingly. In the case of the 'regrets of the dying', we may not recognise what really matters until it is too late. And in the case of addiction, the consequences can be fatal.

In the remainder of this chapter, we will see that there is a range of less extreme goals which have a similar structure to addiction and materialism. All these goals seem innocent enough – they are all ways in which we can improve our lives. However, they loom large in our minds because they are the things we can readily control and not necessarily because they are the things that matter most.

Of course, it is hard to pursue things that are not under our control. If everyone around us is using social media, for example, we are likely to be less connected by going against the grain, even if we would all be better off by spending more time face-to-face than on our mobile phones. We often pursue the things under our control out of necessity, not out of choice. In showing the downsides of the control strategy, I am not suggesting that it easy to do otherwise – we only need to look at addictions to see how difficult this can be. We can, however, recognise the limits of our control, and begin to understand what we are missing out on.

Controlling the future

So far, we have seen the problems with short-term temptations – things that are immediately rewarding, but end up causing more harm than good in the long term. These short-term temptations are more appealing to people who have less hope in their future. The economist Carol Graham, in her book *Happiness for All? Unequal Hopes and Lives in Pursuit of the American Dream,* shows that poverty affects people's expectations for the future, to the extent that they are less likely to invest in it.[23] Graham shows that, without hope, poor white people in the US are far more likely to live in the moment, focused on the day-to-day, and less likely to make investments in their own and their children's future. At its extreme, Graham shows that this loss in hope leads to an increase in mortality rates due to preventable causes, such as suicide and opioid addiction.

But what about those who are more fortunate – who have the opportunities and resources to invest in future rewards? These people are more able to resist the pull of short-term temptations and instead focus on the long-term goals, projects and commitments over which they have more control.

Commitments are often good for us – they provide us with the grounds to form rich connections, develop our skills and engage in meaningful projects. For example, marriage is a commitment device that is intended to help us maintain a relationship through thick or thin, in sickness or in health.[24] We may not be able to develop deep, intimate relationships without committing to working on them over time, no matter what happens. However, *all* commitments come with opportunity costs, even the most worthy ones. Engaging in any activity over time prevents us from pursuing other goals and activities that matter too.

We tend to recognise this when thinking about childhood. We celebrate this time of life as a chance for children to explore their interests and enjoyments without have to think (too much) about the utility of these activities in the long term. In a word, it is at this stage in life where we value *play*. Of course, we also think of childhood as a time for education – learning the skills and capacities that will best equip children for their futures. But we acknowledge that there is a balance to be struck: between educational commitments and other activities that matter, such as curiosity and exploration, spontaneity and emotional security.[25]

For individuals who have reached maturity, however, we tend to think differently. If someone can fully commit to a worthwhile career and a meaningful relationship then they should. For example, in our culture of 'authenticity' people are encouraged to find careers and relationships that can be prized as truly self-expressive. Another example is how various religious and political views encourage people to commit to their family and community. If we commit our lives to something – to collecting it, taking care of it, cheering for it, striving to achieve it and so on – and other people see it as valuable too, then our lives also become worthwhile. Valuable commitments are one of the tools people use to have control over the recognition and approval they receive from others.[26]

The limits of this strategy often become apparent when it is finally successful. As the philosopher Kieran Setiya points out, in his book *Midlife*, people can reach their 'prime of life' having achieved all their long-term goals and ambitions only to realise that lasting happiness – or simply some peace of mind – does not ensue.[27] This, Setiya argues, is the dilemma at the heart of people's so-called 'midlife crises'. For these people, life goes on, only now it continues without the committed focus that has been guiding their activities for the majority of their adult lives.

The advantage of having a mid-life crisis is that it makes the opportunity costs of our commitments all too apparent. This may not be the case for most of us, whose commitments are all too demanding to be able to see past them. It is at middle age that we take on ever-greater responsibilities in our careers and family lives – the burdens of jobs, children and ageing parents. Controlling all these things to our liking is near impossible. Our commitments provide us with some sense of control within all these overwhelming pressures and demands.

It should come as no surprise, then, that middle age tends to be the unhappiest period of people's lives. Happiness researchers refer to this pattern as the 'happiness U-curve': with the highest levels of happiness experienced in childhood and old age and the lowest in middle age.[28] Life satisfaction declines with age for the first couple of decades of adulthood, bottoms out somewhere in the forties or early fifties, and then, until the very last years, increases with age, often reaching a higher level than in young adulthood. Looking at the same phenomenon from a different angle, being middle-aged nearly doubles a person's likelihood of using anti-depressants.[29]

The happiness U-curve emerges even after controlling for stressful variables, such as children, income, employment and marriage. This suggests that our ambitions and commitments play a key role in our middle-age slump. As the developmental psychologist Laura Carstensen notes, 'As people age and time horizons grow shorter ... people invest in what is most important, typically meaningful relationships, and derive increasingly greater satisfaction from these investments.'[30] With age, as people perceive the future as increasingly constrained, they set goals that are less ambitious and that they care about more.

This is what children and older people have in common – unlike middle-aged adults, they are able to prioritise the things they really care about. And they tend to be happier as a result. Why, then, can those who are middle-aged not do the same?

The reason is that modern societies aren't set up that way. Our societal structures reflect what middle-aged individuals can do and achieve. Unlike children and older people, middle-aged adults have more control over their future. For those of us with the opportunities and resources to form long-term goals and commitments, we are encouraged to sacrifice our happiness now in order to gain some control over how our lives will look like in the future.

The philosopher Cheshire Calhoun, in her book *Doing Valuable Time*, emphasises how our commitments give us a sense of stability and familiarity over time. To know what will fill today and our days to come, where we will live, what places we will go to, with whom we will interact, what activities will engage our time and so on, is to know where we are in time and, as Calhoun puts it, 'to not be lost in our lives'. Commitments, according to Calhoun, lock-in the future in a way that mere intentions and provisional plans do not. This can create a sense of control that we often lack in the face of our ever-changing situation. The problem is that, by locking ourselves into the future in this way, we miss out on opportunities for spending our days doing more meaningful activities and other valuable pursuits.

Although our commitments and ambitions are often heralded by others as valuable, they can also be another source of *overdoing* – in this case, a kind of *over-achieving*. The more we focus on achieving long-term goals, the less time and energy we have to spend on other things that matter and make life worthwhile. We live in a world obsessed with huge achievements and uninterested in modest goals. And yet, as the philosopher Alain de Botton notes, it is a good thing 'to be able to have a so-called ordinary life, to take pleasure in holidays and to place friendship and love at the center of things. We should, on occasion, dare to feel rather sorry for over-achievers.'[31]

Controlling ourselves

Many of the same societal forces that emphasise the value of ambitious goals and commitments also glorify ideas of productivity and perfection. Again, these are seemingly innocent things – who wouldn't want to be more productive, change ineffective habits or develop a more efficient routine? These things become problematic, however, when we consider the opportunity costs involved. When no amount of increases in productivity is enough, people become overly stressed and busy. In our desire to achieve perfection, we can miss out on the other things in life that matter. On a more fundamental level, the more we try to constantly improve our lives – to be better, healthier, happier – the less we feel they are already good enough.

We now have a range of products and services that have been designed to help us control ourselves – to make us more productive, healthier and happier. For example, the 'quantified self' movement centres around tracking our states and behaviours in an attempt to consciously improve them: moods apps monitor our state of mind throughout the day; health apps track our physical activity; social media tracks our connectivity, including how many people 'like' the things we are doing, and so on.

There is nothing wrong with gaining this self-knowledge and trying to improve our lives. These quantitative methods are especially useful in contexts where long-term rewards are less salient than more immediate ones, such as eating a healthy diet or doing consistent exercise.[32] But we can end up not having a spare ten minutes in our day in which we cease trying to improve our lives in some way. Everything we do, from the moment we wake up to the time we eventually go to sleep, can become an opportunity for self-improvement.[33]

This is made worse by two things. First, in order to know how well we are doing, we must compare our progress to others. In a hyper-connected society, it is easy to see people who are doing better than we are at anything – people who are more successful at work, who have written more books, who have more friends, who are healthier and happier. Moreover, when we are expected to be successful in every area of life, we are bound to not meet these high expectations across the board. Something has to give.

In some areas we might excel, but that means we are more likely to be achieve normalcy, or worse, in others.

The second problem is that, rather than accepting our limits and lowering our expectations, the more productive we are, the more productive we can be. We do not tend to use the time and resources we save from various technologies or 'life hacks' to simply sit back and relax. In fact, research shows that, the more money we have, the more we feel as if we don't have enough time.[34] This is not due to the fact that those with more money tend to work more. It is because with more money we can do so much more with our spare time. This is also why our efforts to optimise and schedule, plan and streamline, and 'upgrade' ourselves, do not tend to make us feel any less busy. Instead, these things only end up providing us with extra time and resources to do more stuff.[35]

Put together, these two factors mean that our potential to improve our productivity is seemingly endless. We look around us and see how productive everyone is being and follow suit. The more control we gain over ourselves and our circumstances, the more productive we can be, which, upon looking around, is also what everyone else is doing. The result is ever-increasing levels of busyness and stress. Again, this may be harmful in itself, but it is also harmful because of the things we miss out on. We can end up focusing so much on how to be the best version of ourselves that we fail to stop and think about what being so productive is ultimately for.

This is most obvious in the case of perfectionism. Perfectionism is a psychological trait characterised by a desire for flawlessness, combined with harsh self-criticism. Perfectionists need to be told that they have achieved the best possible outcomes, whether that's through scores and metrics, or other people's approval. When this need is not met they experience psychological turmoil because they equate mistakes and failure with inner weakness and unworthiness. It is associated with a range of mental health problems, including depression, anxiety and suicide ideation.[36]

Perfectionism, like the overuse of digital media, is on the rise in young people in modern society. 'Millennials' tend to spend less time doing group activities for fun and more time doing individual activities for a sense of personal achievement.[37] This is the kind of impact perfectionism can have on a generation. Ultimately, it can cause young people to lead busy, stressful lifestyles, with a sense that they are wasting their lives. At its most extreme, trying to completely control ourselves and our circumstances can become addictive, as is the case with obsessive compulsive disorders and body dysmorphic disorders, which are also on the rise.

In modern societies, there is no part of life we can turn to that is free from the imperative of improvement and control. In modern medicine, cryogenics and other ways of trying to live forever are now big business. Similarly, a modern form of eugenics that focuses on screening for chromosomal and genetic disorders, aims to give people the best start in life. Modern psychology and the self-help industry are devoted to helping people improve their state of mind, from staying positive to being as mindful as possible. I could go on.

All these technologies and techniques have their merits. But trying to improve our lives in every single respect can not only be exhausting, it can also blind us to the things that really matter, including the value of what we already have. When it comes to ourselves, the constant search for self-improvement can prevent us from seeing that we are already worthwhile. In trying to be the best version of ourselves, we can lose sight of the fact that we are good enough.

Controlling the lives of others

So far, our focus has been on the individual – how trying to control our circumstances, our future and ourselves can blind us to the things that really matter. In this section, we will go beyond the individual, and show how the opportunity costs of control can negatively affect the relationships we have with our partners and our fellow citizens.

Controlling our loved ones

Let us begin with our romantic, or intimate, relationships. The relationships we have with our partners are valuable for a number of reasons. In particular, our intimate relationships provide us with acknowledgement and support. Our partners see us in a different way to how strangers do: they tend to see more of our whole selves and our full potential as an individual. They also tend to support us in realising our potential, giving us valuable feedback and resources.

And we may well do the same for them. Intimate relationships are often formed on the basis of joint pursuits – for example, making a home, running a business or raising children – providing mutual support and recognition. On our own, the world can seem like a very daunting place – our long-term goals and ambitions can be a constant struggle. However, with the help of another, the same challenges can be met with an underlying sense of security that comes from being part of a team. We know that, if all else fails, someone has our back.

This sense of security created by our intimate relationships is also what makes them so terrifying. When we depend on someone so much to help meet our needs, we make ourselves vulnerable to rejection, heartbreak or loss. It is no surprise, then, that we try and control our relationships in a number of ways.

This is the realm of 'attachment theory', which we briefly looked at in Chapter One. Adults with 'insecure attachments styles' try to gain security in relationships in a number of ways that fit into two broad patterns. First, people can be controlling and try to secure connection *within* the relationship – what researchers call an 'anxious' attachment style. Second, people can be distant and seek connection *outside* the relationship – what researchers call an 'avoidant' attachment style. If we are insecure within our relationship, we can either focus on controlling our partner to our liking (anxious) or on making sure we have control of our lives outside the relationship (avoidant).

These strategies of control are associated with different negative consequences. Fully invested in their relationship, the anxiously attached person is more likely to obsess over how it's going and create arguments. They are more likely to want to change their partner to better meet their needs, or be particularly sensitive to any potential signs of changes in affection. In contrast, the avoidantly attached person is more likely to look for affection elsewhere, including having affairs. They are more likely to make comparisons between their partner and other potential partners, including ex-lovers.[38]

None of these behavioural patterns are usually carried out with the intention of spite. They are instead desperate (largely unconscious) attempts at asserting some kind of control over a situation in which our needs are largely dependent on the whims and will of another.

Beyond our attachment styles, there are other ways in which we try to gain control over our relationships. Long-term commitments, such as marriage, can help make our intimate relationships more stable and secure. Another strategy is to try find the 'perfect match' – someone who is both 'like us' and 'completes us', and ideally with whom we will live happily ever after.[39] There are also the countless ways in which we can 'work' on our relationships, from learning how to communicate better to simply being more present in each other's company.[40]

Of course, many of these strategies work to some extent. They become problematic, however, when they are overdone. No matter how much work we put into our relationships, it will never be enough to fully rely on our partner. At some point, we must accept our insecurity and *trust* them. Without exposing ourselves in this way, we will never develop the trust that makes our intimate relationships so special.

A clear example of this is physical intimacy. We typically go throughout our day with an invisible space surrounding our body, which we expect everyone to respect by staying well out of it.[41] Everyone, that is, other than our loved ones. We let the people we are intimate with into areas that we keep well away, and well hidden, from others. With them, we let our barriers down. In the case of sex, we expose the most vulnerable parts of our bodies to our sexual partners and (hopefully) rejoice in the fact that, rather than be repelled by our nakedness, they accept and appreciate our bodies with gentleness, tenderness and joy.

By focusing exclusively on the ways in which we can control our relationships, we miss out on many of the things that make them valuable. This includes not just letting our physical barriers down, but also our mental barriers. We can expose the more vulnerable and seemingly unacceptable parts of ourselves to our partners. In response, instead of seeing us as the terrible person we sometimes think we are inside our own heads, they may reflect back our worth.

To be seen with love can be empowering and enlivening. As the philosopher Troy Jollimore notes in his book *Love's Vision*, 'To be valued in this way, to be installed at the centre of the lover's universe, is to have one's reality and individuality truly and fully acknowledged. Only the lover, after all, looks closely, carefully, and generously enough to truly recognize the beloved in all her individuality.'[42] We cannot force others to see our whole selves in this way. Intimacy is, by definition, largely out of our control.

Controlling our children

We might think that attitudes of care are the antidote to controlling behaviour within our relationships. We try and control our partners partly because we depend on them for acknowledgement and support. Perhaps, if we focused on their needs instead of our own, we would be less focused on being in control?

This isn't necessarily the case, however. The temptation to control people's behaviour can be just as strong from a place of care. This is well illustrated by so-called 'fearful parenting'. In his book, *How Fear Works*, the sociologist Frank Furedi notes that parenting advice used to advocate a sense of risk and fear as making a positive contribution towards a child's character. In contrast, in the culture of today, parents are told there is danger everywhere, and if they don't manage these risks well, they could ruin their child's life. As Furedi puts it: 'we are mightily attuned to children's fears, and strive to blunt them at all costs'.[43]

It is easy to criticise modern parenting practices, such as 'helicopter parenting', and hark back to the good old days of 'free range' childhood – of kids riding their bicycles around their hometowns, unchaperoned by adults, by the time they were 8 or 9 years old. But children (and adults) are fragile. What may be a challenge for one kid may feel like a threat to another – each child's level of resilience and vulnerability is different.

The emergence of child-centred parenting – which aims to be responsive to the interests and enjoyments, as well as the anxieties and concerns, of the child – is no doubt a good thing. We must accept that, if we treat children as autonomous human beings, we will want to protect them from a whole new set of adult-like fears, such as the fear of failure and low self-esteem.

However, this does not mean that parents are responsible for protecting their children from every possible risk to their mental and physical health. Moreover, raising healthy children may require at least some exposure to risk. As the psychologists Jonathan Haidt and Greg Lukianoff note in their book *The Coddling of the American Mind*, the phrase 'whatever doesn't kill you makes you stronger' has some truth to it. It is the stresses and failures that we experience and overcome that help us grow.[44]

We know this on an intuitive level. It is how people build up their physical strength: too much rest and comfort, and muscles begin to atrophy; too much strain and exercise, and they may get pushed too far. The optimal conditions for keeping up our strength are somewhere in between – regularly putting stress on our muscles (in the form of exercise) without causing any physical damage. The economist Nassim Nicholas Taleb calls this the principle of 'anti-fragile' – the process of building resilience through exposing ourselves to new challenges.[45]

The same principle may hold for other forms of growth – constant 'hormetic stress' may build up our resilience and tolerance to potential future threats. For example, organic fruits and vegetables may partly be good for us because of the bio-pesticides they release to fend off soil bacteria and fungi. When we consume these foods, our immune system responds to these natural defences as small stressors and challenges. It may be that one of the problems with highly refined foods that make up the modern Western diet is that they fail to toughen up our immune system in this way. In general, developing anti-fragility may be one of the most effective ways for fragile beings like us to protect ourselves from the unknown threats and demands of the foreseeable future.

There is, then, clearly a balance to be struck. Over-controlling and protecting our children can fail to expose them to the risks they need to develop into well-functioning adults. Too little protection, on the other hand, risks serious cases of abuse, bullying and trauma. Parents are right to be fearful for their children. But they must also be aware of the costs involved in trying to make everything in their environment as safe and as perfect as possible.

Controlling people's potential

The difference between loving relationships characterised by strategies of control and those built on freedom and trust is vast. I believe we can say a similar thing about the relationships we have with others in general.

The mechanisms we use to control our relationships with others are labels and stereotypes – generalisations about particular 'types' of people, how they tend to behave, what they are capable of, and how we should act in relation to them.[46] Whenever we meet someone new, we instantly group them into a number of social categories and roles; they may be a parent, employee, athlete, spouse, friend, patient, religious devotee, conservative or liberal, man or woman, black or white, young or old, and many more things besides.[47]

Many of these labels – like most strategies of control – work to some extent. Stereotypes are built on generalisations about how different groups of people tend to behave. However, beyond these basic generations, they tend to be limiting and potentially harmful. Often, they act more like self-fulfilling prophecies than accurate descriptions of people's nature.

Consider, for example, a child who shows a bit more ability or interest in music than other children. That child might be labelled as 'musical' and, as a result, be given lessons and encouraged to pursue their 'natural musical talents'. The child is likely to receive more training and positive feedback – whatever modest differences there were between them and other children will be magnified. Over time, it may genuinely look as if some children are musical and others are not. We tend to underestimate, however, the role that labels and self-fulfilling prophecies tend to play in this process.[48]

For any stereotype there is a range of expectations that come with it. These expectations, if internalised, can significantly limit people's behaviour – a tendency referred to by psychologists as 'stereotype threat'.[49] The sad thing about this tendency is that intelligence, creativity, athletic ability and many other mental and physical skills are capable of being learned by most people with adequate levels of training. With a suitable amount of time and practice, human beings are able to master a vast range of skills and activities.[50]

This is one of the things that separate us from other animals. As the philosopher Jesse Prinz argues, in his book *Beyond Human Nature*, we are 'general-purpose learners'.[51] With our brains wired for social learning, we have the ability to acquire a countless number of cognitive and motor skills.[52] And yet, our social roles and labels often prevent us from doing so.

An obvious and pervasive example of this are the kinds of goals and activities associated with gender norms. To fit in, boys and girls, and men and women, develop acceptable 'masks'. Men are pressured to be strong and dependable, in the form of physical strength, athletic ability, aggression, domination over others, success and material wealth. Women are pressured to be beautiful and caring, in the form of their physical appearance and sexual appeal, and their emotional dependence and sensitivity.[53]

And yet evidence shows that, despite these social pressures, so-called 'masculine' and 'feminine' traits are shared by both genders.[54] This is why the mask metaphor is so appropriate. Social labels and roles cover up the parts of ourselves that do not fit with them.[55] These masks can be extremely painful when we recognise parts of ourselves that cannot be expressed without running the risk of taking off the masks, and feeling shame and isolation.[56]

This opportunity cost of social labels and judgements is a significant one. We miss out on others – including ourselves – fulfilling their full potential as general-purpose learners and unique, individual human beings. The pressure to conform to social labels and roles can breed a kind of cynicism towards others. Too often, we are overly judgemental of other people's efforts. We tend to judge people we don't know in uncharitable ways – a form of criticism that, as Caitlin Moran says, 'scours through a culture like bleach, wiping out millions of small, seedling ideas'.[57]

Controlling people who are not 'like us'

The social labels we use to control people's potential are not always purely descriptive in nature – they often come with moral undertones. We see this most clearly with the labels and stereotypes we use in the political sphere.

When two groups with different political ideologies disagree, it is unlikely that they will enter into a civil discussion.[58] Instead, both sides are likely to label members of the other side as ignorant, naive, selfish or plain stupid. This kind of stereotyping is a common trope of in-group / out-group dynamics.[59] As the neurobiologist Robert Sapolski notes in his book *Behave*, we tend to think of our group as 'full of noble, loyal, distinctive individuals', whereas outsiders appear 'disgusting, ridiculous, simple, homogeneous, undifferentiated, and interchangeable'.[60] We are right, but they are deeply wrong.

Instead of questioning these implicit group divides, we frequently back up our intuitions by finding rationalisations for them. We employ 'confirmation biases' to rationalise and justify our automatic judgements towards those who are not one of us.[61] We tend to pay much more attention to the testimony of those in 'our tribe' than to those who belong to 'the other side'.[62] We are less likely to challenge the views of people who hold the same moral and political values as us, and look for alternative information. Conversely, we are more likely to explain away contrary facts presented to us from people who hold different values to us. Informed opinion matters much less than who is saying it.

These simple group narratives, talking past each other and demonising members of the other side, come with significant opportunity costs. We are currently seeing this with the identity politics that dominates democratic debate in the UK and the US. On both the political left and right, this moral panic and outrage can make political disagreement more dangerous than it would otherwise be. As the philosopher Martha Nussbaum warns, in her book *The Monarchy of Fear*, 'fear, suspicion, and blame displace careful thought about what the real problems are and how to resolve them'.[63]

The consequences of control

In this chapter, we have seen just some of the ways in which, by focusing too much on what we control, we pay too little attention to the other things in life that matter. In thinking, 'if only we had ___ then we'd be happy' we can end up overdoing things: developing bad habits and addictions, being too ambitious and committed, trying to be endlessly productive or unhealthily perfect, being either controlling or distant in our loving relationships, overly conforming to social labels and stereotypes, and playing out hostile in-group, out-group biases.

All these strategies have a grain of truth to them – they all work up to a point. But as we saw in Chapter One, they will never provide us with enough of what we're looking for. Trying to control ourselves, others and our environment in these ways comes with significant costs – the more we employ these strategies, the less time we can spend doing the things that really matter.

In Part III of the book we will see how the same dynamics play out on a societal level. We try to control things on a societal level, on issues such as crime, poverty, health, democracy and the environment. By focusing on the things we can readily control, we spend too much time adopting simple narratives, temporary solutions and quick fixes. We miss out on better understanding the underlying causes of these problems and the wider social changes required to solve them in the long term.

The implications of this way of thinking are serious. It is not just that we are left unhappy at the end of centuries and millennia of material and social progress. We are also rapidly creating mass inequalities and destroying the planet. Thinking differently about happiness will not solve all our problems. But it does get to the heart of how we have ended up where we are now. We can continue to try and control entire nations and environmental resources, but it will never make us happy. The more we try to control things, the less we focus on what really matters. The sooner we realise this, the better.

Which raises the following question: why *don't* we realise the limits and problems of control? This will be the topic of Chapter Three.

THREE

Certainty

Let's take stock. In Chapter One, we looked at why trying to control everything in our lives doesn't make us happy. We can do all sorts of things to improve our circumstances – be healthier, work on our relationships, find our 'tribe' and our life's purpose, accumulate more resources and so on. But no matter how much progress we make, it will never be enough. We will still be insecure: vulnerable to disappointment, loss and suffering. These insecurities are a necessary part of the things that make life meaningful – we cannot have love without loss, success without failure. We would do better to acknowledge our insecurity and work out how to live within it, rather than going to war with reality and trying to get everything in our lives just right.

In Chapter Two, we looked at the kinds of problems that come from pursuing happiness through the means of control. By trying to constantly improve our lives – be better, healthier, happier – we miss out on appreciating the things we have. By conforming to our social labels and identity, we miss out on exploring what we most care about and are truly capable of. By trying to be more secure within our relationships, either through being distant or controlling, we miss out on trusting and relying on others. By focusing on the things we can control, we miss out on the other things in life that matter.

If this is correct – that trying to control everything in our lives does not make us happy, and can end up making things worse – then why don't we see this? Why does the phrase 'if only we had ___ then we'd be happy' seem so reasonable? It is, after all, how most of us go about living our lives. We spend our days engaged in activity as if it *really mattered* – that achieving our goals and commitments will significantly change our lives. But they won't. They will only ever be the tip of the iceberg. They might make us happier, but they will never make us happy.

In this chapter, we will see how we continuously fall for this illusion. The protagonists of this story are our *goals and expectations*. We do not see reality as it is. We see the world through the lens of our goals and expectations – how we expect things to go from the perspective of our practical goals and concerns. Our perceptions of reality are more like 'a controlled hallucination'[1] than an accurate description of how things really are.

From the point of view of our minds, we do not care so much about being happy, or even what reality is actually like. Our main priority is to achieve our goals as effectively as possible. The result of this process is often unwarranted *certainty*. We may only have a narrow view of what the world is like, but, if it helps us get by, we will adopt it with the utmost confidence.

We typically go about our days confident in the knowledge of what we need and how we can achieve it. In actuality, however, our knowledge of what really matters is extremely limited. We might know enough to effectively achieve our goals. But this doesn't mean we are achieving them in the most effective way we can, and it doesn't mean they are worth achieving in the first place.

In this chapter, we will see some of the key ways in which our knowledge of what matters is limited. In the first section, we will discover how our expectations determine how we see reality. The following three sections look at what influences our expectations. First, we will look at our *cognitive architecture* – how our emotions, moods and personality traits dictate how we see the world. Second, we will look at our *social context* – how we see reality through the lives of others. Last, we will look at how our cultural values and norms shape our *personal narratives* – the stories we use to navigate our lives.

By the end of the chapter I hope to have convinced you that we know less about ourselves, others and our environment than we typically think we do. It might really seem that if only we could control our lives to our liking – get everything just right – then we'd be happy. This is, however, an illusion. We do not know what really matters. Finding that out is a lifelong process, and will be the subject of Part II of the book.

Expectations of reality

Living in the future

On a typical day, we often know what is likely to happen: we will wake up in the morning already with our minds full of what is required of us – who we need to talk to, what tasks we need to perform, what problems we need to solve and so on; we will travel to work knowing pretty much what it'll be like – we will take our usual route, try to ignore all the hustle and bustle around us, let our minds wander for a while; by the evening, we will rest and entertain ourselves somehow, maybe watching some television or spending some time with friends – neither of which will be that exciting; hopefully we will get an early night.

We may take all this knowledge for granted, but it is really a phenomenal achievement. Compare, for example, the above description of a typical day with the typical day of a baby. None of the events described would be as concrete and knowable to an infant: waking up, going from one place to another, performing tasks, being entertained, spending time with others – all of these things would be deeply fascinating; none of their meanings would be set in stone.[2]

What distinguishes us from infants is that we have learned to predict what most of the stimuli we encounter mean.[3] We can wake up in the morning and, assuming that nothing has gone wrong overnight, we can ignore most of the bodily sensations we are receiving, and can continue to do so throughout our day. We can travel to work and pay little attention to almost everything we can see, hear, touch and smell, knowing that such a cacophony of activity around us is unlikely to affect us; we can focus on performing tasks and solving problems, again predicting how we might go about doing so; we can see friends or watch television, expecting that neither activity will be too stressful or threatening. Our world, unlike that of a baby, is one that we can predict with relative accuracy – instead of a 'busy, bustling confusion',[4] it is a world of order and certainty.

77

We see the world relative to our practical goals and concerns. This includes the problems we are currently trying to solve, the tasks we are trying to complete and the questions we are trying to answer. A nice example of this is a well-known experiment on 'attentional blindness'.

Note: the following will spoil the experiment for those who don't already know about it. If you want to give it a go, watch the experiment video before reading any further; search for 'selective attention test' on YouTube.

In the experiment, participants are asked to watch a short video of two teams each passing around a basketball in a small area. The participants are asked to count how many times one of the teams passes the ball during the length of the video. It is a reasonably difficult task – one that requires not getting distracted by the other team passing around another basketball in the same space.

Typically, participants complete the task with close to the correct answer and a sense of satisfaction. However, most of them fail to realise that, about half way through video, someone dressed in a gorilla suit walks straight through the scene and waves at the camera (the experiment has been dubbed 'the invisible gorilla' experiment). To anyone not concentrating on the basketball passes, this is blindingly obvious. Yet the majority of participants were blind to it.[5]

To many, this experiment seems shocking, especially if you've watched the video and failed to see the gorilla. And perhaps it should be. But it is no more shocking than failing to see the faces that pass us on the street on the way to work; or the different trees that line the pavement; or the architecture of the buildings we walk past.[6] In trying to achieve our goals, we block out most of reality.

We fail to see all these things because they are not relevant to our practical goals and concerns. We are always trying to predict what is going to happen based on the things we care about. When we want to count how many passes the team makes, we expect only to encounter basketball players, balls and passes. When we want to think about how we're going to spend our evening while on our way to work, we expect only to encounter our thoughts on different options and scenarios. What we expect from our situation determines the things we see. We live in the future, which blinds us to most of the present.

We are prediction machines

The idea that we are prediction machines is supported by an emerging theory of the mind: predictive processing theory (PP). PP has been used to describe a wide range of cognitive capacities, from vision to decision making, and, as a result, has gained near consensus among cognitive scientists.[7]

According to PP, we are constantly predicting how we will feel from one moment to the next. Before I pick up my cup of coffee, for example, my mind has already made a complex array of predictions about the sensory information that will come from extending my arm, lifting the half-full mug, smelling the coffee's aroma and so on. What takes up my attention are the predictions I get wrong – perhaps the mug was more/less full or hotter/colder than I expected. Instead of wasting our precious cognitive resources attending to what we already know, it is more efficient to only pay attention to the predictions we get wrong – what are known as 'prediction errors'.

A silly yet wonderful example of PP in practice is tickling. It is well known that we cannot tickle ourselves. PP, and a clever experiment, provides us with an explanation of why this is the case. When we try to tickle ourselves, we can too accurately predict how it will feel. Researchers found that this is true even if we are in control of a mechanical hand – unlike another person, we can still too accurately predict its movements. But when the movements of the mechanical hand are automatically delayed by a fraction of a second, people are then able to tickle themselves – suddenly the sensations caused by the mechanical hand's movements become unpredictable.[8]

Once we understand the role that expectation plays in dictating our feelings and attention, we begin to see it everywhere. (In fact, this itself is a feature of our predictive minds, commonly known as the 'confirmation bias': when we expect something to be the case, we tend to look for evidence that confirms our expectations and downplay evidence that goes against them.[9])

I will briefly consider a few more examples here. The first is our perception of threats. Our expectations work largely unconsciously and automatically to filter the information we pay attention to – making some features of our situation more salient than others. When we expect our partner to be angry, for example, we tend to look for signs of anger in their facial expressions and bodily posture. We might end up 'seeing' their anger where others would see irritability or frustration.[10] This is a relatively innocuous example. More serious are cases where policemen in a violent area see a young adult holding a firearm where the rest of us might see them simply taking their hands out of their pocket.[11] It matters whether our expectations help us see reality more or less clearly.

This example points to the influence that contextual cues have on our expectations. The 'situationist' literature in psychology is made up of numerous studies that show the importance of situational factors – in particular, other people – in us predicting what is going on.[12] For instance, the infamous 'bystander experiments' show that our tendency to help someone we cannot see but who is screaming in pain (played by an actor), drops from 70 per cent to 7 per cent in the presence of another person (also an actor) who is not helping.[13]

In fact, it may be that a similar process underlies the well-known placebo effect. Researchers have found that taking a sugar pill can make us feel better even if we have already been told that the drug is a placebo.[14] It may be that the act of taking a dose of treatment prescribed by a medical professional is enough to make us more confident that we will get better soon. These changes in our expectations may make us more likely to switch on the body's natural healing processes.[15]

When our expectations of getting better are low, it makes sense to stay in 'fight–flight–freeze mode' and deal with the threats and demands of our environment. But when our expectations of getting better are high, it makes more sense to switch to 'rest-and-digest mode' and use stored energy to repair ourselves. This process may underlie the fact that healing and longevity are influenced by non-medical factors, such as having close relationships or a sense of purpose.[16] When we expect that getting better (and staying alive) is going to be worth our while, we may be more likely to devote our internal resources towards doing so.

Which brings us to our final example, to do with our perceptions of usefulness and worth. We use contextual cues and other generalisations to predict whether any given activity is worth our time. For instance, the psychologist Carol Dweck, in her book *Mindset*, shows how students with a 'fixed mindset' use external feedback and labels to predict their success at a given task.[17]

For example, if a student has previously been told they are good at maths, they are more likely to try harder in their maths class. However, on receiving a bad score in a maths exam, they are also more likely to assume they are not as good at maths as they thought they were, and give up. In contrast, Dweck shows how students with a 'growth mindset' do not use external feedback and labels in the same way to predict their future success. Instead, they take negative feedback as a sign that they need to work differently in order to succeed in the future.

I imagine you have had a similar experience with issues of procrastination and self-control. Self-control is costly – it sacrifices immediate rewards in favour of uncertain rewards in the long term.[18] If our expectations of long-term success are low – in other words, if we're not confident that we will achieve our long-term goal – it makes sense to seek more reliable forms of gratification in the short term. This is one of the main reasons we so frequently procrastinate. It is also why breaking up our long-term goal into more immediate, achievable goals can be such an effective way of overcoming it.

Getting by

All these examples show how our expectations can either help or hinder us in seeing the world as it really is. But surely we can't get things too wrong? Wouldn't we cease to function if we were always under this illusion?

Yes and no. On the one hand, our expectations effectively guide us through the world. Our expectations make us experts at living our own lives. They help us respond to the world with a repertoire of sophisticated, fine-tuned behaviours that we have built up over time according to our best guess of reality.[19]

On the other hand, we do not always need an accurate picture of reality. Evolutionary biologists know this well – our perceptions of reality only have to be accurate enough for them to be sufficiently adaptive.[20] We don't need to flourish. We just need to get by.

Consider, for example, the evolution of the eye. In the initial stage of its evolution, a single sheet of light-sensitive cells means that an organism can see the difference between night and day, which gives it an advantage over diurnal and nocturnal predators. In later stages, the formation of a shallow cup over this sheet means that an organism can detect the direction of light via shadows on the single sheet of light-sensitive cells, and therefore can detect the direction of potential predators. In the most advanced stages, the eye evolves a much deeper cup until it resembles something much like a pinhole camera, which means the organism can detect a faint image.

At each of these stages of evolution, the eye that's formed creates an evolutionary advantage for the organism.[21] Even if none of these eyes comes close to the accurate images formed by our fully developed human eyes, they nonetheless give the organism an advantage over their prey, predators and competition.

The point is that our expectations could, at least in principle, work the same way. Our predictive map of reality may help us see reality more clearly than we would without it. However, like the primitive versions of the eye, it could still be extremely inaccurate in comparison to the complexities of the human and natural environments we live in.

Cognitive architecture: you are what you see

Seeing with our bodies

In Chapters One and Two, I argued that our achievements will not bring us lasting satisfaction – they will never be enough; they are only the tip of the iceberg. We don't see this, however, because we see reality through the lens of our expectations, which reflects our practical goals and concerns. We are too busy predicting what will happen next and how we can adjust our behaviour accordingly to achieve our goals more effectively. In short: we live in the future, stuck in our problem-solving bubbles.

But where do our goals and expectations come from, and how much should we trust them? That will be the main topic of the rest of this chapter. I will show that our goals and expectations provide us with a narrow and limited view of what's possible. We will begin with our emotional bodies. Our embodied emotions are the foundations of our cognitive architecture.[22]

When we look out at the world we do not tend to see it in a dispassionate way. We imbue features of our environment with meaning depending on how they make us feel. Once we attach an emotional meaning to something, it can be very hard to see things differently. For example, on recently breaking up with your partner, you may feel awful and heartbroken. Those around you may know that you will soon get over it, but you cannot so easily see things that way. The other good things in your life, including the prospect of having another, more suitable relationship, seem more like abstract ideas than a likely reality.

We do not tend to realise just how closely our emotions are linked to the way we see the world. Advice from others to 'get over it' or logical reasons to see things differently are often insufficient because, so often, we simply take how we see things to be how they really are. When we see the straight stick bent in the water, we may know that it is an illusion caused by the refraction of light, but we still *see* the stick as bent. Our emotional experiences of the world, shaped by our largely unconscious expectations, are the same.[23]

Not only do we see the world through our emotions, we *feel* it. As we saw in Chapter One, we experience our emotions in our body: physiological changes (hearts racing, guts churning[24]), facial expressions (frowning, smiling[25]) and behavioural tendencies (moving towards, turning away[26]). Returning to the example above, you do not just see your break up as a bad thing for you; you also feel it as gut wrenching and heartbreaking. Likewise, we do not just see a situation as dangerous; we are motivated to fight, flee or freeze in response. We see the world through how it feels in our body.

Our physiological changes and behavioural tendencies are built upon the totality of our lived experience – even if our emotions can go widely awry, they still represent *possible* ways of seeing the world. We might irrationally worry that we left the gas on when we left the house, for example, and feel the tension in our bodies created by the desire to go home and check. Even if there's only a slim possibility that we did in fact leave the gas on, it is nonetheless possible.

It is possibilities and probabilities – our expectations, with varying degrees of certainty – that dictate how we see the world. According to PP theory, we never see things as they actually are. We only ever see our best guesses of reality. Normally our bodies are quite accurate predictors – reliably informing us of when we are hungry, sitting down, standing up or in pain.[27] When the tension in our bodies is telling us what's possible, we tend to listen to it.

This is why our bodily state can have such a profound impact on our lives. When our bodies feel good, we tend to perceive the world as good. The converse is also true. For instance, even mild bodily infections make us feel confused and fatigued. Conversely, a good, exhausting bout of exercise can lift our mood and make us feel, at times, euphoric.[28] Our body and mind are not separable. They act in sync, continuously updating our predictive map of reality.

Stuck inside our problem-solving bubble

Of course, we do sometimes see past our emotional, embodied perceptions. We like to think that we are above our more 'primitive' or 'basic' emotions, such as anger, fear, disgust and jealousy, as well as so-called 'recalcitrant' emotions such as phobias and other irrational fears and dislikes.[29] In response to occasional 'outbursts of passion' we fall back on our cold, hard capacities for reason, which seemingly provide us with a more 'objective' view of reality.

Although I agree our emotions often get things wrong in this way, I think it's a mistake to think our capacities for reason do much better. The distinction between emotion and reason is not as clear-cut as we like to think it is. We may use thoughts and beliefs to regulate our emotions, but our cognition is also strongly influenced by our emotional states.[30] In particular, the way we see and think about the world is heavily influenced by our *mood*.

Our moods are subtle. In contrast to our emotions, which tend to be caused by discrete events in our lives, and motivate us to quickly respond to them, our moods are much more pervasive.[31] We may feel anxious about having to give a talk in the afternoon, for example. But we may feel in an anxious mood about nothing in particular – life *in general* may simply seem threatening. Our moods can be such an all-encompassing and pervasive way of seeing the world that we often don't notice them. They form the background colour of our lives.[32] They are the lens through which we see reality.

(For instance, what mood are you in now? Do you feel expansive or compressed? Do you feel connected to your environment or separate from it? And, before answering these questions, did you know what mood you were in?)

There is a tragic irony here: the fact that moods colour the way we see ourselves, others and our environment is the reason they are so hard to spot. This is perhaps most tragic when it comes to stress. We have already seen how bad chronic stress can be for our physical and mental health. And yet, prior to having health problems or a mental breakdown, we have a remarkable ability, on a conscious level, to adapt to chronic states of stress. It is in the nature of stress to be all consuming, but in a way that focuses our attention elsewhere – to all the demands and pressures on our time, and all the problems we have to solve.

As the philosopher Dan Haybron notes in his book *The Pursuit of Unhappiness*, one of the defining features of stress is that it 'compresses' us – makes us narrow our focus and 'hunker down'. We have too much to do in too little time. Our bodies may feel 'small and pinched'. But, somewhat tragically, we tend to be too busy and preoccupied with 'insane' demands to notice.[33] It might not be until we catch our facial expression in the mirror or notice how sluggishly we're walking up the stairs at night that we get an idea of the mood we've been in throughout most of the day.

Haybron argues that this inability to see past our moods can happen to all of us, on a mass scale.[34] Consider, for example, two environments. The first is a busy, noisy, congested urban environment in which people tend to be stressed, tense, irritable, distracted and self-absorbed. The second is a slower, quieter, spacious coastal town in which people tend to be at ease, untroubled, quick to laugh, expansive and self-assured. The difference between these two environments is vast. Most of us, if given the choice, would say they'd prefer to live in the latter. And yet, if you asked people in the more stressful environment how they were doing, they might say they were doing just fine – busy, and a bit stressed out, but getting on with it nonetheless.

This is supported by life satisfaction surveys. When people are asked how satisfied they are with their life as a whole, they tend to report being satisfied – neither overly satisfied, nor too dissatisfied (things could be better, but they could also be worse). However, national health statistics tell a very different story. In the US, for instance, 43 per cent suffer adverse health effects from stress. Moreover, the one-year rate of mental illness in the US, which includes depression, anxiety, substance abuse and impulsive control disorders, is 26 per cent – over a quarter of the population.[35]

These are shocking statistics. We may think that our lives are going okay without realising that we are stuck in our own problem-solving bubble. We are often more concerned with our own internal to-do lists than our overall health and wellbeing. Occasionally, we might catch a glimpse of life outside our bubble, such as when we go on a relaxing holiday and our mood is temporarily elevated. But, for those who don't have the luxury of taking such a break, they are likely to continue focusing on the things they can control at the expense of their ongoing physical and mental health.

When our problem-solving bubble becomes who we are

One thing we can say about our moods is that, eventually, they will change. We may wake up in a different mood to the one we had before we went to sleep. Or an unexpected event may be put us in a different mood, such as the kindness of a stranger or a friend asking us for help. This is not the case for our personality. Our personality traits can be viewed as relatively permanent mood states that we apply to most of the situations we face. Although our personality can change over time, it tends to be a more stable part of who we are.

Personality psychologists make a big deal of what they call the 'Big Five' personality traits: extroversion, openness, neuroticism, agreeableness and conscientiousness.[36] Unlike popular personality tests that tell you about your personality 'type', it is only how people score on the Big Five dimensions of personality that has been shown to have a significant impact on their lives. For instance, those who score highly on the trait of agreeableness tend to do well at work. People high in conscientiousness tend to live five to six years longer than people low in conscientiousness. And people high in extroversion tend to be happier and have better quality relationships.

It's important to note a few things about what the Big Five personality traits are (and are not). First, they are dimensional. Everyone falls somewhere along each of the five dimensions of personality – scoring high or low on any dimension does not necessarily mean the same thing as having a good or bad personality. For example, people high in agreeableness may do better at work, but are less likely to start a revolution.

Second, personality is not destiny. Although the Big Five predict some stable life outcomes, they do not dictate everything that happens to us. As we saw in Chapter One, in some situations, we may have acquired what Brian Little calls 'free traits' – generalised habits that go against our personality traits, which we have developed in order to achieve a long-term goal. Little gives the example of himself as a staunch introvert who nonetheless developed the trait of speaking in front of large numbers of people as a lecturer and public speaker.[37]

Last, our personality traits do not act independently of our situation. If we are more agreeable in nature, this does not mean we'll act nicely to everyone, no matter what mood or context we're in. In fact, our personality traits may work partly by putting ourselves in particular kinds of situations. For instance, people with high levels of self-control do not just have stronger willpower. They are also better at selecting situations where there are no temptations to be found.[38]

These three points all suggest that our personality traits are more flexible than we might think. However, despite this flexibility, they still have a large impact on our behaviour and how we see the world. The psychologist Daniel Nettle gives the following example of a fictional character called Julian:

> Julian is typically enthusiastic. He is drawn to fusion music, psychodrama, self-sufficient farm living, and travel writing all within a short life. It is as if there is a constant quest for new ways of experiencing the world and expressing his experience of it. He finds a new domain and becomes tremendously, infectiously excited and activated by it. Over time, though, these feelings fade, and in place of enthusiasm come doubt and worry about the future.[39]

To Julian, all of these things may have seemed very real at the time. Like the previous example of suffering from a recent break up, it may have been extremely difficult for Julian to have seen things otherwise in each situation. However, to the personality psychologist, Julian has simply seen his circumstances unfold through the lens of being open to new experiences (high in openness) but without the discipline and self-control to turn them into more concrete, long-term projects (low in conscientiousness).

The takeaway point, again, is that we don't see things for how they really are. Our personality traits determine the *general concerns* we are highly sensitive to, from arousal and reward (extroversion) and the new and unfamiliar (openness) to dangers and losses (neuroticism), social intimacy (agreeableness) and achievement (conscientiousness). These may be good general strategies for dealing with many of life's problems. However, any amount of employing one strategy detracts from employing alternative strategies. By definition, this is what our personality traits do – they prioritise one set of concerns (for example, the new and familiar) over another (for example, achievement).

Like our moods, our personality traits are subtle. As we saw in the case of Julian, they dictate what we see as valuable and what is under our control. This, in turn, blinds us to many different ways of seeing our situation. Instead of noticing the impact our personality, moods and emotions are having on our view of reality, we tend to simply accept things as they appear.

This may work for a while, or even most of the time. But it is still a narrow and limited way of seeing ourselves, others and our environment. As a result, in both the short and long terms, we may end up being consumed by many issues and problems that don't really matter, and blind ourselves to many of the things that do.

Social context: we see reality through the lives of others

Our social realities

So far, we have seen where our goals and expectations come from, with a focus on our cognitive architecture – our emotions, moods and personality traits. These things make some parts of reality more salient to us than others. On the one hand, this helps us effectively achieve our goals. On the other hand, it leaves us with a narrow and limited view of reality. We are confined to our embodied, problem-solving bubbles, and we rarely see outside them.

We do not, however, live in a vacuum. Even if we can't see outside our problem-solving bubbles, our bubbles are still formed by the outside world. In particular, our goals and expectations are formed by our *social context*.[40] In this section, we will look at the social forces that shape our expectations – how we see reality through the lives of others.

This is most obvious at the beginning of our lives. As we saw in Chapter One, when we are infants, we are entirely dependent on our caregivers for our survival and wellbeing.[41] We see the world through their eyes (as well as their facial expressions, tone of voice, smell and touch). Is the world a safe and secure place, or is it scary and threatening? Can I rely on others for support, or are other people, including those closest to me, not to be trusted?

In modern, individualistic societies, we like to think that as we mature, we become self-contained individuals – rational, autonomous and self-sufficient. This is not the case, however.

Instead of losing our attachment relationships, we *distribute* them. We still see reality through the lives of others. We just have relationships with a greater number of people. In addition, the people we are in relationship with also look towards us to find out what's possible.

So, let us begin at the beginning. As infants, we are attuned to seeing faces from birth, and quickly learn how to imitate them.[42] We do not simply demand things from our caregivers – we soon learn how to see the world through their eyes. It is through this process, for example, that a state of confusion caused by a loud noise can turn into a smile after being comforted by our caregiver and imitating their positive coos and exaggerated facial expressions.[43]

This process of learning how to see the world through the eyes of our caregivers grows in sophistication over our infancy. By nine months, infants can follow the gaze or pointing gestures of their caregivers, again using imitation to grasp the emotional meanings of the objects being pointed to. By 12 months, infants can initiate this activity themselves, pointing towards objects that might seem surprising, funny, scary and so on, and learning more about the reality of those objects through the reactions of their caregivers. In fact, by 14 months, by which time children are more independently mobile, they already avoid objects that their caregivers have shown fear towards, even in their absence.[44]

Our tendency to imitate and learn from the behaviour and feelings of others never goes away. Consider, for example, how it feels to enter a room where everyone is quiet and sombre. We are likely to automatically 'catch' the emotional atmosphere and feel something similar. This is not simply because we want to fit in or are easily susceptible. Instead, like infants, we are constantly trying to grasp the reality of our situation and use the people around us to learn what's going on. (An unfortunate consequence of this phenomenon is the effectiveness of canned laughter used in TV sitcoms – we're more likely to be attuned to the funniness of a joke in the presence of laughter.[45])

This does not mean we suck up the atmosphere of whatever is going on around us. We are still selective in our imitation. Research shows that we are more likely to imitate people who we think are authoritative.[46] For instance, we are more likely to mimic the panic of airplane assistants than the panic of our fellow passengers. We also tend to imitate people less if we deem them to be of lower status, and vice versa – all those nods, smiles, and unconscious mimicry of bodily postures and tone of voice we do when talking to someone, establishing how much they are like us, how comfortable we can feel in their presence, and, most importantly, how much we can learn from them.[47]

Of course, we direct the majority of our attention towards the people we are in caring relationships with – our friends, family and partners. It is from these relationships that we learn most about the world around us – who we are, what we are capable of, and how much support we have in achieving our goals. Research shows that we literally 'sync up' with our loved ones, imitating not just their expressive behaviours, but also their physiology, such as heart rate. Through this process of synchronisation, we literally gain a shared perspective with our loved ones, seeing and feeling the world in the same ways they do.[48]

These effects are subtle because, like our moods and personality traits, they are pervasive. Social mimicry and synchronisation happen quickly and unconsciously, and they happen all the time. In the same way that we are always using our bodies to find out what is important – tracking and regulating our levels of hunger, thirst, energy and so on – we are always using the behaviour and feelings of others to understand the world around us.

Consider the following example described by the philosopher Tom Cochrane in his book *The Emotional Mind*. You are walking along the street with a friend and come across a person vomiting. To you, this may seem disgusting or worrying. But your friend may find it amusing. This might instantly down-regulate your initial emotional response – you might take the episode less seriously, or even 'take on' your friend's amusement. Or your friend might adjust their initial emotional response to match yours. Either way, within a matter of moments, a new equilibrium is likely to form – one that is not entirely your own.[49]

This dance of emotional synchronisation – remarkably similar to the one between infants and their caregivers – extends to more abstract levels. Social norms and values, which we will look at in more detail below, can be viewed as ways in which people mutually adjust their feelings and behaviour to fall in sync with each other.[50] We should be sad at funerals, but happy at weddings. In these situations, we don't need to work out what to feel entirely on the fly – the social groups we belong to have already prescribed their meanings for us.

Under the influence

Once we understand how much we see the world through the lives of others, we can begin to see how powerful our social contexts can be. From social network research, for instance, we know that one of the best predictors of a wide range of life outcomes – from obesity to suicide – are the people you are connected to (in other words, whether you know other people who are obese, or who have committed or attempted suicide).[51] The lesson from such research is a harsh one: if you want to change your behaviour, change your friends.

As a specific example, consider something that matters to most people: money. In Chapter One, we briefly looked at findings from the study of subjective wellbeing on the relationship between income and happiness. After having enough money to meet our basic needs, it seems that further increases in income don't make us any happier. We can see this on a national scale, where average levels of life satisfaction have stayed constant over the past 50 years, despite a threefold increase in GDP (what is known as the 'Easterlin Paradox').[52] And we can see this on an individual level, where, in the US, increases in annual income above $75,000 do not tend to make people lastingly happier.[53]

To many people, these findings ring true. Of course, money can't buy you happiness! (But it can certainly help meet your basic needs.) And yet, when it comes to our goals and concerns, we tend to always want more of it. According to one study, when asked the question, 'How much more money would you need to be satisfied?' both rich and poor people tend to provide the same answer: they all desire about three times the amount of money they currently have.[54] This is astounding. Why would a billionaire – in the top 0.1 per cent of the wealthiest people on the planet – not be satisfied with their financial situation? Why are the super-rich – or, for that matter, the middle class – just as concerned about making more money as those with very little in comparison?

The answer is to do with who we compare ourselves to. We do not see the world from an objective standpoint. Instead, we see it through the behaviour and feelings of those around us. We do not just want to keep up with the Joneses to look good. It is the Joneses who inform us of what *is* good. From the people around us – who typically have the same level of resources and opportunities, or beliefs and values – we find out what is desirable and what is possible.[55]

We are constantly motivated to improve our lives and we look towards others as a guide to both what and how much we can achieve. What matters in this process is our 'social reference group' – the group of people who are sufficiently 'like us' that we can model our goals and aspirations on what they do.[56]

In fact, this is why good role models can be so empowering – and why bad role models can be the complete opposite. When it comes to understanding what's possible, seeing is believing. For example, children from a deprived background can be told repeatedly that if only they tried harder at school then they could go to university and get a good job. However, without contact with people who have done exactly that, this advice is hard to take seriously. They only need to look around to see that such advice doesn't seem to apply to people 'like them'.

In working out our goals and concerns, we look towards the people around us to find out what's possible. This strategy makes sense. However, our social reference group can sway us in less healthy ways. For example, wanting to be and look as healthy as our friends do is often a good thing. However, the same kinds of influences can also make us think it is good idea to go on extreme diets and be dangerously thin. Looking towards other people to find out what's possible is only a good strategy if the people around us are doing good things.

This is how we can end up adopting goals and concerns that are in conflict with our personal interests and enjoyments. Individuals in our social networks may not have the same interests and enjoyments that we do. In adopting similar behaviours to those around us, we can feel as if we are doing them because we 'should' rather than because we really care about them. We can feel 'alienated' from ourselves, as if we are not the authors of our own lives.[57] Our wider community can shape us in ways that do not fit with who we really are.

One of the ways in which we work out who we are is by internalising social roles and labels. We may think of ourselves as a parent, employee, young, old, black, white and so on. These labels can often act as a double-edged sword.[58] On the one hand, being given a particular label can inspire us to live up to it. If we think of ourselves as musical, for example, we are more likely to engage in musical projects, to practise more, not give up so easily and so on. On the other hand, the same label can limit us. We might not engage in other artistic practices, such as drawing and painting, as much as we do with music. We might also react badly to any sign that we might not be musical, such as doing badly in a music exam.

Of course, this trade-off is not necessarily a bad thing. We can learn to endorse our labels for as long as they serve us, and then update our conceptions of ourselves when they no longer do. But there is always the danger that we will conform to the labels we have been given without testing whether or not they are true.

Personal narratives: who are we, anyway?

I hope you are beginning to see that we don't really see the world as it is. Instead, we see reality through the lens of our goals and expectations, which make us fall for the illusion that, 'if only we had ___ then we'd be happy'. How we fill in the blank is determined by our personal histories – our emotions, moods and personality – and by our social context – in particular, people who are 'like us'. Still, we might think that underneath all these things we know what's important. Perhaps in our more reflective moments, we can still see what is valuable in the world and what we care about. In the remainder of this chapter, I will show that even our values and identity are narrow and limited in scope. We do not see the world as it is, and that includes what we care about.

Stories of ourselves

One of the ways in which we simultaneously discover and create what we care about is through our *life story* – the narrative that ties together many of the distal, fragmented parts of our personality, such as our needs, personality traits, goals and commitments. When we elaborate on the question 'what do you do?' we give people part of our life story. For example, we may tell people that we're a baker, but came to the profession late after first trying to be a doctor only to realise that working in a hospital was too stressful. When we create our life narratives, we do not simply recall the exact chain of events that led to where we are now – that is not how narratives work. Instead, we pick out the most important events and omit the less important ones.

Much like memory, this is a constructive process.[59] Each time we tell our story, different events will seem more or less important, depending on our current context. It is, ultimately, more of a fiction than a factual record. Nonetheless, it is the fiction we tell to make sense of our lives.[60]

Our life stories typically show how our lives have been, and are likely to continue to be, worthwhile. They are often redemptive in nature: for example, how we overcame a setback early on in life to create the life we have now – a failed relationship, not trying hard at school, having a difficult background and so on. Not only does this highlight the things of value we currently have in our lives, it also shows the value of our agency in bringing them about.[61] We use our life stories to communicate the worth of our lives and ourselves to others.

But from where do we get our stories of value and worth? In the previous section, we saw that our practical goals and concerns are often the result of social comparisons. We may think that we really need three times the amount of money we currently have. But that might largely be the result of comparing our current situation to a particular social reference group. It is hard to see outside our social bubble and take a more objective point of view of what we need.

We can say a similar thing about our values and norms. Our ideas about what makes our life worthwhile are largely a product of our wider social context. This is something we tend to resist in more individualistic cultures, where we like to think that we can be our most 'authentic self', following our own passions and desires, free from the shackles of community and conformity.[62] This is, however, not true. To flexibly cooperate on a large scale, we follow norms and shared values. This is the case in all cultures, even though the predominant kinds of norms and values differ from culture to culture.[63] The result is that even our most authentic selves and life stories reflect the social contexts we live in.

We can see how our values reflect our social context by looking at data from the World Value Survey, which tracks changes in values across the world.[64] Values can be mapped onto two broad domains. The first is 'survival' versus 'self-expression' values. Survival values concern physical and economic security, whereas self-expression values are about personal growth and creativity. The second domain is 'traditional' versus 'secular rational' values. Traditional values concern authority and community, whereas secular rational values are about individual rights and autonomy. People might value all these things, but tend to care about some sets of values more than others.[65]

What determines the kinds of values we have? The simple answer is our wider socioeconomic circumstances. Within deprived circumstances, people largely care about economic and physical security (survival values) and depend more on others and their community (traditional values). The wealthier that nations become, the more people drift away from survival and traditional mindsets. Within affluent Western nations, people begin to care about things beyond financial and material security, such as authenticity and self-development (self-expression values), and become more independent of the group, putting more emphasis on the individual (secular rational values).[66]

These divides also exist within nations. For instance, within Western nations, those living in poverty, who tend to live in more rural areas, still have more survival and traditional values. In contrast, rich people, who tend to be concentrated in cities, care more about personal autonomy and human rights.

These changes are not to be underestimated. Without having to worry about securing food, shelter and protection from violence, we can instead focus on developing our interests and enjoyments, having intimate relationships and making the world a better place. As the economist Christian Welzel puts it, in his book *Freedom Rising*, 'Fading existential pressures open people's minds, making them prioritize freedom over security, autonomy over authority, diversity over uniformity, and creativity over discipline.'[67]

Now, I am not saying that these changes in our values are necessarily good. As we will see in Chapter Eight, the affluence of modernity was built on the back of mass human and environmental exploitation, and continues to be so. My point is merely to show that changes in socioeconomic status bring about significant changes in the things we care about. In constructing our life stories, it may feel as if we are discovering and creating what really matters – what makes our lives and ourselves worthwhile. And yet, the values that make up our life stories are limited to our wider social contexts. They are, ultimately, a useful social fiction.

The things we care about

Changes in our values can literally change our minds. For instance, research shows that people in more 'individualistic' cultures think differently to people in more 'collectivist' cultures.[68] The difference between individualism and collectivism maps onto the domain of 'traditional' versus 'secular rational' values, described above. Collectivist cultures are all about the group: valuing harmony, interdependence and conformity. In contrast, individualistic cultures are all about the individual: valuing autonomy, personal achievement and uniqueness.

These cultural differences have an impact on a wide range of attitudes and behaviour, from how people think about their identities to how they praise and blame others. For instance, when people in individualistic cultures are asked to draw a diagram of how their self relates to the others (what is known as a 'sociogram'), they typically represent their self with a large circle in the centre of the piece of paper, surrounded by other, smaller circles representing their loved ones, friends, acquaintances and so on. In contrast, people in collectivist cultures tend to represent their self with a small circle on the edge of the piece of paper, which is part of a much larger circle in the centre that represents the group. Similar studies show that, 'individualists' consider themselves to be separate from their friends and family, whereas 'collectivists' see themselves as inseparable from the group.[69]

Again, these cultural differences in how people see the world reflect their material circumstances. Collectivist cultures have typically been built on large-scale cooperative endeavours, such as rice farming. In contrast, modern individualistic societies rely on large-scale cooperative behaviour, but via specialisation and trade, not communal work and collective labour.[70] To a member of a more individualistic culture, it may simply seem as if they are the centre of their own universe – that they should spend the majority of their days thinking about their own goals and achievements, their intrinsic attributes and the quality of their own efforts. This way of seeing reality, however, is a direct result of their social context. Someone in a more collectivistic culture would see things completely differently, thinking first and foremost about the group.

Another distinguishing feature of social norms and values is how 'tight' and 'loose' they are.[71] Both kinds of norms regulate cooperative behaviour, but differ in the extent to which they can be broken. 'Loose' social norms are guidelines for what people should care about and how they should behave, but still allow room for individual flexibility and autonomy. In contrast, 'tight' social norms are much more strict – the costs of nonconformity, or simply thinking otherwise, tend to be severe. An example of 'tight' social norms is the set of values found in 'honour cultures' in the Southern states of the US. These cultures were typically built on herding and pastoral practices – a mode of production that is vulnerable to stealing from outsiders. As a result, cultures of violence, honour (including hospitality and chivalry) and revenge emerged.[72]

The tighter our social norms are, the harder it is to see beyond them. The way we see reality becomes fixed and rigid. The same thing can happen on an individual level. Some theorists have argued that particular mental disorders – such as OCD (obsessive compulsive disorder), depression and addiction – can be characterised as 'over-rigid' mental conditions.[73] A depressed person, for instance, is trapped in a narrow way of thinking, often ruminating over negative thoughts about their self, the world and the future. In fact, SSRIs – a common type of anti-depressant that increases serotonin levels in the brain – may work to the extent that serotonin temporarily frees up people's over-rigid cognitive system, creating room for more flexible thoughts and behaviour.[74]

The rigidity created by 'tight' social norms is, however, a matter of degree. All norms and values, to some extent, make us see the world in a fixed, narrow way. As do our personal narratives – our relatively stable views of ourselves, the world and the future. These things determine how we see reality, and are largely a feature of our social context. Instead of seeing ourselves as independent of our circumstances, we should acknowledge that we are a product of them. We may think that we see the world as it really is – that our values are right and that our lives are worthwhile. But the fact is, if we had grown up in a different social context in another part of the world we would have thought that a different set of values were right and that our lives were worthwhile, despite looking vastly different.

This failure to see outside of our problem-solving bubbles and our social context can have dramatic consequences. This was the idea behind the infamous 'obedience experiments' conducted by the social psychologist Stanley Milgram.[75] The experimental set up is simple: the experimenter – who is wearing a white coat, much like a scientist or a doctor – asks the participant to deliver an electric shock to a fellow participant as part of a learning exercise. The participant being shocked is, in fact, played by an actor and is not receiving any electric shocks. Milgram found that most participants did as the experimenter asked. Moreover, the majority of participants in Milgram's series of studies delivered electric shocks that were shown on the dial to be potentially dangerous, and continued to do so despite hearing the screams and protests of the other participant/actor.[76]

Milgram's obedience experiments were designed to show how ordinary people could do terrible things as a result of blindly conforming to authority – what Hannah Arendt referred to as the 'banality of evil'.[77] Typically, we trust and adhere to the authority of people in white coats – scientists and doctors. In most circumstances, this is a reasonable thing to do. The problem is that we don't always have the cognitive resources available to go against our habitual responses when necessary – to question whether or not they are appropriate in our current situation.[78] Milgram's obedience experiments show just how damaging this lack of awareness and flexibility can be.

The social contexts we are in can be viewed as Milgram's obedience experiment writ large. We think that what we care about is what really matters. But our values and norms largely reflect our wider material circumstances. To find out what's possible, we don't normally look outside these contexts. Instead, we read the same newspapers as those around us, we spend our time with likeminded others, and largely confirm our pre-existing opinions and beliefs. Instead of going about our lives thinking that we are mostly wrong, we tend to think the opposite – that how we see things is how they really are. It is this certainty and confidence in what we already know – including who we are and what we care about – that blinds us to what really matters.

Waking up

Over the past three chapters, we have looked at the wrong way to think about happiness – that happiness comes from control.

First, we think that happiness is about getting everything in our lives just right – the perfect job, relationships, family, home, body, mind and so on. With these stable circumstances in place, we will have a lasting sense of meaning and satisfaction. The problem with this way of thinking about happiness is that it is simply untrue. No matter what circumstances we have, we will still be insecure.

Second, we think happiness comes from controlling everything in our lives to our liking – to solve all our problems, protect ourselves from our fears and achieve all our goals. The problem with this way of thinking about happiness is that, by focusing only on the things we can control, we miss out on the other things in life that matter. All the achievements we make will merely be the tip of the iceberg.

Third, we think we know what we need to be happy – what feels good and bad, who is right and wrong, what is acceptable and unacceptable. In this chapter, we have seen how this sense of certainty is illusory. The problem with going to war with reality is that, in the process, we blind ourselves to what really matters. We hold on to a limited and narrow view of reality and fail to see the bigger picture.

The alternative is to wake up: to acknowledge our insecurity and embrace uncertainty. We need to rethink happiness – switch our focus from control to understanding. This will be the subject of Part II.

Part II

FOUR

Uncertainty

> To be a good human being is to have a kind of
> openness to the world, an ability to trust uncertain
> things beyond your own control.
> *Martha Nussbaum*[1]

In Part I, we looked at the wrong way to think about happiness. We want more security and stability than is possible. We try to achieve it through power and control, which is limited. And we are overly confident and certain in the face of complexity and uncertainty. The control strategy doesn't work. The problem with going to war with reality is that reality will ultimately win.

In Part II, we will look at an alternative way of thinking about happiness. Before doing so, however, it is worth understanding the appeal of the control strategy and going to war with reality. We only need to look around us to see that the strategy works to some extent. You are probably reading this somewhere comfortable – safe from any immediate danger, and hopefully in reasonably good health. When you stop reading this, you will probably have food to eat, water to drink, a place to sleep and so on. These circumstances of relative security have come about through a long process of control and a certainty mindset. If we go to war with reality, with enough (literal) blood, sweat and tears, we will win some of our battles.

It is also important to realise just how appealing – and necessary – going to war with reality can sometimes seem. After witnessing a significant loss, for example, in the grips of great suffering, reality can be unbearable. Of course, we would do everything in our power to change our circumstances. The fact that such suffering is inevitable at some point in our lives may be of little consolation.

In offering an alternative way of thinking about happiness, therefore, I do not want to rule out the control strategy completely. The war metaphor is a deliberate one. Despite the problems and atrocities of war, it may sometimes be necessary. We should, however, only engage in war and conflict as a last resort – when all other options have been fully explored. This is how we should think about happiness and our relationship to reality. Yes, life can sometimes be unbearable and we need to do everything we can to change things. But we do have an alternative. Instead of going to war with reality, we can strive for peace within it. The first step of this process is not control, but *understanding*.

Understanding reality may well be much harder than controlling it – there are no guarantees. Nor does it promise us a lasting sense of meaning and satisfaction. The outcome of the understanding strategy is not happiness in the way we normally think about it. It includes sadness as much as it includes joy, frustration as much as satisfaction, loneliness as much as connection, and so on. We can strive to alleviate the suffering we experience in our lives, but suffering will continue to pervade our experience. Instead of security, we can think about happiness as living well within insecurity.

Now, I understand that this may not seem instantly appealing. So we'll build up to it. Over the next three chapters, we will look at the three parts of the understanding strategy – the *outcome*, the *process* and the *mindset* – in the opposite order to how we did things in Part I. In that section, we looked at the three parts of the control strategy: the outcome as security and stability; the process as control and achievement; and the mindset as certainty and predictability. Put together, this way of thinking about happiness may help us improve our lives, and even be a bit happier as a result, but it also blinds us to what really matters.

In Part II, we will look at the outcome, process and mindset of the understanding strategy in reverse. This is deliberate. Instead of first thinking about the outcomes we want to achieve, understanding reality begins with how we can see the world as it is – ourselves, others and our environment. In this chapter, we will look at how to view reality – the mindset of happiness. We can replace our certainty with uncertainty. Instead of being confident in knowing what we need, what others and ourselves are like, and what is important, we can pay attention to what we don't know.

The mindset of uncertainty naturally leads on to the process of curiosity. This will be the topic of Chapter Five. Instead of controlling everything in our lives to our liking, we can be curious about our lives. We can appreciate and explore our whole selves and discover what we most care about and are truly capable of.

This process of curiosity is an ongoing one and will take us to unknown places. As we have already noted, the outcome is not one of security. In Chapter Six, I will show that, through the process of curiosity, we can learn how to live well within insecurity – how to improve our lives while acknowledging our insecurity. The unstable circumstances that we create may not provide us with a lasting sense of meaning and satisfaction, but they will give us the continual need for care and compassion. This is how we should think about happiness.

From control to understanding

In this chapter, we will look at how we can begin to switch our focus from control to understanding. We can go beyond our problem-solving bubbles, our habitual ways of seeing the world, and our narrow views of reality, and gain a deeper understanding of what really matters.

The divided mind

We have the option of making this switch – from control to understanding – because we have a divided mind.[2] On the one hand, we have capacities for control: they are about certainty, order, judgement, objectification, habit, achievement and stability. On the other hand, we have capacities for understanding: they are about the opposite – uncertainty, chaos, openness, connection, attention, curiosity and flexibility.

We need both capacities to successfully navigate our lives. We need certainty to act in ways that will reliably meet our needs. But we also need to remain open to new ways of thinking, feeling and acting well.

As an example, consider the writing of this book. Without some certainty that I could write it, and that doing so would be worthwhile, it wouldn't have made sense for me to take on such a project. I had to read a lot of books and sit in front of my laptop for a very long time. At times (mostly when it was sunny outside) it was awful. Instead of spending my time doing other valuable things, I decided to commit to this project. Without some degree of certainty over its success, it would probably have been better to commit to something else.

However, at no point did I know that writing this book would work out. I still don't know whether doing so will be worthwhile. At any point during the writing process, something could've happened that would've made it impossible. I could've been hit by a bus, or had a mental breakdown; or either of these things could've happened to someone I care about and had to look after. Alternatively, the idea for the book might have ended up being a bad one – what seemed interesting in my own mind may not be so insightful once written down. Or I might not be skilled enough to translate what is in my head into a book-length narrative that is both clear and intriguing.

Writing this book, then, requires being both sufficiently certain of its success and sufficiently open to it not working. Without the former, I would have given up writing it a long time ago. But without the latter, I wouldn't have been so open to the bits that are badly explained, to the gaps in my own knowledge, and to new ideas. In general, the lesson I learned was to discount a lot of my habitual thoughts, which continued to provide me with reasons to give up and do something else, or at least rewrite the whole thing. These thoughts seemed to be certain enough – the scenarios of failure they presented me with appeared very real. But I continued to learn that these judgements were never the whole story. There was always more I could do, and different ways of seeing things, which eventually made writing this book possible.

This is contrary to how the well-known Stoic philosopher, Seneca, put things over two millennia ago. He argued that:

> Putting things off is the biggest waste of life: it snatches away each day as it comes, and denies us the present by promising the future. The greatest obstacle to living is expectancy, which hangs upon tomorrow and loses today. You are arranging what lies in Fortune's control, and abandoning what lies in yours. What are you looking at? To what goal are you straining? The whole future lies in uncertainty: live immediately.[3]

Seneca is right that the 'whole future lies in uncertainty' – we really could get hit by a bus tomorrow, or befall some other unexpected tragedy. And he is right that, by putting things off, we put ourselves in 'Fortune's control'. But to advise that we should, therefore, live immediately – 'in the moment' – does not straightforwardly follow. Even if we can't be certain of the future, we can still predict that things will turn out in a particular way. Certainty is a matter of degree. Even though I couldn't be certain that writing this book would be worthwhile, I had a sufficient amount of certainty that it would. (Only time will tell whether or not I was right.)

Seneca was wrong to discount the future entirely. But his advice still rings true today because of the benefits that 'being present' provides. As the psychologist Ellen Langer notes, most of the time we are 'not here'.[4] When we are certain of how the future will go and how we're going to get there, we don't need to notice new things. We become less sensitive to our current context; less poised to take advantage of the opportunities all around us.

The divided brain

These differences in our mental state can be seen in different brain networks. The Task Specific Network has been shown to be active when we are fully present, focused on a specific task that takes up all our attention. In contrast, the Default Mode

Network is what is active the rest (and most) of the time. It has been linked with the narrative self – our constant inner chatter, daydreaming and thinking about the past and future (what is known as 'mental time travel'). The expression that we are not really 'present' is to some extent true. When we are not fully focused on the task at hand, we are literally exploring past and future scenarios that might better prepare us for what is going to happen.[5]

In his book *The Master and His Emissary*, the psychiatrist Iain McGilchrist looks in detail at the brain differences that might account for our capacities for control and understanding. He reviews a wide range of evidence in arguing that the two hemispheres of the brain have evolved to provide us with these two opposing, yet complementary, capacities. According to McGilchrist, we literally have a divided mind. He states that:

> The left hemisphere pays the narrow-beam, precisely focused, attention which enables us to get and grasp: it is the left hemisphere that controls the right hand with which we grasp something, and controls the aspects of language by virtue of which we say we have 'grasped' the meaning – made it certain and pinned it down. In contrast, the right hemisphere underwrites sustained attention and vigilance for whatever may be, without preconception. Its attention is not in the service of manipulation, but in the service of exploration and relation – to explore the world for what it is.[6]

McGilchrist shows how our consciousness moves seamlessly back and forth between the brain's two hemispheres, drawing on each as required, and often very rapidly. The difference between our two hemispheres can be summarised by the kind of attention they pay to the world: one type of attention is about control and manipulation; the other is about understanding and exploration.

The idea of the left and right brain hemispheres having distinct functions is a controversial one. Researchers have found exceptions to almost all of the functions that are generally associated with one hemisphere over the other, such as language being a function of the left hemisphere.[7] McGilchrist argues that these generalisations and exceptions can both be accommodated by his theory. But we do not need to accept the idea that our left and right hemispheres have different functions in order to take on what McGilchrist says about the difference between our capacities for control and understanding. Regardless of where in the brain these capacities are situated, we no doubt have the distinct abilities to either narrow our reality down to a certainty or open it up into possibility.

We can think of our capacities for control as providing us with a map and our capacities for understanding as helping us see the actual terrain. We typically take our map of reality for granted – as being accurate enough to predict the future and make realistic goals and plans. To be constantly aware of our present context – much like how a baby finds wonder in one moment to the next – is simply not necessary to achieve many of our goals. In fact, being continuously present would get in the way of staying focused on our goals and plans. As long as our map is good enough, we can get by on what we already know.[8]

However, sometimes we get stuck. In these contexts, we need to look up from our map and actually look around us. We will probably be surprised by what we see – after all, it is unlikely that our map of reality is completely accurate (as Seneca rightly noted, we can never be certain of the future). From looking at the actual terrain, we can hopefully learn enough to flexibly overcome the barriers we're up against and get ourselves unstuck. We can then update our map accordingly and continue merrily along our journey.

This analogy makes the process of switching between our capacities for control and understanding seem easy. It is anything but. The defining feature of our map of reality is that we can rely on it to act effectively – it provides us with a sufficient degree of certainty. This is not something to give up lightly. We do not know when to look down at our map and when to look up at the world around us – when to act on what we already know and when to think differently.

For some people, paying more attention to the unknown and thinking differently may come relatively easily. For others, it may be much harder to go beyond their stable ideas and practices. These differences in personality may be one of the most fundamental personality traits we have. Researchers who study the Big Five personality traits – which we looked at in Chapter Three – have shown that they map onto two 'meta-traits' of personality, which they call 'stability' and 'plasticity'. People who score high in the meta-trait of plasticity are more likely to draw upon their capacities for understanding. Conversely, people who score low on plasticity are more likely to seek control.

The meta-trait of plasticity is made up of two of the Big Five personality traits: extroversion and openness. Openness reflects people's tendency toward the new and unfamiliar. Extroversion reflects people's tendency toward arousal and reward. Together, plasticity is the general tendency toward *learning* and *exploration* – the creation of new goals, interpretations and strategies.

The opposite to plasticity can be seen clearly in what psychologists refer to as 'absolutist thinking styles'.[9] People with an absolutist thinking style are more likely to be dogmatic, with an all-or-nothing outlook on the world; they tend to place totally rigid demands on themselves and those around them; and when confronted with stresses and misfortunes, they often magnify and fixate on them. They are more likely to use words such as 'completely', 'totally' and 'definitely'.

We are constantly trying to work out how plastic or rigid we should be – when to open ourselves up to nuance and complexity, and when to be certain in what we already know. In Chapter Two, we looked at the problems involved in focusing too much on the things we can control. The remainder of the book is an attempt to redress the balance. We will begin by looking at the kinds of cultural practices that help us move away from trying to control our lives and instead cultivate our emotions of attention and understanding.

What we don't know

In this section, we will look at our emotional capacities for understanding in more detail – emotions such as awe, wonder, gratitude, compassion, forgiveness, hope and trust. Although these emotions are often viewed as 'spiritual' in nature, I will argue that there is nothing supernatural about them. Their defining feature is their focus on the 'unseen' – what lies beyond our current level of understanding. In addition to spiritual and religious practices, they are central to a number of other cultural practices, from art and creativity to spending time in nature and with others. These practices help us 'go beyond ourselves', 'lose control' and gain a deeper understanding of the world around us.

Emotions of attention

As we saw in Chapter Three, we see the world through our emotions and moods: fear makes the world seem scary; anxiety makes it seem threatening; joy makes life seem full of opportunity, and so on.[10] We don't just see the world in these ways, we feel them in our bodies: fear is entwined with our fight–flight–freeze response; when we're anxious, we'll feel on edge; when we feel joy, the space around us feels bright, boundless, even springy. Psychologists refer to these bodily interpretations of the world as 'affordances' – our bodily feelings represent possible ways of interacting with our environment.[11]

Most of our emotions are wrapped up in our practical goals and concerns. Fear, anxiety, panic and disgust, for example, are all designed to keep us safe from different kinds of potential harm. Love, sadness, guilt and shame are all designed to regulate our relationships. We have a range of emotions, however, that are less about how well we are doing, and more about paying attention to the world. The objects of these emotions are not necessarily seen as good or bad (like how the object of our fear feels bad). Instead, it is simply the attention we are paying to our surroundings that feels good. We do not necessarily want to have more or less of whatever we are paying attention to, but we do want to pay more attention to it. Just think of a baby, staring with utmost attention to the mobile dangling above them – they don't know whether the mobile is something that is either good or bad for them, but they know it is fascinating.[12]

We have a number of these 'emotions of attention': wonder, awe, interest, curiosity, delight, gratitude, contentment, serenity, bliss, ecstasy, peace of mind, tranquility, compassion, forgiveness, hope, trust, love. They tend to occur when we momentarily drop our practical concerns, and become open to *glimpses* of understanding – new possible ways for interacting with our environment. The philosopher and author Iris Murdoch called these experiences of 'unselfing':

> Our minds are continually active, fabricating an anxious, usually self-preoccupied, often falsifying veil which partially conceals our world ... The most obvious thing in our surroundings which is an occasion for 'unselfing' is what is popularly called beauty ... I am looking out of my window in an anxious and resentful state of mind ... Then suddenly I observe a hovering kestrel. In a moment everything is altered. The brooding self with its hurt vanity has disappeared. There is nothing now but kestrel.[13]

As Murdoch describes, these glimpses of what's possible often take up our full attention – this is the realm of beauty, wonder and other experiences that take us beyond our current limited understanding of the world and focus our attention on what we don't know.

Our emotions of attention, like other emotions, come with distinct physiological profiles and behavioural tendencies. In the 18th century, the philosopher and economist Adam Smith wrote that wonder arises 'when something quite new and singular is presented ... [and] memory cannot, from all its stores, cast up any image that nearly resembles this strange appearance'.[14] Smith went on to describe the distinctive bodily feeling associated with wonder: 'that staring, and sometimes that rolling of the eyes, that suspension of the breath, and that swelling of the heart'.[15] Wonder makes us stare and widen our eyes. The object of our attention is perplexing because we cannot rely on past experience to comprehend it. This leads to a suspension of breath, similar to the freezing response that kicks in when we are startled: we gasp and say 'wow!'

These kinds of experiences are often described as 'spiritual', 'transcendent' or 'mystical' in nature.[16] This makes sense – when we are attending to something that goes beyond our current understanding of the world, it can rightly seem mysterious. But even if the objects of our emotions of attention are mysterious, there is nothing mysterious about the emotions themselves. As we saw in the previous section, these capacities are what help us understand what's possible – they focus our attention on what we don't know: the 'unknown' or the 'unseen'. By drawing on these capacities, we can temporarily drop our habitual patterns of thought, feeling and behaviour and see reality more clearly.

This need not entail anything supernatural. We can always deepen our understanding of the world, including a hovering kestrel. Everything that makes up reality is infinitely complex. We can impose order on the world through our concepts and ideas, but reality will always have the power to surprise us.

These forms of heightened attention are often at the heart of spiritual teachings and practices.[17] However, they can also be taken up by naturalised, secular views of reality.[18] We can always see more in our situation, including things that we would typically classify as bad for us. Even in suffering, there are unknown possibilities.[19] This is, perhaps, what is at the heart of the religious concept of 'holiness' – seeing something in its entirety (its 'wholeness') – the possibilities that arise from its connections with everything else. The infinite complexities of reality are what make the unseen world vast, whether that world is natural or supernatural. 'There is another world, but it is in this one.'[20]

For naturalised, secular views of reality to ignore the unseen would be a big mistake. We may know much more about reality than we did in the Middle Ages. But there is still plenty of reason to be humble about the limits of our knowledge.

Practices of attention

As Iris Murdoch's example of 'unselfing' suggests, our experiences of going 'beyond ourselves' and paying full attention to our surroundings are often out of our control.[21] This makes sense – we cannot have control over losing control. Instead of grasping the world, we tend to be grasped by it; much as Murdoch's attention was grasped by the hovering kestrel.

And yet there are numerous cultural practices that have been designed to cultivate our emotions of attention. In this section, we will briefly review these kinds of practices. In the following section, we will look at the kinds of conditions that bring about similar experiences in our everyday lives. It can often seem as if we have no option other than to control our circumstances. I hope that by the end of this chapter you will see that there is a wide range of practices and conditions which helps us better to understand our lives, instead of trying to control them to our liking.

The most obvious practices of attention are religious and spiritual practices. These practices are often non-cognitive in nature – they aim to take people outside their usual cognitive understanding of the world, beyond analysis and judgement, and instead connect with the more subjective, unpredictable nature of reality. To a secular mind, these practices may seem irrational or superstitious. For example, prayer as a way of talking to God may seem like a waste of time to someone who does not believe in God. However, we can also view prayer as a form of attention towards our deep human needs and the limits of our understanding, including the myriad of connections between things that can work out in our favour.[22] Paying more attention to these connections and the possibilities they provide may be a very rational thing to do, albeit in a way that bypasses the slow and deliberate machinery of our cognitive minds.

Many religious and spiritual practices are based on ritual. Rituals are often collective in nature, such as group singing, chanting or dancing. They involve a heightened state of attention towards things that are deemed to be important, such as a creation myth, a particular time of year or time of life. By paying attention to these things, participants are encouraged to refamiliarise themselves with them and reorient their lives accordingly.[23] They may gain a deeper understanding of the subject of the ritual and its importance. What previously might have seemed like a relatively profane or mundane object, place or person, may now appear to be sacred or profound.

Rituals are especially appropriate for common experiences that are nonetheless rich in meaning and vital to keep in mind. Perhaps the most important kinds of rituals in this respect are rites of passage. In cultures around the world, significant times of life – such as birth, going from adolescence to adulthood, and death – are navigated through a number of collective rituals.[24]

These rituals cement the importance of individuals within their community. They provide individuals and the community as whole with a deeper understanding of someone's value and worth, as well as the recognition and support they need.

Consider, for example, three different types of ritual. Through often-arduous 'coming of age' rituals, individuals can come to feel 'held' in their community, and 'called' to use and develop their unique gifts to contribute positively towards it. Through 'grief' rituals, the wider community acknowledges the tragedy of someone's loss, as well as the significance of the process of grief and readjustment that must take place. In land-based communities, through 'seasonal rituals', people pay attention to the changing rhythms of their environment and the new demands and opportunities these changes bring. These rituals may all serve a bigger, overarching purpose: they remind people that our insecurity is part of what it means to be human – that no one's life is easy; our vulnerabilities to suffering and loss are something we all share.

Of course, we no longer lead ritualistic lives. We have either lost these kinds of rituals or replaced them with consumption-rich events, such as birthdays and holiday periods. More traditional rituals are often viewed as throwbacks to more primitive ways of life steeped in irrational beliefs and superstitions.[25]

But this does mean that modern cultures are devoid of practices of attention. Practices of play and humour, art and creativity, sport and entertainment, and spending time in nature are all things we engage in to 'go beyond ourselves' and 'lose control'. Each of these practices focuses our attention on what matters.

In play, we explore possible realities through the safety of our imagination. For instance, for many animal species that live in groups, the young engage in play fighting, which helps them develop their hunting and social skills in a nurturing environment. In a similar way, children pretend to be doctors and nurses, robbers and policemen, and other social roles they may end up filling or encountering in their adult lives. In 'deep play', people can lose themselves entirely in their own imagined fictions, paying attention to things that otherwise might seem too risky, or simply a waste of time, to explore.[26]

Humour has much in common with play. In fact, some theories claim that laughter originated from the mock distress calls involved in play fighting. According to other theories, laughter may be an essentially communal practice, having evolved out of the vocalisations involved in group mobbing.[27] Among hunter-gathering societies, social anthropologists have shown that humour and laughter function as a levelling device – bringing people down to size. Humans have a tendency of going above their station. Prior to punishment, humour may act as an initial warning.[28] In modern societies, humour may still serve this grounding function. We tend to go about our days being *serious* – thinking that our thoughts, feelings and behaviours are all very important. Moments of humour can help us see the funny side of our situation and bring us down to earth. We can see ourselves from an external perspective and realise how our well-intentioned efforts are perhaps not so important after all.

We engage in play and humour throughout our lives, but these things often take a more formalised structure in adulthood, through practices of art and creativity. In contrast to play and humour, art and creativity tend to be less practical and social, but still involve using our imagination to see things differently. As the poet Jane Hirshfield notes, the aim of art is 'to perceive the extraordinary within the ordinary by changing not the world, but the eyes that look.'[29]

Art can change the way we see things. For example: we may no longer categorise things the same way; we may begin to see what we have in common with people who we thought were different; and we may recognise emotions and values in us that we hadn't considered to be important before. Although art is often appreciated as something valuable in itself, it also has the power to help us gain a deeper understanding of what is possible and important in life.

The practice of art is similar to the practice of science. As Albert Einstein noted, mystery, awe and wonder 'stand at the cradle of true art and true science'.[30] Scientists may use the methods of prediction, experimentation and observation rather than tastes, words, sounds and sights, but their intention – of revealing the mysteries of life – is the same. Of course, we can say a similar thing about the practice of religion and spirituality – different means, same end.

An essential difference between art, on the one hand, and science and religion, on the other, is that art does not attempt to resolve the mysteries it reveals. When both science and religion claim to have all the answers, they risk becoming stale and dogmatic. In contrast, art encourages the viewer/listener to stay questioning – to live on the edge of mystery. We can continue to pay attention to our lives, understanding in it in greater depth and complexity.

So far, we have just looked at the viewing of art. Creative practice is another structured form of attention, from arts and crafts to other skilled activities, such as games and sports. What these practices have in common are states of 'flow' – being fully absorbed in a skilled activity.[31] We experience flow from challenging activities that are neither too easy, nor too difficult – at the limits of our capabilities, requiring our full attention. For example, a downhill skier must make constant micro-adjustments in response to particular obstacles and contours. Running on autopilot – utilising just habitual patterns of behaviour – is not sufficient to deal with the challenges at hand. They must also stay fully absorbed in the activity, making split second decisions about how to act. Psychologists sometimes refer to experiences of flow as 'optimal performance'. In flow, we are often at our most flexible and creative.

In states of flow, we 'lose ourselves' in the activity at hand. But it is not only in challenging, skilled activities that we can witness this dissolution of our selves. We can experience similar kinds of ego-loss from being part of a crowd, such as being a fan in a football stadium or a spectator at a political rally. These are examples of what the sociologist Emile Durkheim called 'collective effervescence'.[32] Such experiences involve synchronised behaviours and feelings – something that can happen through a range of activities, from having sexual intercourse to being part of a choir, sports team or military platoon.[33] Temporarily becoming part of something larger than ourselves can help us gain a deeper understanding of what reality is like outside of our usual problem-solving bubble. Like religious and spiritual rituals, these experiences redirect our attention away from ourselves and our practical concerns, providing us with a completely different perspective on what's important.

The final practice of attention worth mentioning in this respect is spending time in nature. Natural settings are well suited to states of awe and wonder, and gratitude and contentment, for a number of reasons. First, they exist on a different timescale to human affairs. As Oliver Sachs noted, this sense of timelessness brings a deep peace with it, 'a detachment from the timescale, the urgencies, of daily life'.[34] Second, natural settings are cyclical, helping us appreciate the ups and downs of our own lives – the necessary cycles of action and rest, birth and death. Third, they are wild and complex, presenting us with new possibilities for expression and understanding – of how order can arise from chaos. Last, natural settings are often vast and open, allowing us to feel more expansive. We experience awe, for instance, within places that make us feel simultaneously small in comparison and larger in connection, such as volcanic mountains, storms at sea, powerful cascades or expanses of desert.

This last kind of aesthetic experience has puzzled philosophers in light of being so pleasurable and profound despite making us feel fearful and inferior. For the philosopher Emmanuel Kant, the experience of nature's sublime power prompts us to realise we are weak and existentially insignificant in the grand scheme of nature.[35] However, by paying attention to the great spatial and temporal expanse of our natural surroundings, we can take solace in two things. First, like being fully absorbed in an activity or being part of a crowd, we can exist in connection with it. Second, despite the fact that it appears threatening, by connecting with it, and paying attention to it, we can begin to understand it better, incorporating the vastness of natural settings into our view of the world.

Learning through living

So far, we have seen how a number of practices focus our attention on what we don't know and help us gain a deeper understanding of the world. These practices of attention are useful. But it's important to realise that they work by taking our natural capacities for understanding and applying them to a particular form or context; for example, through ritual or art. We can also, simply through the practice of living, be given plenty of opportunities to drop our practical goals and concerns and pay more attention to our surroundings.

Learning in the short term

As we saw in Chapter Three, we typically enter into a situation with a number of expectations about how it will go and how it will bear on our future. For example, we might think that a difficult discussion with our partner will end up in an argument, which might in turn have serious consequences. Often, these expectations can help us respond skilfully to our situation – only focusing on the parts of it that are unexpected. However, they can also be overly certain, blinding us to parts of our situation that are worth paying more attention to.

To continue the example, we might be able to have the difficult discussion with our partner without getting upset or angry, or have an argument without it being destructive. By paying more attention to what we don't know, we are less likely to react in habitual ways: getting angry or upset, or trying to end an argument as quickly as possible or not ending it without a resolution. All these strategies may have worked for us in the past, but may no longer be appropriate in our current context. Without these forms of certainty, we can remain open to the possibilities of our situation. When we do enter into a situation in this way, we often find we are more adaptive, creative and spontaneous in response.[36]

This is often referred to as being 'present', which suggests a complete lack of expectation for the future or learning from the past. I don't think that's necessarily possible. But it's a useful term nonetheless, as an indication that we are toning down our expectations about what the meaning of the current situation is and what our reactions to it will be.

We can either practise being in this state or we might simply find ourselves being more open to our situation. The above example is similar to what social psychologists call 'deep listening'.[37] Deep listening involves opening ourselves up to what we don't know about what someone is telling us, even if it sounds problematic or challenging. Instead of making assumptions about what someone is saying – based on our past experiences – we can assume that we don't know. And instead of trying to quickly work out how to respond – such as trying to fix their problem – we can listen with an open mind. The idea is that we can listen to someone *nonjudgementally* – without assumptions, and without instantly categorising what they're saying into something that is either good or bad.

The term 'deep listening' reflects the fact that the emotional tone behind what someone is saying is often equally, if not more, important than the content of their words. When being listened to with full, nonjudgemental attention, people can feel more heard, appreciated and respected than they normally do. This alone can make all the difference, alleviating some of the weight of their problems, feeling they no longer have to deal with them by themselves. The person listening may also realise that the act of deep listening – simply acknowledging the weight of the other person's problem – is all that is required in the meantime. They may also come up with a particular response or solution that would not normally occur to them in such a situation.

Deep listening shows that we can tone down our expectations and certainties about what someone is saying to us, and pay more attention to what we don't know about the situation. When we do so, we can end up acting with greater flexibility and responsiveness.

This does not, however, just hold for listening. We can be more mindful in all our activities, as advocated by 'mindfulness'-based practices and therapies.[38] With an open mind, we can face our problems and challenges in more resourceful and adaptive ways than we might at first think. By paying nonjudgemental attention to our situation, including our thoughts, feelings and behaviour, we can find ways of responding to it that neither rely solely on our habitual reactions nor on distracting ourselves and ignoring the problem at hand.

Of course, we will not always act smoothly and spontaneously in response to all the problems we face. Sometimes things will go wrong. But this can be also an opportunity to pay more attention to what we don't know and learn from our situation. This brings us back to the distinction between having a 'fixed mindset' and a 'growth mindset', which we briefly looked at in Chapter Three.[39] When people with a fixed mindset make mistakes, they very quickly take that as an indication that they aren't going to succeed in the particular task in question. In contrast, people with a growth mindset view their mistakes as good learning material – what went wrong and how could things be done differently next time?

People with a growth mindset tend to do better in the long run. Although people with fixed mindsets often do well at the things they believe they are good at, they also encounter greater doubts and a lack of motivation when things go wrong. In contrast, people with growth mindsets, more open to failure, are more likely to stay confident in light of inevitable mistakes and setbacks.

Sometimes this learning process can be instantaneous and almost effortless. There is a strong tradition within ancient Chinese philosophy on how we can, by paying attention to the whole of our situation, be more skilful and spontaneous within it. This tradition has influenced the more recent psychological study of 'flow', briefly described above. According to Confucian philosophy, for instance, a virtuous life is one of constantly breaking old habits and forming new ones, which better respond to the particularities and complexities of our situation.[40] Through this process, we can be constantly aware of our capacities and limitations – both using our learned behaviours to respond skilfully to our situation and being open to better, more spontaneous, forms of action.

Situations that initially appear to be difficult can also be rich sources of learning. We may be surprised that, when we remain open to what we don't know about our situation, we can respond to it with greater flexibility and resilience. This is the power of being 'in the moment', 'present' or 'mindful'. Even when things are not to our liking, we can still pay attention and learn from them.

Learning in the long term

We cannot always be mindful. In some situations, being instantly flexible or spontaneous may not be appropriate. Within a major life crisis, for example, we cannot – and should not have to – immediately adapt.

Going back to ancient Chinese philosophy, there is a well-known story of grief experienced by the renowned philosopher Zhuangzi from the loss of his wife.[41] When he is found being his usual cheerful self, only a day after losing his wife, he is asked why he does not grieve. He replies saying how he wept and suffered more than he could ever have imagined, and as much as any other man would have – though, only for one day. After this short period of grief, he reminded himself that the nature of all things is change, and that, although he loved his wife very much, no further amount of grieving will bring her back. So, instead, he began to focus again on the other things in life he found worthwhile.

Now, Zhuangzi's experience is all very well if you want to go about life that way. For many us, however, we don't. The idea of being so easily detached from the things we care about – so readily equipped to deal with loss and adversity, to learn from it, and then move on – is not so desirable.

But it's important to realise that most of us do move on from loss and adversity, albeit on a longer time scale. Over time, we may be stronger and more resilient than we tend to think we are. This is essentially the same process we looked at above – paying more attention to our situation and learning from it. Only, this time, patience is required for it to happen.

Grief is a powerful example of this process. The beginning of grief is typically a very difficult time. People tend to withdraw from the world, are lethargic and spend much of their time reflecting on their loss. This may include ruminating over particular losses: experiences they had with their loved one, which they're never going to have again; the ways in which they built their life together, and how that's no longer possible; how their loved one protected them in ways that now leave them feeling exposed and vulnerable, and so on. This may even include losing their sense of identity if it was significantly wrapped up in their loved one's wellbeing and their joint projects. To some extent, they may question whether they want to be whoever they have now become.

This grieving process is potentially one of the most difficult things we will experience in our lives. And yet, for most people, it eventually transforms into something else. The grieving process itself may never end – we may never find 'closure' and forget the loss of our loved ones.[42] But it's also well documented that this initial grieving period, full of sorrow and rumination, eventually dissipates. The rest of life moves on, including our other responsibilities. We cannot continue to grieve intensely without dropping our other concerns, such as caring for the people we love who are still with us.

As part of this process, are various realisations and insights – things we learn from paying attention to our loss. For example, we may come to realise, at some point through the grieving process, that our pain is partly what makes us sensitive to the love we had for whom we've now lost. Only from the joy of our relationship could we now be experiencing so much sorrow from being separated. When our loved one was alive, we might have known they were important to us, but that we also had various other important things in our lives; we may now come to realise they meant the world to us, and that's a beautiful thing to have had. Our grief may help us realise how much we want to prioritise our relationships with the other people we love, now that we know how dear and precious life and love can be.[43]

Similarly, we may find a newfound sense of compassion with those who have gone through a similar process of losing who they love.[44] We may not have known just how tragic and difficult that was before having experienced it for ourselves. In general, through grief we can come to learn about what it means to love and be ourselves – perhaps what it means for life to be worthwhile.

Like grief, a personal crisis or mental breakdown might be terrible at the time, but in hindsight may come to be viewed as a blessing. We may look back, and see it as something that showed us that how we were living our lives was not sustainable. We might have been running away from some very scary things that we didn't want to confront. Only through the process of crisis or breakdown did we eventually find the support we needed to face those things head on and reprioritise the parts of our lives that were most important.

Both crisis and grief seem like some of the worst things in life that can happen to us. However, they can also end up being some of the most meaningful. Psychologists refer to this process as 'post-traumatic growth' (in contrast to post-traumatic stress). Numerous studies have found that people can not only live through adversity, but they also live better lives as a result.[45]

This is perhaps most striking when we consider people's life narratives – the stories people tell about their lives. Our lives are made up of many positive and negative events. However, from connecting past and present events, as well as potential future events, we can come to see that many of the negative events we experienced are causally related to the things that have gone well in our lives. Often, we see that we've learned from them.[46] Perhaps the breakdown of our marriage showed us what it means to truly communicate and love someone, and helped us find a much better relationship. Or perhaps a similar thing happened from losing our job – it gave us the opportunity to really look into the ways we want to most spend our time.

Through the power of our stories, we can come to see that periods of struggle and adversity can nonetheless be of worth. Often, our personal stories emphasise not just what happened to us – the lucky and unlucky breaks, the failures and successes – but also how we responded to them. For example, despite all the anxiety and pain we have experienced in our lives, we are still here, still standing. In looking back over our lives, we cannot only see how things panned out, but also the active part we have played in it all.

Our personal narratives then, if taken seriously, can provide us with a sense of personal strength and agency, much like knowing we can be more adaptive and spontaneous within a given situation. Our current situation might seem hopeless, and one that we want to get out of as soon as possible. Yet, over time, with great patience, we may come to see it as worthwhile.

With this sense of meaning, we can endure much of what life throws at us. Consider, for example, someone climbing a mountain. They are able to endure extraordinary depths of hardship knowing that, eventually, it'll all be worth it. The pain they experience as they climb may even be seen as a something valuable – it is part of the satisfaction they hope to experience on the summit. The commitments we set ourselves can make us incredibly resilient in the present, even without the certainty that they will pay off in the future.[47]

Just to be clear, I am not suggesting that we need to experience grief, breakdown or crisis to understand what really matters in our lives. Instead, my point is that, if we are unfortunate enough to experience tragedy in our lives, we may come, over (a potentially long period of) time, to learn from it. It is through the practice of living that we can come to gain a deeper understanding of what matters, either in the short term or the long term.

Letting go of control

In this chapter, we have seen how we can step outside of our problem-solving bubbles and see things differently. Practices of attention, and the practice of living, can help us gain a deeper understanding of what really matters.

But why do we sometimes take these opportunities to see things differently and at other times ignore them? When do we try to control our situation and when do we try to understand it better? This choice is not a random one, nor is it purely a consequence of personality. It often reflects the situation we are in. In this section, we will see the kinds of conditions that make us more likely to embrace uncertainty and pay attention to what we don't know.

The kinds of experiences we have been looking at are more likely to occur within two broad kinds of conditions – both of which have to do with control.[48] First, we are more likely to pay attention to what we don't know when we *lack control*; for example, during a mental breakdown or at the end of life. Second, we are more likely to embrace uncertainty when we have *no need for control*; for example, during times of rest or no immediate demands or concerns.

These two conditions are extremely different from each other – they are the times in which we have the least and most control over our lives. The first is characterised by hitting rock bottom – when we've exhausted all our options and feel helplessness in response to our situation. We need to see things differently out of *necessity*. In contrast, the second set of conditions are those in which we feel safe and secure enough to go beyond our practical concerns and open up to new forms of understanding. We can, at least temporarily, *afford* to let go.

When we lack control

We have already seen how periods of grief and personal crisis present people with opportunities to gain a deeper understanding of what really matters. From paying attention to their loss over time, they can begin to see the world differently. One of the reasons these experiences can be so transformative is because there are few other options. In the case of grief, there is nothing we can do to bring back our loved one. We need, instead, to spend some time trying to incorporate the significance of our loss into our lives and our view of the world.

There are two other notable situations in which we lack control over our lives. The first is the most striking: situations of extreme loss and deprivation. The well-known Jewish psychoanalyst Victor Frankl famously wrote that 'Everything can be taken from a man but one thing: the last of the human freedoms – to choose one's attitude in any given set of circumstances, to choose one's way.'[49] This dramatic statement is supported by the fact that Frankl wrote it in reflection of his time spent as a prisoner in a concentration camp during the Second World War. The conditions Frankl experienced were unimaginable in their terror. And yet, within them, he managed to find meaning and worth.

Frankl's experience is testimony to the power of our emotions of attention. Being in a concentration camp could easily lead to despair and hatred. No doubt Frankl experienced these things too, but he also experienced hope and love. The fact that we can have such different attitudes in response to such horrific circumstances shows that the meaning of a given situation can almost always be interpreted in different ways.

Of course, not everyone responded to the same situation as Frankl did. Deprived conditions do not always help people see things differently and gain a deeper understanding of what matters. We should not fetishise suffering. However, this does not mean that we cannot also recognise its potential for transformation.[50]

In conditions of extreme depravity, people's opportunities are severely limited. This is common to the second notable situation in which we lack control: at the end of our lives. Despite the fact that we know, for sure, we are going to die, we can spend most of our days conveniently ignoring this fact. However, when confronted with our own mortality, either through old age or from terminal illness, we must acknowledge our limitations. Again, this can lead to either hope or despair depending on how people interpret the meaning of their situation. We shouldn't glorify the dying process any more than we should glorify suffering. But we can still recognise the power it has to change people's perspectives and gain a deeper understanding of what matters.

For instance, in his memoir *We Know How This Ends*, Bruce Kramer notes how, after being diagnosed with motor neurone disease, he found faith in the fact that things will be what they will be – that his disease will go about what it does, inexorably, and without a cure. From embracing the fact that it is what it is, Kramer describes how he was able to perceive great beauty and great joy in his life.[51] The political consultant Philip Gould, who also suffered from a terminal illness, described this as the 'death zone'. Gould notes how, only when you are aware that you are definitely going to die, that life 'screams at you with intensity'.[52]

All these situations have something in common: an extreme lack of opportunities and control. There are similar accounts of people who have suffered debilitating health conditions or who lived through times of disaster, conflict or oppression. For instance, Rebecca Solnit notes that in most disasters most people are calm, resourceful and creative. Reflecting on five major disasters in the US, from the 1906 San Francisco earthquake to Hurricane Katrina in New Orleans in 2005, she says:

> What startled me about the response to disaster was not the virtue, since virtue is often the result of diligence and dutifulness, but the passionate joy that

shined out from accounts by people who had barely survived. These people who had lost everything, who were living in rubble or ruins, had found agency, meaning, community, immediacy in their work together with other survivors. [53]

These extreme situations stand in stark contrast to the circumstances of ordinary life. However, many ordinary situations are also out of our control. As Kramer himself notes, after writing about his experience, people began writing back to him, describing their own struggles. One person described the breakdown of their marriage – how they felt similarly out of control. They did not expect their marriage to suddenly come back together, in much the same way that Kramer did not expect to be cured of his disease. Kramer claims that we all carry this phenomenon of 'dis-ease' within us, which we cannot run away from. The flipside is that this lack of control provides us all with the opportunity to embrace it and learn from it – this is the freedom of which Frankl spoke.

When we have no need for control

We do not have to wait for tragedy to strike to embrace uncertainty and pay attention to what we don't know. We also tend to be more open during times of rest, such as taking a quiet walk in the woods or having a long shower.[54] In fact, most of the practices of attention described above involve people being in a safe and secure space – a place that helps them let go of their practical goals and concerns, and devote their full, undivided attention to the activity at hand.

It is no surprise that religious and spiritual traditions all emphasis sacred spaces, full of hush and splendour, where people can temporarily feel transported outside of their normal practical lives.[55] The same goes for aesthetic and cultural institutions, such as grand music halls, reverent art galleries and sport stadiums. The idea of the 'sacred' may not just be to mark out objects and places worthy of our attention, but also to signal that we are safe to stop our daily routines and slip into a place of abandonment and astonishment.[56]

In addition to these practices of attention, there are two other notable situations in which we have no need for control in our lives. The first is perhaps surprising: elderhood. Much of our need for control comes from wanting to achieve our goals and prevent things from going wrong in the future. By old age, however, we have done most of what we can do, and most of what could happen to us has already happened. Although old age brings new fears and concerns, we may reach a place of greater acceptance and security – of knowing what we can and cannot achieve, and that we can handle what life throws at us.

This is why elderhood and wisdom often go together.[57] It is through bitter experience, and the safety and security of hindsight, that elders can gain a deeper understanding of what matters. They may see, for instance, how the good and bad things in life are intrinsically linked. They can see clearly that loss is an inevitable consequence of having cared for something, or that failure is an essential part of taking on challenging projects – they have lived through both. They know that their losses and failures have contributed to who they are now. They can see how everything is part of what makes life worth living.

Acknowledging the connections between the good and bad things in life is one of the hallmarks of wisdom. Wise individuals simultaneously accept what is horrendous and embrace what is good about the world. The blossom, the brief moment of sunshine, the warmth of a family gathering or the love of a relationship – these things all come to have a profound sense of value for the wise because they are so aware of the tragic backdrop against which they stand.

Seeing the connections between the different parts of our lives is a defining feature of the kinds of experiences we have looked at in this chapter – often referred to as religious, spiritual, mystical,[58] transcendental, ecstatic,[59] peak[60] or enlightenment[61] experiences. Exploring these heightened experiences is the second notable situation in which we have no need for control. Proponents of psychedelic experiences, for instance, emphasise the importance of having the right 'set' and 'setting' – to undergo such experiences within a safe setting and an undisturbed mindset. Without these conditions in place, it may not feel possible to let go of control and pay attention to the experience as it unfolds.

These experiences are now a serious subject of science.[62] Cognitive scientists have begun to investigate the psychological and neurological effects of psychedelic drugs and other mind-altering experiences, including religious and spiritual practices such as meditation.[63] Within these experiences, participants report a heightened sense of attention and a profound sense of connection. They may feel fully connected to the present moment – attuned to their environment, knowing exactly what to do, without any need for conscious deliberation. And they may feel connected to their whole selves, as well as their past, present and future – their weaknesses as essentially connected to their strengths, and their past sorrows connected to their present and future joys.

If we take the realisation that everything is connected to its logical conclusion, nothing is straightforwardly good or bad. If everything is connected to everything else, then everything has a valuable part to play – we cannot have any of the good things without the bad things that are causally connected to them.[64] This is necessarily true. From an historical point of view, we literally cannot have all the good things that currently exist without also having the things that causally preceded them – famines and wars, disease and poverty. From a deterministic point of view, we literally cannot have anything that currently exists without also having everything else that is causally connected to it.

This might be why individuals who undergo a psychedelic experience sometimes report seeing the world as 'perfect' – everything is necessarily as it is, and full of possibility. The difficult part of psychedelic therapies is turning these momentary insights into long-lasting impacts – for individuals to use this window of opportunity to change their goals and priorities. Not just to marvel at the universe, but to then come back to ground and change things for the better.

We can view this kind of experience as a temporary, supercharged shot of wisdom. Individuals who undergo a psychedelic or transcendental experience of any kind see how the things in our lives are connected. This gives them the flexibility to reinterpret the good and bad events in their lives, their strengths and weaknesses and their relationships to others. The difference is that this may all happen in a single, profound moment of insight, rather than over a lifetime of hard work and experience.

Giving up control

On the one hand, the two different kinds of conditions we have looked at in this section are about as different as things can be – just compare Victor Frankl's experience in a concentration camp with going for a quiet walk in nature. On the other hand, conditions in which we have the least and most control may have more in common than we might think.

First, we often have less control than we think we do. This was the key lesson of Chapter One – we are inherently insecure; nothing we do to improve our lives and make ourselves more secure will be enough to protect us from tragedy. As Bruce Kramer noted, we may not be immediately dying or have a physical or mental disease, but we will all die eventually and we all suffer from some forms of 'dis-ease' – hardships in our lives that we can do nothing about.[65]

Second, we may, within our insecurity, have less need for control than we think we do. This was the key lesson of Chapter Two – by focusing on the things we can readily control we miss out on the other things in life that matter. When we give up control we can connect with, pay attention to and gain a deeper understanding of the things in our lives that matter.

It is possible, therefore, that in any given moment or situation, we can benefit from embracing uncertainty and paying more attention to what we don't know. The conditions may be in place, whether we recognise them or not.

In the following two chapters we will explore the benefits of embracing uncertainty and acknowledging our insecurity. In the next chapter, we will see how, through this process of curiosity and exploration, we can discover what we most care about and are truly capable of.

FIVE

Curiosity

We are hardwired with curiosity inside us, because life knew that this would keep us going even in bad sailing.
Anne Lamott[1]

In Chapter Four, we looked at the first part of how to think about happiness differently. According to the understanding strategy, the mindset of happiness is one of uncertainty and possibility rather than certainty and predictability. Trying to control everything in our lives requires us to narrow our vision and live in our problem-solving bubbles. In contrast, trying to understand ourselves, others, and our environment requires us to be humble, widen our perspective and pay attention to what we don't know.

In this chapter we will look at how we can use this mindset to switch our focus from control to understanding. This is the second part of how to think about happiness differently – the process of happiness. We will explore the idea we presented at the end of the previous chapter: what if, in any given moment or in any given situation, we could embrace uncertainty and benefit from paying attention to what we don't know? This is the process of curiosity.

We will see that, from being curious about our lives, we can open ourselves up to experiences of beauty and gratitude. We can also respond with greater flexibility to the challenges we face, less stuck in our habitual ways of seeing the world. With these inner resources, instead of having fixed ideas about our 'authentic' self and adhering to our limited personal narratives, we can continue to discover what we most care about and are truly capable of.

This process does not eliminate the strategy of control completely. We will often need to act on what we already know – the benefits of embracing uncertainty can be outweighed simply by the need to get stuff done. However, the limits of trying to control our circumstances will eventually become apparent again, and we will need to resort back to curiosity, exploration and understanding. This negotiation between understanding and control is one that never ends.

The process of curiosity described in this chapter is how we can achieve both *breadth* and *depth* within our lives. First, from being curious towards our lives we can better understand our whole selves, in all our diversity and humanity. Instead of having fixed ideas about 'who we really are', we can continue to surprise ourselves. This process of curiosity and exploration is what gives our lives breath – a wide range of things we care about and are capable of. Second, with this understanding of what matters, we can commit to the things we care about, limiting our opportunities and creating new challenges. And yet, by remaining curious towards our lives, we can discover what's possible within our commitments. This process of commitment and curiosity is what gives our lives depth – the process of living up to what really matters.

Curiosity as an inner resource

In this section, we will see the three major benefits of curiosity. First, by being curious we open ourselves up to the potential value of the things that would otherwise pass us by – this is the realm of beauty. Second, we become more aware of the potential value of the things we already have – we feel gratitude and contentment. Third, we can respond to the challenges we face with greater flexibility, less stuck in our habitual ways of seeing the world. Together, these three benefits of curiosity are an inner resource we can draw upon to explore and commit to what really matters.

Beauty

We have all experienced moments of beauty in our lives. For me, the experiences that stand out are listening to music and walking across mountains. Despite these two activities being very different, they both made me feel the same way: for a while, everything stopped; nothing else mattered other than the sounds or sights that I was experiencing; my mind was so full of those things that I felt there was nothing to do, nowhere to go; there was only awe, wonder and beauty.

These experiences are certainly nice to have. It is why many people engage in the kinds of practices of attention we looked at in Chapter Four – from art and creativity to spending time in nature. When we feel safe and secure, and temporarily able to drop our practical goals and concerns, we can open ourselves up to new ways of seeing the world. We might do this in an art gallery or at a music concert. Or we might dedicate our lives to these kinds of experiences through the creation of art or other forms of creativity and entertainment.

We do not need these practices, however, to experience beauty in our everyday lives. Once we open our eyes and become curious about the world around us, we will find it full of delights to feast on.[2] Every morning on our commute to work, for example, we can notice the sky, the air around us, the scent of freshness, the different shades of each house on the street, the trees lining the pavement, the faces and stories of those we meet throughout the day.

Beyond our immediate environment, we have opportunities to be interested in an infinite amount of phenomena that make up our universe: how the cosmos was formed, including earth and life on it; the weird and wonderful creatures and plants we share the planet with; the workings of natural and designed ecosystems and so on.[3] Life is rich with beauty and wonder – we just need to let ourselves see it.

This has much in common with Buddhist practices of meditation and mindfulness. Through the process of meditation, we can gain a sense of detachment, or distance, from our internal and external circumstances. By simply paying attention to the sensations, thoughts and feelings they arouse in us, we can accept how things are right now, without judgement; without trying to either 'escape' negative feelings or 'hold on' to positive ones.[4]

Instead of being a state of neutral indifference, this state of complete attention is typically pleasant, sometimes even ecstatic. As we saw in Chapter Four, our emotional capacities of attention are not entirely neutral – they are designed for us to see things differently, to gain a deeper understanding of whatever it is we are paying attention to. This is partly why practices of meditation and mindfulness have recently become so popular in a Western secular context. In contrast to most people's busy and stressful lifestyles, it provides them with an opportunity for finding some peace of mind. As Pico Iyer notes, 'Sitting still as a way of falling in love with the world and everything in it.'[5]

When we let ourselves observe how things are, without judgement or wanting things to be otherwise, we realise there is much to appreciate and enjoy. The same is true for other 'mindful' practices, such as spending time in nature, engaging in art, sport, dancing, singing, contemplation, prayer or sex.

Through being mindful we can let ourselves, as Stephen Batchelor says, become 're-enchanted with the world'.[6] With this capacity, we become free to appreciate the world around us, as if for the first time. And often, we are grasped by it. The world is full of possibility, and our experiences of wonder are responses to its suggestions. What was once simply an ordinary tree among others now appears to us as something beautiful and special – a living creature we can learn from, spend more time with and care for. As the philosopher Alexander Nehamas notes, in his book *Only a Promise of Happiness*, beauty is a kind of beckoning, 'an invitation for further exploration and interpretation'.[7]

Sometime we experience intense moments of wonder, where our minds are completely filled by the things we are appreciating, such as the example I gave at the beginning of this section. Often, in such moments of awe, we experience something much greater than ourselves, simultaneously feeling small in comparison and part of something greater. This may be physical: seeing an expansive landscape, or comprehending the cosmos itself. Or it may be temporal: contemplating the generations of humans that have got us to where we are now, or seeing an ancient woodland that has stood the test of time. From these larger perspectives, our practical concerns are made small by comparison. In their place, we may appreciate possibilities for action that we hadn't previously considered, or had perhaps forgotten the importance of.

Which is the important point: when it comes to beauty and wonder, it is not the world that is limited, but ourselves. It is our practical goals and concerns that stop us from seeing the beauty all around us and all the hidden depths of wonder. It is easy to be curious about the world because the world is full of interesting and beautiful things to be curious about. The issue is whether we can let ourselves stop and smell the roses – to stop what we're doing, temporarily put down our problems and concerns and pay attention to what we don't know. As the poet Kahlil Gibran puts it: 'beauty is life when life unveils her holy face. / But you are life and you are the veil.'[8]

Gratitude

We can say a similar thing about gratitude. We can always appreciate what we already have, in much the same way as we can appreciate the world around us. But it is our practical goals and concerns that prevent us from doing so. When we have stuff to do, it doesn't seem worth stopping and being grateful. Again, the process of curiosity reverses this trend. By being curious about our lives, we open ourselves up to the potential value of what we already have: to gratitude and contentment, as well as awe and wonder.

We may ask what the practical benefits are of appreciating what we already have and already know the value of. After all, the reason why we adapt to our circumstances is so that we can focus on making them better – to move on to the next goal and achievement. The problem with adaptation, however, is that we sometimes take it too far. We may end up taking the things we have for granted and fail to respect and care for them properly. Gratitude does the opposite. It makes us pay attention to the valuable things in our lives that we otherwise might overlook. It gives us a sense of perspective over what matters.

For instance, gratitude exercises – promoted by religious teachings and modern psychology[9] – encourage people to count their blessings. This can help people appreciate, on a deeper level, the value of what they already have.[10] With this deeper understanding, they may put more effort into maintaining or protecting the good things in their lives, such as spending more time with loved ones, caring for their possessions or making their home beautiful.

These practices and states of appreciation counteract our tendency to pay less attention to what we have achieved and be captivated instead by what we don't have. They are perhaps more needed than ever. Our desire to move on to the next thing is amplified by a bombardment of cultural messages – all trying to convince us that our lives are not good enough; we must have bigger, better, more luxurious things and more exciting experiences.[11] In contrast, experiences of gratitude can help us 'rediscover' the things we already have, of which we have many, and mostly take for granted.

We are saliently reminded of this fact whenever we temporarily lose the things we have. This can happen when we are in an unfamiliar situation. For example, we may witness a power cut ('What, no wi-fi?!'), go on a camping holiday ('So where's the toilet?') or find ourselves alone in a hotel room on business. At these times, we can be reminded of the gifts we have in our lives. Similarly, when we become temporarily ill or injured, we viscerally see what we no longer have. After lying in bed for days, the joy of breathing fresh air or walking around the garden can make us feel like a child again – seeing the familiar with new eyes.

Perhaps the most profound version of this experience of appreciation happens when we are reminded of death. On hearing about a tragedy in which people have died, or witnessing the near death of someone we know, we may appreciate the simple fact that we are alive – life is short, and it is worth living fully. This can help us approach our goals with a new sense of urgency and purpose. Alternatively, we may realise the value of what we already have and that we need to focus our efforts on caring for those things.

As with wonder, feelings of gratitude vary in their intensity. When we experience intense forms of gratitude, the things in our life do not just seem good, but also good *enough*. These moments of contentment involve seeing our lives as having enough goodness in them that, at least for the time being, we do not need anything more. Such feelings may make us more inclined to protect the things we already have, or make us simply rest and maintain our energy.

It is important to note that feelings of contentment need not be inconsistent with ambition. Contentment is about seeing the life we have lived *so far* as good enough.[12] Things will inevitably change in the future, and we will be forced to see things differently again. Nonetheless, there is nothing irrational about feeling content in recognition of the fact that our lives are currently sufficiently good for us, helping us to simply appreciate all of what we have.

This is an important lesson, which we have already touched upon with experiences of beauty. We can experience either beauty or gratitude at any given moment, in any given situation. There is nothing irrational about experiences of gratitude and contentment. We can be content with our lives right now if we wanted to – to simply appreciate the immense value of what we already have. What makes gratitude and contentment so elusive is the fact that they have to compete with our certainties: the goals and concerns we think we need to focus on instead. Curiosity is the opposite of these certainties. It rests on the attitude that there is much we don't know and that it's worth trying to find out.[13] This includes the things we already have and care about in our lives.

Flexibility

We are very unlikely to be able to spend all our time smelling the roses and counting our blessings. The process of curiosity may open us up to beauty and gratitude, but we will still have practical goals and concerns that get in the way. We have needs to meet and people we care about. We will, at some point, stop appreciating the world around us and get to work.

Curiosity does not have to stop there, however. We can bring the same openness and interest towards the challenges we face. Instead of assuming that we know how to achieve all our goals, we can embrace uncertainty and pay attention to what we don't know. This has much in common with the notions of presence and 'flow' discussed in Chapter Four. Through paying non-judgemental attention to our situation, we can more flexibly respond to its demands.

This level of flexibility is easier said than done. Our habits and traits are ingrained parts of our personality. They are designed *not* to make us see things differently. The whole point of these automatic patterns of behaviour is that they are reliably rewarding forms of action – we can engage in them without having to think about how to act otherwise. We don't need to be aware of how we are cleaning our teeth, for example – having adequately cleaned our teeth thousands of times we can now do so on autopilot and think about other things.

And yet we can still pay attention to our habitual ways of seeing the world, and start to see things differently. This is what the practice of mindfulness is all about. We can even practise paying attention to mundane activities, such as cleaning our teeth. Doing so can help us remain curious towards everything in our lives, which we can then apply to our more ingrained habits.

This practice pays off in situations when our habits get us stuck. There are countless examples of our habitual behaviours getting in the way of what we most want to do: we may want to be in a trusting, loving relationship, but always get overcome with jealousy and suspicion; we may want to exercise regularly, but manage to convince ourselves out of doing so when the time comes; we may want to be kind and considerate of others, but get angry and annoyed when people act in ways that are not to our liking and so on.

All of these habitual ways of seeing the world have been learned through practice – to some extent, they have worked for us in the past and we are using that knowledge to predict the future. Through being curious about what we don't know, we can learn new tricks. We can pay attention to the whole of our situation, which includes the parts of ourselves, others and our environment that our minds have learned to automatically and effectively filter out.

By seeing things differently we can begin to act in different ways – more spontaneously and adaptively. Of course, we have no guarantee that acting differently will be better. But when our habitual ways of seeing the world are so rigid and stuck in their ways, we often have no other choice.

This is most obvious when our habits become so fixed and rigid that they ruin our lives. Addiction and depression are extreme cases in point. When people get addicted to a particular drug or behaviour it is hard for them to see things differently. They cannot think of ways to relieve their craving other than getting their next fix. This is not the same as impulsive behaviour – people can be very flexible and creative in finding new ways to feed their addiction.[14] The problem is being incapable of imagining life outside their addiction. Their addicted and habitual ways of seeing the world become so fixed and rigid that other possibilities are almost impossible to see.

Similarly, individuals with depression often get caught in habitual patterns of thoughts, feelings and behaviour fuelled by the process of rumination. A negative event can spark off a cascade of automatic, seemingly uncontrollable, negative thoughts about themselves ('I'm worthless'), the world ('No one values me') and their future ('Things can only get worse').[15] The more people interpret the world in these ways, the more each thought and feeling feeds off each other, making it very difficult to see things differently.

Depression and addiction are extreme cases of our habitual ways of seeing the world being too fixed and rigid. We all suffer from less extreme versions of this process. When we encounter a problem we often try and fix it by going through all the options in our minds, only to get more confused and make things worse – this is a mild form of rumination. And, as mentioned in Chapter Two, up to 50 per cent of the US population may suffer from a recognised form of addiction.[16] Many more of us suffer from addictive relationships towards our mobile phones, emails, to-do lists, diets and other forms of distraction.

The process of curiosity challenges our habits by paying attention to the possibilities we automatically and impulsively ignore. We go about our lives constantly making 'good versus bad' judgements.[17] We judge other people, ourselves, our relationships, our actions, our situation and so on – we habitually see everything as either good or bad. In doing so, we divide reality in half. We try to avoid half of it – the bad bits – as much as possible, and we try to seek out the other half – the good bits – as much as we can. Curiosity takes a different approach. It sees the whole of reality as worthy of our attention. We may not like half of what we see, but we may find some value within it. It is through this appreciation and exploration that we become more flexible. With enough curiosity, we can find better ways of responding to the challenges we face.

Finding ourselves

So far, we have seen how being curious can open us up to the world around us: to the value of what we already have (gratitude) and what would otherwise pass us by (beauty); and to new ways of responding to the challenges we face (flexibility). These three things are all resources we can draw on when trying to change our lives for the better.

In the remainder of the chapter we will look in more detail at the process of curiosity and how we can improve our lives – what do we most care about and what are we truly capable of? In this section we will look at the limitations of trying to improve ourselves without being curious about who we are.

We are often told to just be ourselves – to worry less about what other people think, and be our 'true' or 'authentic' self. But who we really are is far from straightforward. We are made up of multiple habits, personality traits, emotional dispositions, coping strategies, goals, ambitions, commitments, values and so on. Figuring out which ones are the 'real' us and which have been imposed on us from the outside is an endless, and potentially futile, process.

There may be no good answer to who we really are. We may be too complex to 'find ourselves'. Consider, as an analogy, whether or not we've had a good day. We may have had all sorts of experiences throughout our day – from being tired and grumpy to having a sense of achievement and connection. When someone asks us how our day was, we might be able to instantly come up with answer – 'okay, thanks' or 'ugh, rubbish'. But this will be a gross simplification of how things actually went. It is similar to how our holiday photos might sum up our actual holiday experience. As snapshots of our holiday, they might show the kinds of activities we got up to. But they say nothing about what our holiday was actually like: how we felt in the mornings, what we were like in the company of others, the thoughts that preoccupied us, the sense of vitality we had from doing something new and so on. Knowing who we really are might be like trying to sum up our holiday with a set of photos or sum up our day in a single sentiment.

We can, of course, still do things to improve our lives. For instance, according to modern personality psychology, and self-determination theory in particular, we can improve ourselves by becoming more *coherent*.[18] Yes, we are a complicated jumble of habits, traits, goals, values and so on. But we can bring these different parts of ourselves in line with each other. Instead of fighting against each other, we can find ways in which the different parts of ourselves can form a coherent whole.

To illustrate what achieving self-coherence involves, consider the difference between the things that bring us happiness and the things that bring us meaning. Although these things often coincide, subjective wellbeing research shows that happiness and meaning can systematically come apart. Happiness is about meeting our needs, developing our skills and achieving our goals in the short term. In contrast, meaning is about our long-term goals and projects and creating a narrative that links our past, present and future.[19]

An example of where happiness and meaning come into conflict is parenthood. Parents who are living with children usually score lower on measures of happiness.[20] And yet, despite this fact, parents typically report to be very happy that they've had children. This 'parenting paradox' can be resolved by making a distinction between the happiness and the sense of meaning that people get from being a parent. Raising children may decrease people's day-to-day happiness but it also tends to increase their sense of meaning.[21]

We make this distinction in our lives all the time. Whenever we put in hard work towards a long-term goal or commitment, we sacrifice our present satisfaction (happiness) for a future pay-off (meaning). There are, however, ways in which we can bring happiness and meaning together. The philosopher Thaddeus Metz, in his book *Meaning in Life*, notes that once we understand the things in our lives that give us happiness and meaning, we can better integrate them. As he puts it, we can pursue, 'happiness with labour and meaningfulness without sacrifice.'[22]

For example, athletes may receive happiness from developing their athletic abilities on a daily basis and also receive meaning from the long-term achievements that hopefully come from all their hard work and determination. Finding this sweet spot between happiness and meaning is what it means to spend our days doing the things we love.

We can create coherence between the different parts of ourselves in two ways. First, we create goals and projects that go 'with the grain' of our personality. For example, if we were a shy and analytical person but wanted to campaign against climate change, we would be better off working behind the scenes than being a public speaker. It helps to know ourselves – our habits, personality traits and coping strategies – so that we can work with them, not against them.[23]

Alternatively, we could go 'against the grain' of our personality. To continue our climate change campaign example, after working behind the scenes for a while, we might want to step up and talk to more people about what we think matters. This would involve acting out of character, engaging in ongoing social activities. Over time, and with considerable effort, grit and determination, we could slowly change our habits to be more in line with our values.[24]

These two ways of achieving self-coherence – of knowing ourselves and changing ourselves – are all very well. However, they both assume that greater coherence is possible. This is not obviously the case. As the parenting paradox illustrates, some of the things we care about are simply in conflict with each other. We cannot expect to raise children at the same time as having a relaxing lifestyle.

More importantly, the idea of self-coherence assumes that we already know what we most care about and are capable of. We might want to have children, for example, but also want to focus on being an athlete. How do we weigh up the relative importance of the two? Which part of ourselves should we bring in line with the other? Alternatively, we may know that we would prefer to focus on being an athlete if we thought we had a reasonable chance of being successful. Of course, we can ask our coach and our friends if they think we have what it takes, but we cannot know for sure unless we try. How can we decide which part of ourselves to go with or against if we don't know what we can achieve?

These questions highlight the problem with the idea of being our 'true' or 'authentic' selves. We don't know who we really are. As the poet David Whyte puts it, 'Self-knowledge is not fully possible for human beings ... Half of what lies in the heart and mind is potentiality.'[25] Creating a more coherent self relies on the idea of there being parts of ourselves that we know are more important, or 'central', to our personality than others. But finding out what makes up our 'core' self is no different from the problem of knowing ourselves in general. We can tell ourselves a story about who we really are, and which parts of ourselves are more central or peripheral to our 'core' self. But, in doing so, we limit our potential – both what we care about and what we are capable of.

There is a different approach, however, that gets around this problem. Instead of trying to find definitive answers to the question of who we really are, we can engage in an ongoing process of creation and discovery – a process of *appreciation* and *exploration*. Instead of trying to create coherence between our core self and the other parts of ourselves, we can be curious towards each part.

We can be curious towards our *whole self*, not just its most important or central elements. And we can be curious towards each of our *multiple selves*, none of which is more important than any of the others.

This is a different way of viewing ourselves. When we are curious towards our whole self we no longer see ourselves as made up of central parts versus peripheral parts – parts of ourselves that we are happy with versus the part we want to bring into line. Instead, we pay attention to each of our multiple selves, curious about where they came from and what we can learn from them.

Another way of putting this difference is that, instead of changing ourselves from the 'top-down' – trying to achieve coherence between the different parts of ourselves – we can create change from the 'bottom-up'. We can be curious towards our whole selves and explore the possibilities that each of our habits, personality traits, goals, values and so on, provides us with. This process of change is largely unknown and out of our control – without a 'top-down' image of our identity, we don't know where we're going to end up. All we can know is that, wherever this process takes us, we will have gained a deeper understanding of what we most care about and are truly capable of. It is then that we might be in a position to change ourselves from the 'top-down' and commit to the things that we believe really matter.

Appreciation

This process of curiosity is one of discovery and creation. By appreciating our whole selves, we discover who we are. Then, by exploring our multiple selves, we create who we are. By creating new whole selves, we can then discover who we are again, which we can then explore further and so on. At each stage, we get a better idea of what we most care about and are truly capable of, even if the definitive answers to these questions remain a mystery.

Discovering ourselves

Marion Milner described this ongoing process of discovery and creation in her memoir *A Life of One's Own*. After fruitless attempts at trying to find her life's purpose, she began instead to see her life, 'not as the slow shaping of achievement to fit my preconceived purposes, but as the gradual discovery and growth of a purpose which I did not know'.[26]

Milner found that her attempts to reduce the complexities of her whole self and the world around her to preconceived ideas about what makes life meaningful were unhelpful. Instead, according to Milner, a meaningful life requires a wide-open attentiveness to reality, a curiosity about all that life has to offer. In trying to 'find meaning' in our lives, we may miss the fact that meaning is all around us, if only we cared to look.

We can begin by looking at ourselves differently. Instead of having preconceived ideas about our strengths and weaknesses, we can be curious about the multiple selves we are usually so quick to label. This is often what happens to us over time with the help of our personal narratives. For example, looking back at our lives, we may realise that what we thought was our greatest flaw (for example, our addictive personality) was in fact the thing that took our lives in a positive direction (for example, that forced us to seek help from others and then pledge to help others in return). This is the idea of 'post-traumatic growth' – that whatever doesn't kill us, makes us stronger.[27] What we now judge to be our flaws or weaknesses – parts of ourselves that we would probably get rid of if we could – can end up being our greatest strengths.

These are the kinds of realisations people have when undergoing the kinds of transcendental experiences described briefly in Chapter Four. With a heightened sense of attention and curiosity towards our multiple selves, we can gain a deeper understanding of their potential value. We do not have to wait until we have reached the end of our lives to realise our hidden strengths.

For instance, according to the analytical psychology developed by Carl Jung, transcendental experiences often help us confront our 'shadows' – the seemingly unacceptable parts of ourselves, which correspond to our scariest beliefs about reality.[28] Jung claimed that, even if we are not consciously aware of our shadows, they are in the background, motivating us to think, feel and behave in the ways we do, typically to protect ourselves from some threat or danger.

During a transcendental experience, instead of trying to avoid our shadows, we can begin to see them differently. For example, we may have previously seen one of our multiple selves as flawed or weak (for example 'I'm not a people person'). But through a heightened sense of curiosity, we may now view it as an ally (for example 'I can help other people who are shy or introverted' or 'I love working with animals'). These experiences of new possibilities can be so freeing and profound that people often take them on as their 'personal vision' or 'life mission'.[29]

In psychotherapy, this process is referred to as 'sublimation'. With the unconditional regard of a therapist, patients are encouraged to see how a usually unhelpful impulse can be converted into a noble ambition.[30] For example, an aggressive instinct to kick or hit can be channelled into sporting prowess, or a feeling that no one listens can give birth to a literary career.

This is also what happens in a loving relationship. We give our loved ones a more generous form of attention than we do to strangers. We see their habits, traits and weaknesses in a generous light – not as character flaws, but as the coping strategies they have developed to deal with challenging situations in the past. In a more loving and supportive context, these habitual patterns of behaviour could be beneficial.

For example, unlike others, we may charitably see our loved one's stubbornness as grit and determination, or we may see their shyness as humility and sensitivity. We may even feel that in seeing our loved one's whole self we see them more clearly – we see the best version of themselves, in all their potential. In doing so, we can inspire them to become that person.

Being seen in this way can be a powerful and profound experience. The world can become full of possibilities waiting to be explored. The unconditional regard we receive from a therapist, or the insights gained from a transcendental experience, can have a similar effect. Instead of seeing ourselves as a fixed set of habits and personality traits we can appreciate our full diversity and humanity.

These experiences, however, tend to be rare. We do not tend to view ourselves with curiosity and attention. For example, instead of being open to the possibilities presented by our thoughts and feelings, we tend to instantly assign meanings to them – typically, judging them as either good or bad. We try to keep hold of the good ones and get rid of the bad ones. But this shuts down any further inquiry into their nature – we don't pay any further attention to what they mean and how we might think or feel differently.

Being curious – and paying nonjudgemental attention – towards our feelings goes strongly against cultural norms. In modern individualistic societies, people are encouraged to feel good as much as possible, and feel bad as little as possible – what some critics have called the 'Tyranny of the Positive'.[31] We can see these norms at work even at the level of everyday greetings, such as someone asking, 'How are you?' In response, it is appropriate to answer, 'Fine,' without having to explain ourselves ('Oh, you're fine – nothing to worry about there, then'). But if we reply saying, 'Not great,' people tend to ask why ('Oh no, you're not great – is there anything I can do?'). Of course, this is a relatively trivial interaction, and is often laced with good intentions. But it still rests on the assumptions that feeling bad *is* bad, whereas feeling fine *is* fine.

Seeing our thoughts and feelings as presenting us with new possibilities is hard. As practices of meditation and mindfulness are testament to, it can take a lifetime to go beyond the embodied expectations wrapped up in our emotions.[32] But these practices also show what we have to gain from viewing ourselves differently – as constantly changing, complex, unknown entities. By being curious towards our whole selves, we can discover the potential strengths within our weaknesses and the possible new ideas within our negative feelings.

This process of curiosity and appreciation may sometimes be painful and uncomfortable. And, of course, we cannot spend all our time getting to know each and every one of our multiple selves. But without paying attention to what we don't know about ourselves, we will remain stuck in our preconceived ideas of what we do and do not care about, and what we can and cannot do.

Exploration

What do we do with a better understanding of our whole selves? How do we know whether our ambitions are realistic, or coherent with our other multiple selves? We cannot know the answers to these questions in advance. But we can endeavour to find out. By remaining curious, we can – through hard work and by learning from our mistakes – explore what we are truly capable of.

Creating ourselves

As soon as we start exploring the possibilities presented by our multiple selves, we open ourselves up to what the philosopher L.A. Paul calls 'transformative experiences'. For many of life's choices – such as where to live, what job to have or who to be in a relationship with – it is only by choosing a path to go down that we can discover what such a life is like. We cannot know beforehand how our choices are going to go. It is only through the process of making a choice, and living with that choice, that we become the kind of person who can then discover the value of having made such a choice. As L.A. Paul notes, we must 'choose based on whether we want to discover who we'll become'.[33]

For example, in choosing whether to be a doctor or a ballet dancer, it is only through becoming a doctor that we can understand what being a doctor will be like for us – whether it 'fits' or not. The same goes for being a ballet dancer. Of course, we can do our research – we can talk to doctors and ballet dancers about what their lives are like, we can volunteer at a hospital or a theatre, or we can look at which profession makes people happier. But, without knowing what our own life would be like as a doctor or a ballet dancer, we cannot know whether these ways of living are worthwhile for us. Our lives are too complex to know beforehand whether many of our choices will be right or wrong.

We naturally engage in this process through our relationships with others. Our different friends bring out different sides of us – through our relationships with them, we become different people. Our friends see us and the world in a different way, they give us feedback, they show us what's possible and they encourage us to pursue similar interests. In exploring these possibilities, our lives can take a completely different and unexpected direction. Our friendships – and other relationships – can be transformative experiences.

Not all of our choices involve transformative experiences. We often want to explore things that we already know are good for us. But this process may still be a complex one – one that requires our ongoing curiosity. We can explore our goals, projects and relationships with the overriding expectation that, whatever happens, we will probably be surprised. We can learn to expect the unexpected.

This is very different from the strategy of control, where we try to avoid and pre-empt failure at all costs. As part of this strategy we often create elaborate predictions about what will happen if we do something and fail. For example, should I continue writing this book into the evening? The honest answer is that I don't really know. But instead, I might reason with myself that I would be more productive if I worked on it at another time, perhaps when I'm less tired and can concentrate better. Of course, this might turn out to be true. But these thoughts can also stop me from ever finding out. In general, our predictions about what might happen can stop us from discovering what we are actually capable of.

It is understandable that we don't want to spend all our time making mistakes. But there is a balance to be drawn here. As Tim Harford notes in his book *Adapt*, failure is often the key to progress.[34] In light of the uncertainty and messiness of life, it is often better to place little bets and constantly adapt to their success or failure, than to be certain of the way forward and go for broke.[35] Life is too complicated to know how our pursuits are going to go. If we really want to understand what's possible, we must continue to act and adapt.

This is what people with growth mindsets do. We briefly looked at the distinction between 'growth' and 'fixed' mindsets in Chapters Three and Four. People with a fixed mindset believe they are good at some things and not good at other things – often supported by the idea of talent. In contrast, people with a growth mindset believe they get good at something through a combination of ongoing effort and feedback. In response to failure, people with a growth mindset do not assume they are no good at the activity and give up. Instead, they take failure as an invitation to change course, to try harder, and to grow.[36]

This relates to the psychological literature on 'deliberative practice', which has become well-known partly in opposition to the infamous '10,000 hour rule'. According to the 10,000 hour rule, achieving mastery in any activity, no matter how talented you are, requires at least 10,000 hours of practice.[37] But research into deliberative practice shows that simply putting the hours in is not enough.[38] Achieving our goals is a much less straightforward and much messier affair. Instead, we must develop our skills through practice that involves a constant series of experiments, failures, feedback and learning from our mistakes. As an example of how important failure is to achieving our goals, consider Edison's attempts to create a feasible light bulb. During the process, he is known to have said, 'I have not failed, I've just found 10,000 ways that won't work.'[39]

Humans are general-purpose learners. With a suitable amount of deliberate practice, we are able to master a wide range of skills and practices.[40] But this process requires exploring what we are capable of. Like individuals with a growth mindset, we need to shift our focus away from control and the desired outcomes of our actions, towards understanding and learning what's possible.

Understanding and control

This process of discovery and creation is ongoing negotiation between of our capacities for understanding and our capacities for control. With a better understanding of what we care about and are capable of, we can try to improve our circumstances. Eventually, however, we will come across barriers and get stuck. We must embrace uncertainty and pay attention to what we don't know. With an even better understanding of what we care about and are capable of, we can try to improve our circumstances again. And so the process continues.

This process involves constantly breaking old habits and making new ones. Habits can be viewed as forms of control based on *learned probabilities* – our unconscious, automatic knowledge of rewards that are likely to follow from particular cues and behaviours. As we saw in Chapter Three, our learned probabilities blind us to *unlearned possibilities* – the other potential cues, behaviours and rewards out there. The process of breaking old habits involves becoming more open to learning these new possibilities.

The ongoing development of our habits is central to theories of 'virtue ethics' in both Western (Aristotelian) and Eastern (Confucian) philosophies. Virtues such as courage and honesty are habitual dispositions to act in the right way, at the right time.[41]

This requires not only developing appropriate habits, but also continuously breaking them to understanding new possibilities for right action. For example, an honest person will not just reliably act honestly in all contexts, but also be able to perceive when honesty is and isn't required. Due to the complexities of social life, this is a process that never ends – even the so-called 'honest person' must continue to cultivate the virtue of honesty, and other virtues, throughout their life.[42]

Different philosophies, traditions and practices across the world have come up with different ways of breaking our habitual patterns of seeing the world and responding to it. Confucian philosophy emphasises performing constant 'rituals' as deliberate attempts to break our habitual behaviour in a familiar context.[43] For example, Confucius endorsed an ancient Chinese ritual whereby family members would temporarily swap roles. This, Confucius argued, helped the family members appreciate each other's thoughts and concerns. With this understanding, they could then act more appropriately within their own identified roles – father, daughter, brother and so on. Confucius was also well known for straightening his sitting mat every time before he sat on it. This tiny ritual broke up even the most familiar of gestures – an ongoing practice of opening up to the possibility of doing things differently, no matter what the activity.

Other traditions and practices create the potential for new patterns of thought and behaviour by deliberately invoking states of randomness. If you sit quietly and let your mind wander, you can get a glimpse of this randomness at work. Your daydreams put together odd combinations, relying on randomness and chance to come up with creative solutions to vexing problems. Studies from neuroscience have shown that whenever our attention is not fixed on a demanding task, we are combining and reorganising the contents of the mind, trying to make better sense of the world.[44] This is what Albert Einstein called 'combinatory play'.[45]

Practices such as the I Ching, or Tarot card readings, deliberately engage people in combinatory play by making them interact with random patterns and symbols, many of which come loaded with cultural meanings and significance. It may be that shamanic practices also rely on similar methods. Shamanism often arises among people exposed to uncertainty. For instance, following the collapse of socialism in 1989–91, the Buryat people in Upper Mongolia faced poverty and starvation. Within these conditions, the practices of Buryat shamans flourished as people sought new ways to control the uncertainties in their lives.[46]

All this bustling, largely unconscious, activity nonetheless has rules. (This is true even for shamans: shamanic peoples, just like the majority of Western Christians, prefer Western doctors when they can find them.[47]) For example, when trying to figure out a relationship problem we have, we don't tend to think about cats or dogs – such combinations are irrelevant to the problem at hand.

But who knows, maybe there is something useful in there? Maybe thinking about the calm dependence associated with cats, or the unquestionable loyalty associated with dogs, does have some relevance to our relationship problem after all? This may seem absurd, and is certainly unlikely, but it's an example of what psychologists call 'divergent thinking': combining fragmentary thoughts and concepts into new – often wacky, sometimes genius – ideas.[48]

In fact, randomness and combinatory play may be one of the defining features of genius. As Ralph Waldo Emerson noted, 'In the minds of geniuses, we find – once more – our own neglected thoughts.'[49] By this, Emerson means that the genius doesn't have different kinds of thoughts from the rest of us. They are simply more open to them, and take them more seriously. Genius can partly be defined as paying closer attention to our thoughts and feelings (curiosity) and being brave and tenacious enough to hold onto them even when they seemingly have no immediate place in the world (exploration).

We tend to disavow so much of what passes through our minds either because of its seeming lack of utility or through fear of seeming strange to ourselves and others – genius is, after all, often associated with madness. In comparison, consider how small children are, in their own way, so much more interesting than the average adult – they have not yet become experts in what not to say or think. When we censor and close down our thoughts is exactly the moment when the so-called genius starts to take note of what is happening within them.

Of course, this is simplifying the nature of genius – randomness and combinatory play is only part of what distinguishes a genius from the rest of us. In addition, genius involves: a) assessing the unfiltered subconscious combinations of the mind as either good or bad forms of novelty; b) collaborating with others to build on novel ideas, yet sticking with personal inclinations if others wrongly disagree; and, c) not going mad with all the chaos and the mixture of criticism and positive regard. Personally, I'd prefer to be mundane.

We all have our own small moments of genius when we loosen our learned predictions and make room for divergent thinking and the emergence of new ideas. We call these 'aha' or 'eureka' moments. You may have been working on a problem for a while and it's doing your head in – no matter what you try, you just can't figure out how to solve it. Then, while taking a break, having a shower or going for a walk – suddenly the answer pops into your head. Eureka! You've solved it and you weren't even trying. These moments of effortless insight and inspiration are well documented and now the subject of psychological study. One of the key factors in their occurrence is rest.[50] We often neglect downtime in favour of doing work and being productive, but it may be an essential part of creativity and problem solving.

To make room for rest and randomness, and expecting the unexpected, we may need to go a little easier on ourselves. This process of curiosity and exploration cannot be rushed. My aim in this and the previous section has been to show that being curious towards our lives is, nonetheless, often worth it – perhaps more so than we tend to think. Discovering what we care about and are capable of is an ongoing negotiation between understanding and control. But we often need the more of the former, not more of the latter. Making room for this process of curiosity to unfold may not be easy – it is difficult to be uncertain and to make mistakes – but it is how we come to gain a deeper understanding of who we are within all the complexities of the world. In the next section, we will see that with such an understanding we can begin to live up to what really matters.

Commitment

So far, we have seen how, through the process of curiosity, our lives gain *breadth*. Instead of having fixed ideas about 'who we really are', we can continue to appreciate our whole selves and explore a wide range of goals and concerns. This is how we discover what we most care about and are truly capable of.

In this section, we will see how we can use this understanding to give our lives *depth*. When we care about something enough, we commit to it. Our commitments limit our opportunities and create new challenges. But by remaining curious towards our lives we can discover what's possible within the limits of our commitments. Through this process – of commitment and curiosity – we can live up to what really matters.

Going deeper

We've already looked at the downside of commitment in Chapter Two. We saw that, in committing to a long-term project or relationship, we miss out on engaging in other meaningful and satisfying activities. We must make sure that our commitments are the things we really care about. Otherwise we might regret not having committed to something (or someone) else, such as having children instead of having a career or getting married instead of prioritising our friends.

We also saw how people often commit to things for the wrong reasons. We might commit to something because other people see it as valuable and worthwhile – it is something we feel we 'should' commit to, rather than something we really care about. Alternatively, we might commit to something because it gives us a sense of familiarity and security over time – we lock down our future so that we can be confident in what we are doing in the present.[51]

These commitment traps are what make the processes of appreciation and exploration described above so important. We should not enter into commitments lightly. We all know this, of course. We know, for example, that marriage is a serious business – that it means sticking by someone through thick and thin, in sickness and in health. Very few of us marry the first person we see. And yet, marriage and other commitments – such as long-term goals and ambitions – are so prized in our culture that we often assume we are going to get married or commit to a lifelong project *at some point*. It is perhaps no surprise that we end up doing so before we've fully appreciated what we care about and explored what we're capable of.

If commitments are so problematic then why should we make them? Entering into commitments for the right reasons is worthwhile because they provide us with the grounds to form rich connections and achieve our most ambitious projects. Without committing to something, we don't really know what we are capable of. It is too tempting to give up and focus our efforts on something else. Commitments require our continual striving and effort even when doing so feels hopeless – when we would normally give up. They rest on the optimistic assumption that, over time, all our attention and actions will pay off.

Of course, we may sometimes doubt whether our commitments are worthwhile. But most of the time we are certain of their value. Many philosophers consider this to be one of the hallmarks of meaning and personal identity.[52] For instance, the philosopher Harry Frankfurt, in his book *The Reasons of Love*, notes that our loving commitments – such as being a parent – give our lives meaning because they provide us with a kind of 'restful certainty'.[53] According to Frankfurt, our commitments are like finding a mathematical proof – we no longer have to struggle to make up our minds, the issue is settled.

The hard part is maintaining this sense of contentment. We may enter into our commitments convinced of their worth. But over time we may not feel we can live up to them. We may also feel the opportunity costs of the limitations they impose on us. In the remainder of this section, we will see how overcoming these problems requires, somewhat paradoxically, for us to continue being curious, no matter how certain we are in what we care about.

Simplicity

The limitations that our commitments impose on us can make us doubt whether they are in fact worthwhile – whether the things we care about are good enough. We often experience this concern in the form of an experience we know all too well: boredom.

Boredom exists for a reason. It motivates us to do something more valuable than what we are currently doing.[54] It is telling us that our present situation is out of tune with our interests: we are not content with where we are; we feel restless and wish to be doing something else; we desire to escape. How, then, can we reconcile our commitments, which are limiting by default, with our desire to do what is most important?

The answer is to continue being curious. The philosopher Bertrand Russell spoke of monotony and boredom as gateways to imagination and curiosity.[55] Instead of distracting ourselves with our phones or other forms of escapism, we can use boredom as an opportunity to see our situation differently. Curiosity can help us experience beauty and gratitude in response to our situation, no matter how limited it may be.

For example, doing the washing up can be astonishing once we pay attention to how well choreographed our arm and hand movements are, the different forms of energy that have been used to heat up the water, the care and effort that went into the manufacture of the dishes (and into the preparation of the meal we just ate off them!) and so on. If we accept our boredom, and let ourselves be curious about our situation, we can find beauty and wonder even in the most mundane of tasks.

Our capacities for curiosity, met by the complexities of the world around us, create a kind of *psychological abundance*. We can always open ourselves up to experiences of awe and wonder, gratitude and contentment. This form of abundance has inspired groups and individuals throughout history to seek out lives of simplicity. From Epicurus to Thoreau, people have intentionally based their lives around cultivating a sense of appreciation towards the world: to see the beauty all around them; to not constantly push for greater things.[56]

A simple or frugal lifestyle is a confident one. It assumes that no matter how limited we are in our standard of living, we can spend our time immersed in daily activities such as sleeping, eating, breathing, moving, sitting, listening, connecting. We can apply the same principle to the limitations imposed on us by our commitments. When our commitments stop us from doing other meaningful activities, we can still appreciate the things that make up our daily lives.

In particular, we can appreciate 'small pleasures' and 'quiet values' over dramatic experiences and grand achievements. Ordinary enjoyments are part of what makes life worthwhile: eating fresh food, having a bath, whispering in bed in the dark, talking to a grandparent.[57] If properly grasped and elaborated on, these sorts of activities may be among the most moving and satisfying we can have.[58] Instead of dismissing these things as minor parts of our lives, we can be curious about them and put them at the very centre.

This process is often a subtle one. For example, the aesthetic value of our immediate environment can be quiet and delicate – it is not as stimulating as an action film, or as entertaining as having fun with a group of friends. Likewise, the value of a peaceful moment, a painting, a long walk or the sensation of being alive – none of these things demands strong responses. Yet, these small enjoyments are available to us when other experiences are not. They come from being curious about our situation, whatever situation we are in.[59]

Advocates of simplicity insist that we can cherish the life we already have and resist the psychological inertia that makes us strive for more. We do not all need to lead monastic lifestyles, however, to learn from this process. The limitations imposed by our commitments force a more simple, frugal way of living on us. We can all learn how to be more confident in our commitments, knowing that the limits they impose on us still leave room for an abundance of small pleasures and quiet values to immerse our attention in.

From the perspective of simplicity, we may look at the busy lives of others – trying to achieve all their ambitions and have as many exciting experiences as possible – as somewhat bizarre. Simplicity shows us that, in our hurry to improve our lives, we can fail to see the wonders at our feet.

Hope and trust

With curiosity, we can live well within the limitations that our commitments create. But how can we live up to the challenges that our commitments create?

Again, the answer is to continue being curious. In addition to beauty and gratitude, curiosity can help us appreciate the value of the things we so often try to avoid – our negative thoughts and feelings, or our vulnerabilities and weaknesses. We can pay attention to these things and gain a deeper understanding of them. This understanding can help us respond with greater flexibility to the challenges our commitments create. In particular, curiosity towards our future can give us hope.

With hope, we can continue to live up to our commitments, even without the certainty that all our efforts will eventually pay off. This is different from simply being optimistic. Optimism is the attitude that, despite our uncertain future, everything will turn out fine. In contrast, hope is neither optimistic nor pessimistic. When we are hopeful, we do not simply assume that things will go well. Instead, we see our uncertain future as something to remain open towards and gain a deeper understanding of.[60]

Hope gives us room to think and act differently about living up to our commitments, even if we are unlikely to succeed. For example, we might actively imagine positive events and scenarios, and stay attentive to potential opportunities to bring them about.[61] This ongoing curiosity can end up making the uncertain outcomes more likely. As the poet Emily Dickinson notes, 'hope inspires the good to reveal itself'.[62]

Because our future is uncertain, hoped-for outcomes may not come about for a very long period of time. From the study of history, we know that change is slow. And yet, from a longer temporal perspective, this gradual change can give us hope. Things have not always been the way they are now. And so, they are unlikely to be the same in the future.[63] No matter how difficult things may seem now, we can always stay curious towards our future, and have hope.

It is difficult to know whether this process of curiosity will pay off over time. We might see no way in which our marriage break-up or serious injury, for example, could be anything other than a bad thing in our lives. But, fast forward a few years or decades, and we may look back at these tragic events as the beginning of a positive new life direction or having created opportunities that we wouldn't have had otherwise. This is the lesson of our life stories, which we looked at in Chapter Four. Over time, we can see how the negative and positive events in our lives are connected – how we learn from everything that happens to us – good and bad – in the process of creating our lives. We may not know what we are going to learn from our current experiences and hardships. But we can take solace from our redemptive life narratives and trust that, at some point in our lives, we will get to a point where we see things differently.

We might reasonably ask when this point will come. How patient should we be? At what point would it be better to lose hope and give up on our commitments? I do not think there is a definite answer to this question. The more hope and trust we have, the longer we can persevere and remain open to new possibilities. At its most extreme, we can have faith. For instance, Martin Luther King, in his fight for civil rights, had faith that, in the end, justice would overcome everything.[64] This faith helped him continue to work towards civil justice even if he had no way of knowing whether such work would pay off in his lifetime.

All our commitments require at least some form of hope and trust – for us to remain curious about the uncertainties of our future. These attitudes help us see the worth of our commitments within difficult and testing circumstances. The more demanding our commitments are, the more hope and trust we need. At their most demanding, our commitments require our faith – the attitude that, despite our uncertain future, it is worth sticking with our commitments and being open to what might happen. Curiosity might just see us through.

As we saw in Chapter Four, we often embrace uncertainty when we have a lack of control over our situation. We looked at grief and personal crisis as examples of tragedies where we lack control. Our commitments are another example. When we commit to something, we cannot so easily run away when the going gets tough. We put ourselves in a position where we lack control. When there is no way out, we have no choice but to continue paying attention to what we don't know until we find a way of dealing with the challenges we face. Living up to our commitments requires us to be curious and hopeful towards our lives.

The process of curiosity

In this chapter we have looked at the process of curiosity – of appreciation, exploration and commitment. Through appreciating our whole selves and exploring our multiple selves, we can better understand the wide range of things we care about and are capable of. This is what gives our lives breadth. Through committing to the things we most care about, we can add depth to our lives. The process of curiosity can help us deal with the limits and challenges created by our commitments and live up to what really matters.

This process does not eliminate the strategy of control completely, but instead acknowledges that we can often focus more on better understanding our lives and less on controlling everything to our liking. In any given moment or in any given situation, we can benefit from embracing uncertainty and paying attention to what we don't know. Outside our problem-solving bubbles, there is a wonderful and complex world for us to explore. The more time we spend there, the better we can understand the value of switching our focus away from control towards curiosity.

There is a major implication of this process, however, that we have so far not spoken about – one that deserves an entire chapter of its own. Opening ourselves up to the world does not just expose us to all the good things. The process of curiosity also exposes us to vulnerability and suffering. We cannot get away from this fact. In contrast to the control strategy, which seeks to eliminate as many forms of insecurity and suffering as possible, the process of curiosity aims to better understand reality before going to war with it. This means spending more time with our vulnerabilities and insecurities – appreciating and exploring them, as well as trying to alleviate them.

In the next chapter, we will look at this implication in more detail. On the one hand, the process of curiosity helps us respond with greater flexibility to the insecurities and challenges we face. On the other hand, the same openness to reality that makes us more flexible and adaptive also makes us more vulnerable. We cannot have one without the other. The kind of happiness created by the understanding strategy involves as much sorrow as it does joy, and as much failure as it does success. This is a straightforward consequence of striving for peace with reality, rather than going to war with it. In the rest of this book, I hope to convince you that, nonetheless, we need to give peace a chance.

SIX

Compassion

Before you know kindness as the deepest thing inside,
you must know sorrow as the other deepest thing.
You must wake up with sorrow.
You must speak to it till your voice
catches the thread of all sorrows
and you see the size of the cloth.
Then it is only kindness that makes sense anymore.
Naomi Shihab Nye[1]

In the past two chapters we have looked at two of the three parts
that make up the understanding strategy – an alternative way of
thinking about happiness.

In contrast to the strategy of control, it does not involve getting
everything in our lives just right and the problems that come
from going to war with reality. Instead, we have seen that through
embracing uncertainty and being curious towards our lives, we
can discover what we most care about and are truly capable of.

The outcome of this strategy, however, is not security. The
process of curiosity is not an alternative means of achieving a
stable set of circumstances that will give us a lasting sense of
meaning and satisfaction. Happiness comes from understanding,
but not the kind of happiness we typically think about in modern
society. In the previous chapter, we looked at how continuing
to be curious towards our lives opens us up to experiences of
beauty and gratitude, and greater flexibility in response to the
challenges we face. This process of curiosity is also what gives
our lives breadth and depth, and the internal resources to live
up to what really matters. These are all forms of happiness we

would naturally recognise. However, in this chapter we will see that the same mindset and process opens us up to experiences and circumstances that we would typically try to avoid, let alone include in our vision of happiness. This alternative way of thinking about happiness is less clear-cut than the control strategy. It involves as much sorrow as it does joy, and as much failure as it does success.

Happiness, according to the understanding strategy, does not come from eliminating as many of our vulnerabilities and insecurities as possible. It acknowledges that our insecurity is here to stay. Instead, happiness comes from learning how to improve our lives within our insecurity. The process of curiosity is part of this picture. It is easier to fall back on our fixed ideas about our 'authentic selves' because discovering what we most care about and are truly capable of is an unknown, difficult and scary process. Each step makes us vulnerable.

First, we often don't appreciate what we care about because there are parts of our whole selves that we don't like, or are unacceptable to others. Paying attention to our multiple selves, including our vulnerabilities and weaknesses, can be a painful and uncomfortable process.

Second, we often don't explore what we are capable of because the potential for making mistakes and experiencing rejection is all too real. We want to be good at the things we do, not a failure. We don't want to waste our time. We want to show our best selves to the world, not a work in progress.

Last, we often don't commit to what we most care about because we don't know whether we can live up to our deepest commitments – the limits and challenges they create. Fully committing to a project or a relationship makes us dependent on something outside ourselves, exposing us to loss and heartbreak.

We cannot remove these challenges. But we can learn how to deal with them well. This is the outcome of the understanding strategy – to learn how to improve our lives within insecurity. Instead of a set of stable circumstances which bring us lasting meaning and satisfaction, this alternative outcome is more of an ongoing process of care and compassion. In this chapter, we will see how, through our capacities for compassion, we can gain a deeper understanding of our suffering as well as the motivation to alleviate it. This dual process of curiosity and compassion can, over time, help us understand the central role that our insecurity plays both in our own lives and in the lives of others. Happiness is learning how to live within insecurity with a sense of care.

Being vulnerable

Taking away and adding on

The process of curiosity is an inherently vulnerable one because it does not straightforwardly seek to eliminate all the insecurities in our lives. In contrast to the strategy of control, which aims to avoid as much suffering as possible, being curious towards our lives involves learning from suffering as well as trying to alleviate it. Through the process of curiosity, our insecurities become opportunities to learn more about the world and ourselves.

Of course, this process may be a more effective means of overcoming many of our insecurities in the long run. In Chapters Two and Three, we saw how our strategies of control are often narrow in scope, based on our personal histories and social context. They may eliminate the symptoms of our insecurities (for example, our social smoking habit) but not the underlying insecurity that caused them (our social anxiety). In contrast, through the process of curiosity described in Chapter Five, we can gain a deeper understanding of what we are scared of and the kinds of coping strategies we employ to alleviate our fears.

Our habitual ways of seeing the world are where we are most likely to get stuck – where we see things as solid and certain. The process of curiosity can provide us with the resources to see things differently. Things might not be as bad as we thought, or we might be able to respond to them in better ways.

Curiosity *takes away* the certainty that we attach to our fears, insecurities, needs and desires. We tend to go about our lives thinking that our practical goals and concerns really matter – that, 'if only we had ___ then we'd be happy'. As we saw in Chapter One, this is not true. We can improve our lives, but no matter how much progress we make we will still be insecure: vulnerable to disappointment, loss and suffering. Whenever we find ourselves thinking that the next achievement will make us happy, we have the opportunity to correct ourselves – to realise how, once again, we have been fooled by the illusion of certainty. This is how our insecurities can be windows into seeing reality more clearly.

The kinds of practices of attention we looked at in Chapter Four are all examples of how, by paying more attention to what we don't know about our situation, we can take away the certainty that we normally attach to it. In a state of flow, for example, where our attention is fully absorbed in the activity at hand, we can go beyond our habitual reactions and respond to immediate challenges and obstacles with a combination of skill and flexibility. Similarly, rituals and ceremonies can make us pay attention to something that we might otherwise take for granted, and gain a deeper understanding of its significance.

In the remainder of this section, we will see how this process of taking away the certainty of our habitual fears and insecurities can often be useful, but that it also a vulnerable one. Taking away our certainties creates room for us to see the world differently. As a result, we often see the world and ourselves in more helpful ways. But this isn't necessary the case.

To begin with, let's consider two dramatic cases in which this process of 'taking away' and 'adding on' often goes well: in the use of psychedelic therapies to treat addictions and death anxiety. Consider addiction, first. After undergoing a psychedelic experience in laboratory conditions, many patients report no longer having their addicted cravings. Instead, they report feeling a strong sense of connection with themselves, others and their environment, and a renewed sense of clarity and control over their situation.[2] Through their experience, the certainty associated with their cravings – that they need the object of their addiction to cope with their situation – is taken away.

Addictions are desperate attempts to gain a sense of agency and control within situations of disconnection and helplessness. We may not all have addictions, but we do all have coping strategies to gain some sense of control over our lives. The psychoanalyst Carl Jung referred to these ingrained parts of our personality as our 'shadows'.[3] They are the unacknowledged and unacceptable parts of ourselves which correspond to our scariest beliefs about reality. Psychedelic experiences can help people confront their shadows.[4] Much like in treating addiction, the certain terror that individuals usually ascribe to their shadows is taken away. Without these fears and concerns, they can prioritise interests and enjoyments that they previously felt too insecure to explore.

These transcendent experiences are sometimes described by individuals as having temporarily 'lost themselves' and then 'found themselves' again, having gone through a significant transformation in the meantime.[5] Alternatively, they might describe the experience as the 'death' and 'rebirth' of their self. In fact, psychedelic experiences can be extremely scary for this reason – confronting our deepest fears and insecurities can literally seem like a matter of life and death.

This is perhaps why psychedelics have also been so effective at treating people with 'death anxiety' – a condition that some individuals experience after being diagnosed with a terminal illness.[6] People with death anxiety are unable to acknowledge their health status without suffering extreme distress. They may excessively worry that that they have no lasting legacy, for example, or that they have been a bad friend or parent. Unable to find appropriate ways of bringing their lives to a close, their final days are full of anxiety and suffering.

After undergoing a psychedelic experience in laboratory conditions, many patients report no longer having the same anxieties over their terminal illness.[7] Having taken away the certainty of their worries, they come to see that their life is still of worth. This is often supported by a realisation that part of themselves will live on, even after the death of their physical body. This is not necessarily due to any newfound belief in the afterlife. They may simply pay more attention to the parts of themselves that are likely to 'live on' beyond their death.

This realisation is something that matters to all of us, not just those close to death. To get a better understanding of it, it helps to see how our selves can be viewed as having multiple *levels*. For instance, the founder of psychology, William James, in his book *Principles of Psychology*, described three different levels of selfhood.[8] According to James, at the most concrete and superficial level, there is the 'material self' – our physical body and material possessions. Then, there is the 'social self' – the recognition and status we get from friends, family and loved ones.

At the most subtle and important level, there is the 'spiritual self' – our deepest values, commitments and attachments.

James noted that our 'spiritual self' was the most expansive, but also the most easily neglected. For example, it is very hard to know the impact of our general interaction with those around us. From being kind and considerate, we may influence others to be the same; from other people being kind and considerate, they may influence others and so on. Our actions create ripples upon ripples that go far beyond our conscious awareness of them. James's point is that these ripples are as much a part of us as our material and social selves are.

By taking away the certainty associated with our material and social selves we can gain a deeper understanding of the more expansive parts of ourselves. The fact that everything is causally connected means that single events can create a long, complex series of unintentional consequences.[9] Our actions and intentions are never inconsequential. Individuals with death anxiety may get a glimpse of just how profound our actions and intentions can be. With this understanding, they can 'add on' more helpful ways of seeing the world, including seeing how the things they most care about will continue to go on without them.[10]

We needn't wait until we are on the verge of death to shift our priorities in this way. Through being curious towards our shadows and insecurities we can take away their certainty and free ourselves up to focus on the things we really care about. This is an ongoing process – the majority of our habits and traits may be distractions from, or distortions of, reality.

This idea is often emphasised within Buddhist thought. For example, the Buddhist monk Thich Nhat Hanh notes that we feel empty – 'a great lack of something' – so we naturally try and fill this lack with material goods, loving relationships or whatever else we feel we need. None of these things, claims Thich Nhat Hanh, will get rid of this feeling of emptiness: 'In everyone there's a continuous desire and expectation; deep inside, you still expect something better to happen. That is why you check your email many times a day!'[11]

Expanding ourselves

The more curious we are about our lives, the less certain we become about the potential threats and dangers within it, as well as the potential opportunities and rewards. This openness and flexibility can have profound implications. Having more material possessions becomes less necessary. We can trust the people we love instead of trying to control their affections. Our weaknesses can turn out to be our greatest strengths. And we can feel okay with feeling bad.

This process of taking away our fears and insecurities and adding on the things we care about can happen in every part of our lives. Consider, for example, the insecurities that come from being in a close relationship. In Chapter Two we saw that one of the hallmarks of intimacy is the generous form of attention we receive. Unlike strangers, our loved ones try to understand us in all our individuality and complexity – they see the potential in both our strengths and our weaknesses, and how we can be our best possible selves.[12] And yet despite this generous gaze, expressing our whole selves, including the parts of us that may be less acceptable, can feel like a dangerous thing to do.[13] Being honest about who we are and what we feel risks losing the affection we receive. As the poet David Whyte notes, the 'fear of loss, in one form or another, is the motivator behind all conscious and unconscious dishonesties'.[14] What if our loved ones don't like who we really are, or what we have to say?

By being curious towards these risks and dangers, we can take away their certainty and explore what it is like to share our whole selves within our relationships. The potential benefits of doing so are significant. We can trust and rely on others more, knowing that our relationships are built on love and acceptance, rather than fear and judgment. The sociologist Brené Brown refers to this process of 'strong vulnerability' as having a 'strong back, soft front'.[15] We can have a soft front and expose the most vulnerable parts of ourselves in our relationship. And we can do this from knowing that we have a strong back: if all goes wrong, we can continue to see things differently, adapt and flexibly respond to our situation.

This shift in priorities – taking away the certainty of our fears and insecurities and exploring other possibilities – is what the humanist psychologist Abraham Maslow emphasised in his conception of 'self-actualisation'.[16] Maslow claimed that after meeting our needs for survival, safety, belonging and recognition, we can feel safe and secure enough to prioritise our intimate relationships, creative pursuits and personal growth. Similarly, the psychologist Eric Fromm claimed that a meaningful life involved gradually taking away our tendencies towards narcissism and property – what he called our two 'human chains' – and replacing them with less self-interested and security-focused goals.[17]

This process is sometimes referred to as one of personal *growth*.[18] It is also described as a process of self-expansion, or 'letting go'. Over time, our main concerns expand away from self-oriented desires for survival, safety and recognition towards more other-oriented concerns and values – towards something 'larger than ourselves'. For instance, the philosopher Thaddeus Metz, in his 'transcendence' theory of meaning, claims that meaning comes from transcending the limits of our animal nature – our instincts, drives and emotions – and realising a more rational, intellectual ideal.[19]

We can see this idea throughout history, in the teachings of the world's major religions. For instance, Buddhism teaches that people can end suffering not by altering life itself, but their reaction and response to it. This is the happiness of Enlightenment and Nirvana – a complete transformation of personality characterised by peace, compassion and joy in response to negative thoughts, worries and anxieties.[20] We can see similarities of this thinking in Islam, Christianity and Hinduism.[21] For Hindus, the satisfaction of physical and material desires is considered to be less important than the three possible paths to happiness: knowledge, duty and loving devotion. The practice of Yoga tells us that happiness is not a condition of self-satisfaction but a dynamic directed outward – towards knowledge of something greater than yourself, duty to your community and loving devotion shown to others. The Sufi mystics believed that the problem self – the unhappy self – is the one enslaved by desire and governed by base instincts and appetites. These desires take us further away from the origin of our being – being in

God's presence. The Christian scholar Thomas Aquinas taught something similar: that perfect happiness consists in being in presence of God in heaven – what he called contemplating the 'beatific vision'.

According to all these religious traditions and teachings, the self – characterised by our fears and insecurities – is seen as a major obstacle to happiness. Spiritual growth is a process of quieting or pruning the self – a process that makes people more vulnerable, but also helps them see reality (and therefore God) more clearly. Of course, the self does not like to be denied – we don't like to be insecure ('Give up my possessions and the prestige they bring? No way!'; 'Love my enemies, after what they did to me? Forget about it'). This is why each religious tradition has its own elaborate and sophisticated forms of practice, ritual and worship to help its followers along this lifelong path of taking away their insecurities and adding on more helpful ways of seeing the world.

These are all nice ideas, and have some truth to them. However, I don't think we can be as optimistic as they suggest. This process of growth and self-expansion can often be a beneficial one. But in exposing ourselves, we can also get into trouble. Consider, for instance, the process of trust. Trust grows slowly over time, as we gradually learn how to expand ourselves and rely on other people for support.[22] The more we trust in others, the more we open ourselves up to further opportunities to rely on others. If this goes well our trust increases, which can create further opportunities for reliance and so on.

However, our levels of trust can also spiral in the opposite direction. The less we trust in others, the more we open ourselves up to further opportunities for independence. Once this process of self-contraction begins, it is difficult to turn it around. Trust is fragile. And so are we. Ideas of personal growth and self-expansion may well be inspiring, and to a large extent true. But they can also romanticise just how risky and exposing the process of curiosity can be can be.

If we are lucky, the process of curiosity can lead us on a positive path of self-expansion and increasing our circle of concern. We may end up being more generous towards others and our whole selves. We might feel more freedom to express our full range of thoughts and feelings. We can find the courage to follow our dreams and passions. And so on. But this process can just as easily go wrong. After all, we developed our fears and insecurities for a reason.

Consider again the above example of being honest and wholehearted within our relationships. By exposing our whole selves to our loved ones, we can end up getting seriously hurt – mentally and physically. Now, through the process of curiosity, we may be able to deal with this pain better than we think. But this may only be minor consolation. Being heartbroken or abused, no matter how curious we are, can still give our self-esteem and trust in others a big knock.

We cannot guarantee that the process of curiosity will be one of continual growth – one in which we increasingly expand our circle of concern, become more caring and giving and less self-interested. To say otherwise – as many new age and self-help gurus do – would be irresponsible.[23] At any point in this process, we can end up experiencing pain and discomfort, failure and rejection or loss and heartbreak. As we saw in Chapter Five, this may be the only way in which we can seriously test our limits and discover what we are truly capable of. But that doesn't make the process any less painful.

From curiosity to compassion

Self-compassion

The process of curiosity that we have been looking at does not provide us with a place of rest. It keeps on going – there is always more we can pay attention to and gain a deeper understanding of. Once we begin to see that uncertainty is at the heart of everything, the possibilities for appreciation, exploration and commitment are endless. We may trust our loved ones, for example. But we can always trust and rely on more people. We may be generous with our time and attention. But we could still experiment with giving more of ourselves away, just beyond what is comfortable. We can continue to push our boundaries and ourselves in these ways – to explore what we most care about and are truly capable of. Embracing uncertainty and paying attention to what we don't know is far from passive. It frees us up to explore life in all its fullness.

This includes the bad stuff. Appreciating our whole selves exposes us to pain and discomfort. Exploring what we are capable of exposes us to failure and rejection. And committing to what we most care about exposes us to loss and heartbreak. These experiences of vulnerability and suffering – that we normally try so hard to avoid – are an unavoidable part of the process.

Which is where compassion comes in. Compassion, like curiosity, is about paying attention to what we don't know and gaining a deeper understanding of our situation. In contrast to curiosity, compassion is exclusively focused on our suffering, and it motivates us to alleviate it. Compassion does not simply seek to gain a deeper understanding of our suffering. We are also moved to do something about it, even if all we can do is simply continue to give it our attention. Compassion combines curiosity with care.[24]

With compassion, the attention we pay towards our suffering gains a different kind of quality – a gentleness and tenderness. At the end of a long day, for example, instead of berating ourselves for all the mistakes we have made or the things we haven't managed to achieve, we can gain a deeper understanding of why the day hasn't lived up to our expectations. Instead of blaming what has happened on our fixed moral character, we can pay more attention to the situational factors that have got in our way and made things too difficult for us. Instead of simply telling ourselves to be more productive the following day, we can explore potential ways of making things easier for ourselves.

This is likely to be the opposite of the usual internal voices and stories that provide an ongoing commentary on our lives. When we grow up, in our efforts to work out what is acceptable and what is not, we tend to internalise the voices and emotional dispositions of those around us. We may, for example, have taken special notice of what makes a parent angry, the ways in which a sibling threatened us or the cutting remarks of a schoolyard bully. Through internalising the grains of truth in these voices, we have managed to act in ways that are acceptable to others and get by to the extent we have so far.

These voices, however, are not always kind. They may be quick to judge and put us down. This is different from how we might speak to someone in need, a child or to a good friend. We may accept their flaws as inevitable outgrowths of the challenges they've had to face in their lives and the resources they've had to deal with them. With the people we care about, we may be quicker to see that they are doing their best.

With compassion, we can gain a deeper understanding of where our inner voices and critics came from and what they need. We might discover, for example, that the more unacceptable parts of ourselves developed not through any fault of our own, but from our needs failing to be met at some point. Our aggression, jealousy or sensitivity may have helped us cope with being insecure and vulnerable in the past. And we may still expect to have to use the same coping strategies in the future. Without compassion, we may simply see these traits as moral flaws and inconveniences – things we need to 'get over'. With compassion, we can appreciate that they are intelligible responses to being scared about what might happen in the unknowns that lie ahead.

Compassion for others

We can also have compassion towards others. One of the reasons we don't tend to treat others with compassion is that it takes time. We cannot get to know everyone we meet well enough to understand the origins of their insecurities and concerns. If someone is annoying, irritable or threatening, it is much easier to take their behaviour as indicative of their moral character – that they are rude, inconsiderate or mean. It takes much more time to pay attention to the contextual factors that might have played a part in their behaviour, such as being tired or having a stressful day. Without knowing someone very well, we cannot understand all the ways in which their background circumstances and personal histories make sense of their actions.

Instead of spending time imagining why individuals are the way they are, we tend to simply expect people to behave in 'reasonable' or 'appropriate' ways in particular situations. When people fail to live up to these expectations, we quickly pass judgement on them. We rarely show them compassion.

Psychologists refer to this tendency as the 'fundamental attribution error'.[25] When we do something good, we tend to put it down to our stable personal traits, such as being kind or honest. In contrast, when we do something bad, we tend to attribute our behaviour to contextual factors, such as being under pressure or in a bad mood. We do the opposite, however, for others. When another person does a bad thing, they are a simply a bad person.

We do not tend to treat children in this way. Parents, for example, often try and figure out the contextual factors behind their child's behavior – whether they are tired, hungry, lacking attention and so on – rather than simply labelling them as annoying or selfish (of course, parents sometimes do this too!). We don't ascribe the same level of moral responsibility to children as we do to adults – expecting them to always behave 'reasonably' or 'appropriately'. Instead of blaming them for their bad behaviour, good parenting often involves being compassionate and trying to understand why they behaved in the way they did.

Why don't we treat adults in a similar way? It is not just due to a lack of time and background information. We pass judgement on other people because it can be an effective means of controlling their behaviour. Unlike children, adults are seen as morally responsible for most of the things they do. Blaming someone – labelling them as rude or inconsiderate, for example – can cause them to act differently in the future. In contrast, by understanding them better, we may be able to help them act differently – but doing so may also be more difficult. Through compassion, we may not get the outcomes we want. It is often easier to simply moralise or demonise someone as a means of controlling their behaviour, than to understand them and help them get what they need.[26]

We do not always moralise people in order to change them. Sometimes we give people's positive traits and habits labels so that they stay the way they are. Consider, for example, the beginning of a romantic relationship. On meeting someone, we might be attracted to all the ways in which they 'get us' (in other words, are the same of us) and 'complete us' (namely, are how we would like to be). During this heady stage, we might hope that they stay these ways forever. We then get disappointed when they inevitably change, lamenting either their change in personality ('They're a different person now') or our poor judgement ('They aren't the person I thought they were').

Both of these strategies of control – a) fixing people's characters because we want them to stay the same and b) blaming their characters because we want them to change – may both work in the short term. To some extent, we can get away with treating people as objects that we can manipulate to meet our own needs and desires. But these strategies do not work in the long term, nor should they. People are subjects, not objects. They have their own insecurities, dreams and complex inner lives. Intimate relationships require understanding the inner lives of others, which curiosity and compassion make possible.[27]

Compassion can be more challenging than curiosity because we are invested in the outcome. When we care for someone, we don't want to see them suffer. The temptation is to quickly diagnose their problem and find a way of solving it. In contrast, compassion rests on the understanding that people are more complex than we think and that there may be no easy solutions to their problems. We may eventually understand how to help the people we care about, but it may well require paying much more attention to their suffering first.[28]

Forgiveness

This process of compassion may be hardest when someone harms us or someone else we care about. In the face of harm and wrongdoing, seeing someone with compassion may not be possible. We can, however, still see their actions as wrong, while paying more attention to the harm they have caused. We can eventually gain a deeper understanding of their actions, their whole selves and their potential to act differently in the future. This is the realm of forgiveness.

Forgiving is not the same as forgetting. It does not involve dismissing someone's harmful actions as excusable or no longer relevant and moving on. On the contrary, it involves fully acknowledging the extent to which their actions had, and may continue to have, a negative impact. But even with this understanding of what they did, we can still appreciate the potential for them to act better in the future – that who they are is more than their deeds.

A striking example of forgiveness in action is the Truth and Reconciliation Commission in the wake of Apartheid in South Africa. As a form of restorative justice, the reconciliation process sought to acknowledge the injustice and anguish caused during Apartheid, but with ultimate aim of healing and renewing the broken moral relationship between victim and perpetrator. As Desmond Tutu illustrates in *The Book of Forgiving*, the Commission generally had a positive impact on the rebuilding of a peaceful nation.[29]

This does not mean that forgiveness is straightforward. As the philosopher Martha Nussbaum notes in her book *Anger and Forgiveness*, forgiveness can incorporate a subtle form of anger which ceases to restore the relationships between the victim and the wrongdoer.[30] In recognising someone's wrongdoing, we can seek to downgrade their status, rather than encourage them move on with their dignity fully intact. We can use forgiveness as a subtle way of controlling others – we have the power to either bring them back into the moral community or keep them cast in shame. Nussbaum argues that we need to embrace a kind of forgiveness that sees the wrongdoers acts as separable from who they are in an unconditional sense – that they have the potential to act better in the future, regardless of whether we forgive them or not.

Both compassion and forgiveness require a kind of humility. How we initially see someone and their actions – no matter how evil and harmful they may be – is not all there is to the situation. With curiosity and care, we can look beyond people's deeds and see the underlying needs that, in their failure to be met, have caused them to think, feel and act in the way they have. People are not just greedy or selfish, for example. They are also insecure and scared, with various coping mechanisms to avoid experiencing their discomfort and fears.

Last, we can apply this humility and compassion to the way we deal with conflict. With compassion, arguments are less about finding out who is right and how we can solve the problems at hand. Instead, they are more about coming together to gain a deeper understanding of what each other needs and the help they can be given. Compassion – in contrast to control – prioritises connection and understanding over finding quick fixes and temporary solutions. What makes compassion difficult is the very real possibility that no immediate solutions are available. We may not like the understanding we come to, but we will have at least come to it together, and it will at least be closer to the truth.

The cycle of compassion

The more compassion we have for others, the more we can adopt a gentle, kinder approach to life. People are not straightforward – they are neither good nor bad; their actions are not always right or wrong. We can come to realise that everyone is simply trying their best with what they have, which is often very little and involves a great deal of hardship. We can treat people with more tenderness, acknowledging the vulnerable human beings that they are.

Wrapped up in our own practical concerns, we may fail to realise that everyone is going through the same difficult and vulnerable process of being human as we are. Compassion, however, focuses our attention on the undeniable and serious reality of our suffering. Instead of quickly trying to fix our problems or battle through them resiliently, we can understand that the pain we are experiencing is not something to take lightly. We're going through a hard time, and being kind to ourselves can help us along the way.

The more we feel compassion towards ourselves, the more we realise that other people suffer too, and that their pain is every bit as real and important as our own. Each time we realise the weight of our own loss and suffering, it gives us a greater insight into what life is like for everyone. By paying attention to our own suffering, we can feel greater compassion towards others.[31] In contrast to hope and trust, and other forms of curiosity, compassion helps us transform our insecurities and suffering into something with an immediate value. We do not have to wait to see how things pan out. Every time we recognise our own insecurity, we come one step closer to understanding and caring for others.[32]

This creates an ongoing cycle of compassion and self-compassion, and forgiveness and self-forgiveness. What makes this cycle continue is our willingness to expose ourselves, through the process of curiosity, to experiences of disappointment, loss and suffering. With curiosity and compassion, we can learn from these experiences. We can find flexible ways of responding to the challenges we face. We can see how our current struggles might be of some value in the future. Most importantly, we can be more understanding and caring towards others, knowing that we all have to live within insecurity.

As this cycle continues, the deep insecurities that are part of what it means to be human can take on a more central role in our lives. With compassion, instead of ignoring our insecurities or trying to eliminate them as much as possible, we can face them head on. By continuing to expose ourselves to suffering, and by continuing to pay attention to it, we can gain a deeper understanding of how insecurity is at the heart of what we do and who we are.

It is through this ongoing process of curiosity and compassion that we can acknowledge our insecurity and learn how to live well within it. We can begin to discern when to try and alleviate our suffering and when we should try to understand it better. We can learn how to care for others and how important caring for others can be. As Anne Lamott puts it, 'The world is always going to be dangerous, and people get badly banged up, but how can there be more meaning than helping one another stand up in a wind and stay warm?'[33]

Receiving and giving

This is a *very* different way of thinking about happiness than trying to get everything in our lives just right. From the perspective of compassion, we no longer care so much about having the perfect job, relationship, home and so on. What's more important is our suffering and how we help ourselves, and the suffering of others and how we help them. Of course, we do not have an unlimited capacity for care. But through the process of curiosity and compassion we can discover just how caring we can be and find joy in the process.

There is a final implication of this process of curiosity and compassion, which may be the most important. The more we acknowledge our insecurity, the more we realise just how much we rely on others to stay alive. Our wellbeing and survival is dependent on the existence of countless other living things – from the food we eat to the energy we use. Simply being able to breathe, for example, rests on the health of the world's forests and oceans in combination with the smooth and continuous operation of our lungs. This is nothing short of a miracle – something we can be in full awareness of at any given moment in our lives.

This awareness, however, is not always easy to maintain. In saying this, I do not just mean that we have other things to do than pay attention to our breath – that much is obvious. In addition, paying attention to our deep insecurities and our indebtedness to others can motivate us to give something back. Unfortunately, this is not always possible. We may be relatively powerless to save the world's forests from clear-cutting or the world's oceans from acidification. The more we look, the more we see the consequences of our own existence. Our lives are sustained by forms of mass exploitation, animal cruelty and environment destruction. There is no getting away from these facts. We can, however, acknowledge them and try our best to reciprocate the gifts we have received.

When we are unable to help the people and other living things we rely on, we can, at the very least, give them our attention. As the philosopher Simone Weil noted, 'attention is the rarest and purest form of generosity.'[34] From paying attention to all the gifts we receive, we may feel a profound sense of gratitude – a state of attention that, as the poet David Whyte puts it, 'shows we understand and are equal to the gifted nature of life.'[35]

We may also feel a profound sense of grief.[36] Our existence is reliant not just on the gifts of other living things, but also on their death and suffering: the food we eat, for example, often relies on the death of animals; the energy we use often relies on oil from authoritarian regimes, responsible for civil wars and human rights abuses[37] and so on. Grief is the only reasonable response to this situation. It keeps our attention firmly fixed on the forms of suffering we are unwittingly connected to, creating unlimited opportunities for compassion.

Attitudes of empathy and compassion have recently received criticism from philosophers and psychologists who doubt their efficacy in comparison to other moral attitudes such as moral outrage, anger and contempt. For instance, the psychologist Paul Bloom, in his book *Against Empathy*, notes that even if we can empathise with anyone in theory, in practice our empathy is much more selective.[38] Bloom notes that empathising with someone's suffering – feeling their pain – can either make us help them or make us feel too distressed to do so. In addition, we are more likely to empathise and care for someone who is 'like us', who is physically close to us, who has a higher status than us, and who we think is deserving of help. The upshot of these criticisms is that empathy and compassion may be good at helping us care for people we are already disposed to care about, but not those who may need it most.

Grief and gratitude, however, are likely to direct our compassion in a different way. In contrast to the dictates of utilitarianism, the aim is not to consistently widen our circle of concern to include more and more people.[39] Nor is the aim to respect the demands of other moral theories, such as the duties and virtues prescribed by our moral community.[40] Instead, our grief puts us in relationship with the people, groups and other living things that suffer as a result of our existence. The process of curiosity and compassion makes us pay attention to the direct and indirect harms we cause, rather than the abstract amount of good we can achieve. Acting in response to this enduring obligation to do less harm is a lifelong process. It is one where we increasingly push our boundaries of concern and develop our capacities for compassion in unexpected directions.

This process takes us away from thinking about our own satisfaction towards thinking about how we can best be of *service*.[41] It is about acknowledging that our natural and human environments need us. We are not just alive to explore our interests and enjoyments. Instead, our interests and enjoyments are what provide us with the capacities to potentially be of service to others.

Being of service to others is far from easy. This is illustrated by cultures that have elaborate and often dangerous initiation ceremonies to mark the transition from adolescence to adulthood.[42] In many indigenous cultures this is a time of life where individuals must leave the freedoms of childhood behind and devote their adult lives to being of use to the community. The initiation ceremonies that mark this transition are suitably discomforting in nature – they often involve high-risk activities, such as spending time alone in the wilderness, with no guarantee of success or even survival. The reward for going through this transition is to become a needed and valued member of the community. Part of this initiation is about discovering the unique gifts that an individual has to give back to the natural and human environments that keep them alive.

In modern society we do not go through such an initiation. But we are still expected to figure out what we want to be when we grow up. And it is implicitly acknowledged that all jobs within market economies are of some service to others, even if people cannot see the direct impacts of their labour. What we often lack, however, is committing to other forms of service that come from our direct relationships and obligations with the people and other living things that sustain our lives. We are encouraged to work, for example, in order to be financially and materially secure, rather than to give back to the countless living things we rely on. And we are encouraged to develop our interests and enjoyments so that we can find meaning in our work, rather than to be of service to others as best as we can. The point of this section is to show how the process of curiosity and compassion can open us up to this alternative perspective – one of gratitude, grief, obligation and service. This is where we get to from exposing ourselves to the insecurity and suffering at the centre of our own existence.

To live in acknowledgement of our insecurity and the grief and gratitude that comes from it is a profoundly different orientation towards life. Getting everything in our lives just right is no longer what's important. What's important now is living up to our obligations – what we owe to the countless living things that keep us alive. Of course, doing so may not be immediately possible. Many forms of suffering cannot be so easily fixed. Understanding how to best care for others and ourselves is something we will continue to negotiate for the rest of our lives. But it may be the only way in which we can strive for peace with reality. It is an open-eyed and melancholy kind of happiness.

Towards a compassionate society and world

We have come a long way. Over the past three chapters we have looked at a different way of thinking about happiness – one that switches our focus away from control and towards understanding. Instead of going to war with reality, we can strive for peace within it. We can endeavour to improve our lives while acknowledging our insecurity. The outcome of this strategy is far from our usual picture of happiness. It involves as much sorrow as it does joy, and as much failure as it does success. Instead of trying to have as many of the good things and as few of the bad things as possible, we can be curious and compassionate towards all the things in our lives.

I am sorry if this alternative way of thinking about happiness is not what you had hoped for. In other words, I am sorry if the happiness that comes from understanding doesn't sound all that happy. There are, however, two important reasons why we should think about happiness in terms of understanding rather than control. The first reason is personal. It is through embracing uncertainty and being curious towards our lives that we open ourselves us to beauty and gratitude. This process also provides us with the inner resources and psychological flexibility to discover what we most care about and are truly capable of. Even if this way of living is not always a happy one, it makes up for it in its fullness. It may contain plenty of discomfort, rejection and loss. But it is also full of joy, wonder and connection.

The second reason we should think about happiness in terms of understanding rather than control is interpersonal. We have seen that through the process of curiosity we can begin to live up to what really matters. We have also seen that, through the processes of curiosity and compassion, we can gain a deeper understanding of the central role that insecurity plays in our lives. It is from this foundation that we can begin to genuinely help others. This may not always make us happy. But whatever happiness we do receive along the way will at least be the only kind of happiness worth having.

The way we think about happiness has implications that go well beyond our own lives. So far, we have focused almost exclusively on the individual. In this chapter, we have started to see how thinking about happiness differently can also make a difference to the lives of others. In the third and final part of the book, we will go one step further. We will see how this way of thinking about happiness has important implications for how we change society and the world. We can apply the principles of curiosity and compassion – and see the downsides of control and security – to our most challenging societal and global problems.

This is perhaps the most important reason why we need to rethink happiness. By going to war with reality we end up with simple narratives and quick fixes to our social problems, which can often make matters worse in the long run. In contrast, by embracing uncertainty – through the means of curiosity and compassion – we can better understand how to make real social change.

Part III

SEVEN

Changing society

You are the way and the wayfarers.
And when one of you falls down he falls for those
behind him, a caution against the stumbling stone.
Ay, and he falls for those ahead of him, who though
faster and surer of foot, yet removed not the stumbling
stone.
Kahlil Gibran[1]

In Parts I and II we looked at the right and wrong way of thinking about happiness. In Part I we looked at the wrong way, which is how we typically think about happiness in modern society. Happiness is about security, control and certainty. We know what we need to be happy, it's just reality that stands in our way. By having control over our circumstances, we can change ourselves, others and our environment to our liking. We can create the stable circumstances that will give us a lasting sense of meaning and satisfaction.

The problem with this strategy is that its outcomes are impossible and the process involved blinds us to many of the things that matter. We spend our days in problem-solving bubbles, ticking off items from our to-do list, achieving our goals and projects, trying to protect ourselves from our fears, trying to be better, healthier and happier. These things may improve our lives, but no matter how much progress we make, they will merely be the tip of the iceberg.

In Part II we looked at an alternative way of thinking about happiness. Instead of control, happiness is about understanding. Instead of being so sure of the things we need to be happy, we can embrace uncertainty and pay attention to what we don't know. Instead of trying to control our circumstances, we can be curious about ourselves, others and our environment and see the world in non-habitual ways. This process opens us up to beauty and gratitude, and helps us respond with greater flexibility to the challenges we face. Over time, we can discover what we most care about and are truly capable of.

The outcome of this process is an ongoing acknowledgement of our insecurity and learning how to live well within it. With compassion, we can gain a deeper understanding of what matters and how to care for ourselves and other living things. This outcome is far from living happily ever after – the right way of thinking about happiness does not promise a lasting sense of meaning and satisfaction. The process of curiosity and compassion is likely to include as much sorrow as it does joy, and as much failure as it does success. And yet the kind of happiness that comes from truly facing the reality of our lives and striving for peace within it may be the only kind worth having.

In the third and final part of this book we will look at how this alternative way of thinking about happiness has implications beyond how we change our individual lives. We currently think about social progress in much the same way that we think about individual happiness. We think that we can achieve a set of stable circumstances, on a societal scale, which will guarantee that everyone will be better off. Through a combination of technological innovation, economic growth, public goods and services, democracy, rights and so on, we will all have sufficient resources and opportunities to pursue our own version of the good life.

We think that we can achieve these stable circumstances through the means of control. If people get sick, we will find ways of curing them. If people do bad things, we will find ways of changing their behaviour. If people disagree with each other, we will find out who is right and who is wrong. The only thing in our way is reality. The social world is full of problems to solve and battles to fight: corrupt and self-interested politicians; powerful corporate interests; misinformed and dangerous members of the public and so on.

The problem with this process of social change is that by focusing on the problems we can more readily control, we blind ourselves to other kinds of changes that matter. There is, of course, nothing wrong with curing sick people, stopping people from harming each other or finding out the best policies to advance society. But if we focus only on these kinds of issues we can end up with simple narratives, temporary solutions and quick fixes. We miss out on the wider social and systemic changes that can make significant differences to people's lives.

The alternative way of thinking about social progress is to embrace uncertainty and gain a deeper understanding of the kinds of social changes that matter. The social world is full of problems we can learn from: when people get sick, with curiosity and compassion, we can better understand how to help them; when people do bad things, we can pay more attention to the underlying conditions that caused them to do what they did; when people disagree with each other, we can discover the grains of truth in the views of those we disagree with and so on. The more we understand the wider societal conditions that cause our social problems, the better we can be at solving them.

Again, if we know that we can control our social circumstances for the better, without making things worse in the long term, then we should. If we can cure people, change people's behaviour or disagree with others without any serious repercussions then it may well be worth doing so. I am not saying that we shouldn't deal with our immediate social problems. I am saying, however, that our efforts to do so should not detract from the other kinds of social changes that matter. Otherwise, all our well-earned efforts and hard-fought improvements will merely be the tip of the iceberg.

In this chapter we will look at four social issues in particular: crime, health, poverty and democratic disagreement. For each of these issues, I will show how trying to control the thoughts, feelings and behaviour of individuals blinds us to the underlying societal conditions that they need. Instead of being overly certain of what people are like and how we can control them to our liking, we can pay more attention to the wider social conditions that make them who they are. With curiosity and compassion, we can gain a deeper understanding of the challenges that people face and what they need to overcome them.

Crime: understanding 'the bad' and 'the evil'

Bad people do bad things

Appealing to the merits of curiosity and compassion in the face of criminal behaviour seems weak and ineffective, or naive and idealistic at best. It seems obvious that the reasonable response to people doing bad things is to control their behaviour, typically through the use of force. If someone were about to hit you or someone you care about, wouldn't you try to stop them in self-defence? Clearly, curiosity and compassion wouldn't get you that far.

I agree that desperate situations often call for immediate, urgent responses. We sometimes need to control individuals and we need to do so quickly. But we cannot generalise from the above example about how we should respond to all criminal behaviour. When it comes to the criminal justice system, understanding the underlying causes of crime is necessary to reduce crime in the long term.

We typically understand crime on the level of the individual. Bad people do bad things – ruthless drug dealers, disaffected gang members, screwed-up sex offenders, thuggish abusive partners, indoctrinated terrorists and so on. We invest in the criminal justice system to make sure that these people are punished and prevented from doing further harm.

The most obvious means of control we employ in this respect is incarceration. The prison system can be justified on three counts. First, locking people up keeps them out of harm's way (at least for the general public). Second, prison is a sufficiently large punishment that it will, supposedly, deter offenders from doing further harm. Third, the prospect of incarceration will, supposedly, deter other people from doing bad things in the first place.[2]

There may be a significant amount of truth to each of these expectations. However, they are also not without their problems. On the first point, the harms caused by prisoners to other prisoners can be substantial.[3] On the second and third points, there are serious limitations to the effectiveness of punishment as a deterrent. For gang members in deprived urban neighbourhoods, the prospect of greater prison sentences has been shown to have little impact on preventing further criminal behaviour.[4] In fact, incarceration can end up having the opposite effect. High incarceration rates in deprived neighbourhoods can cripple people's opportunities, making a life of crime more likely for those who have been left behind to support their families. And many prisons are more like schools for how-to-be-a-better-criminal than how-to-be-a-better-person.[5]

Of course, we can and should fight hard for criminal justice reforms that could potentially account for these problems. Rehabilitation may often be a more effective means than punishment for preventing offenders from doing further harm. For instance, according to one random controlled trial, people with drug addiction problems were shown to be less likely to reoffend if given treatment than incarcerated.[6] Experiments such as these have also determined effective means of supporting and rebuilding trusting communities affected by criminal behaviour.

Other types of prevention may prove to be more effective means of reducing crime than mass incarceration. For instance, particular types of early intervention in childhood education have been shown to diminish the likelihood that children will become convicted offenders. This includes preschool projects that involved not just classroom education but also nutrition and work with families. These projects increased both employment and law-abidingness in adulthood.[7]

Despite the evidence in favour of these reforms, incarceration and other forms of punishment are often supported on the basis that offenders deserve to be punished. This is the idea of retributive justice. The criminal justice system is founded on the principle that, if we can show that someone intentionally caused someone else harm, we can hold them accountable. When we judge them to be responsible for their actions, we also judge them to be deserving of punishment.

When it comes to this story of individual responsibility and desert, evidence of more effective means of deterrence misses the point. The idea of retributive justice is that offenders deserve to be punished regardless of whether it will deter them and others from doing further harm.

And this story is compelling. Bad people do bad things. How else are we to understand the atrocious things that people do to each other? How can we understand acts of rape and torture? How can we understand people like Hitler or members of ISIS? Surely, in light of their deeds, these people are different from normal people? They must have evil at their core. They must be psychopaths, beyond reform. They must be of less moral value and deserve to suffer for what they have done.

No matter how compelling this story is, like all stories it is overly simplistic. It doesn't account for the bigger picture – the bigger societal story at play. One way to see this is to look at the kinds of people we used to view as 'bad' and 'evil' in the past, but who we now see as morally no different from the rest of us. For instance, the neurobiologist Robert Sapolski, in his book *Behave*, notes that in the 15th century, people living with epilepsy were prosecuted and burned at the stake for being witches or possessed by the devil.[8] We now know this isn't true – that people living with epilepsy are not personally responsible for their seizures. The idea of punishment today seems barbaric.

This is progress. But the problem with progress is that it is often an unfinished process. We can and should ask ourselves what terrible things we are doing today that people in the future will look back on in the same way as we now look back at witch hunts? How about the numbers of people with drug addiction problems, or offenders in general, being convicted with mental health problems? Or the higher crime rate among young adults in US states with anti-abortion laws?[9]

The causes of crime are complex. We may know, for instance, that mental disorders and unplanned/unwanted/deprived/ traumatic childhoods cause criminal behaviour. But we cannot know the impacts that these factors have had, or are likely to have, on the behaviour of any given individual. Or at least, we cannot know with the same level of accuracy as we now know that a particular neurological condition will lead to an epileptic seizure. Instead of saying something complex, like 'some combination of mental disorder, childhood environment, genes and social support predicts 50 per cent of criminal behaviour', it is much easier and satisfying to say that bad people do bad things. Likewise, without the neurological knowledge we have today, it would have been much easier and satisfying in the 15th century to say that people living with epilepsy were evil.

Throughout this chapter we will see how we opt for simple stories of individual responsibility over complex systems of wider societal conditions. We opt for the story that someone is simply bad and deserves to be punished because this provides us with a more complete formula for knowing why they did what they did and how to prevent them from doing further harm. By blaming and punishing people we can control their behaviour, at least in the short term.

In contrast, the alternative, more complex story leaves plenty of unknowns. Even with an understanding of the neurological, biological, situational, historical and cultural factors that cause criminal behaviour, it is far from obvious to know what we can do about it. This alternative way of thinking about social change is more demanding. But the rewards are much greater. Through an ongoing process of curiosity and compassion, we can begin to discover the wider social changes that make a significant change to people's lives in the long term.

Towards a bigger story

Despite our bias towards simple narratives of personal responsibility, we do have the ability to think in terms of complex systems.

For example, in one study where criminal activity across a city was framed either as a 'beast' or a 'virus', people's recommendations about how to reduce crime differed accordingly.[10] Participants who read about the criminal activity framed as a beast were more likely to adopt enforcement measures to stop the beast preying on the community, such as locking more people up. In contrast, participants who received the virus framing were more likely to recommend social reform to stop the virus infecting the city, such as better education and greater economic opportunity. Even a simple metaphor can drastically change how we think about complex social issues.

We already know enough about the wider social determinants of criminal behaviour to know the kinds of changes that can make a significant difference. The philosopher Gregg Caruso, in his book *Public Health and Safety*, shows that the social causes of crime are broadly similar to the social determinants of health.[11] In particular, poverty and other social inequities – including homelessness and lack of educational attainment – have a big impact on health and crime outcomes. Caruso shows how a public-health approach can successfully be applied within the criminal justice system. We have the tools at our disposal to eradicate the virus of crime that is making our society sick.

Of course, this does not necessarily mean getting rid of punishment and incarceration altogether. We may still need to keep people out of harm's way, similar to how we keep people in quarantine if they have a seriously infectious disease. Convicted offenders, if they are deemed to be a significant risk to the public, may need to be forcibly separated from them.[12] Punishment may also be the most effective means of communicating the severity of criminal behaviour to other members of society. However, to be justified on these grounds, punishment would have to be significantly more effective than other forward-looking measures, such as early interventions and social reform.[13]

The difference between these and retributive forms of punishment and incarceration, however, is that they do not come attached with narratives of individual responsibility and blame. This is important for seeing them for what they are. We should adopt forms of incarceration and punishment when doing so is absolutely necessary – an immediate, urgent response to a desperate situation, much like putting people in quarantine during the outbreak of an epidemic. But this should not be our priority in the long term. When we are no longer in the midst of a crisis, we should not focus solely on controlling the behaviour of individuals. We should, in addition, set our sights on the underlying conditions that cause criminal behaviour – its wider social causes.

This strategy may be more complex, unknown and harder to implement. But in the long run, it may well be worth it. Instead of simply blaming and punishing those who are 'bad' and 'evil', we can learn from them. The philosopher Bruce Waller, in his book *Against Moral Responsibility*, likens this approach to the no-blame system model that is used in some workplaces. Waller notes that, 'rather than blaming or shaming an individual worker as the source of the problem, the system model treats errors and mistakes – whether large or small – as learning opportunities that can improve the workplace and the production system. A worker who reports an error ... is thanked rather than blamed.'[14]

I am not suggesting that we should thank convicted offenders for doing terrible things. However, I do believe that we should pay attention and gain a deeper understanding of the conditions responsible for making people act in the ways they do. A curious and compassionate society is one that sees its most terrible acts as an indicator of how much progress has yet to be made. We should treat criminal behaviour as an opportunity to better understand the kinds of systemic changes that we so desperately need to make.

Health: understanding 'the sick', 'the disabled' and 'the mad'

It is not a coincidence that we sometimes call people who do bad things as 'sick'. Like someone who has an illness or disease, offenders must have something wrong with them – things are not how they should be. In the previous section, we saw how we can interpret criminal behaviour in two very different ways – either as a symptom of individual moral character or of the wider social conditions. Calling individuals 'bad' or 'evil', and punishing them accordingly, may help us control their behaviour in the short term. But in the long run we must change the underlying social causes of crime if we are serious about reducing it.

In this section I will show that we can say a similar thing about health. We can interpret individual sickness in the same two different ways – either as a symptom of someone's physical or mental disposition or of the wider social conditions they live in. We may not call people with an illness or disease 'bad' or 'evil', but we do give them labels that are still be unjustified, such as 'mad' or 'disabled'. Medical treatments are aimed at the individual, and clearly help people get better in the short term. However, in the long run, we should switch our focus away from the control of individuals towards understanding the underlying social causes of illness and disease. We can start by paying more attention to wider social conditions that make people sick.

Poor health

One of the most important findings from public health research is what is known as the 'socioeconomic status–health gradient'.[15] In culture after culture, the poorer you are, the worse your health: the higher the incidence and impact of numerous diseases, and the shorter your life expectancy. For every step down the ladder of socioeconomic status (SES), starting from the top, average health worsens.

Why might this be the case? Perhaps the most obvious answer is to do with access to healthcare. Healthcare is a luxury that many people around the world simply can't afford. This, however, does not explain the SES–health gradient. The gradient exists even in countries with universal access to healthcare, is independent of how much people access healthcare, and has an impact on diseases unrelated to healthcare access.

About a third of the SES–health gradient can be explained by differences in factors that increase the risk of contracting various illnesses and diseases. Poorer individuals tend to live in more toxic environments, in which they are exposed to greater amounts lead or air pollution. The lower a person's SES, the more likely they are to take up harmful behaviours such as smoking and drinking. Poorer individuals also tend to have less access to protective health factors such as shops that sell nutritious food and green spaces to do physical exercise.

How can we explain the other two thirds of the SES–health gradient? One major candidate is the role of stress.[16] We know that stress has adverse effects on people's health, increasing the likelihood of adult-onset diabetes, obesity, cardiovascular disease, ulcers, impaired fertility and infectious disease.[17]

As we saw in Chapter One, the poorer a person is, the less control they have over their lives. With less material and financial security, it is more likely that if one thing in our lives goes wrong, everything else will fall apart. Conversely, the more resources and opportunities we have, the more we can buffer ourselves against these negative knock-on effects. The continuous lack of control caused by poverty is stressful on a daily basis.[18]

This is different from what we might call 'good' stress. Stress is a normal part of our daily lives and our well-functioning.[19] It is stress hormones that wake us up in the morning. Throughout the day, we constantly switch back and forth between our parasympathetic nervous system (rest-and-digest mode) and our sympathetic nervous system (fight–flight–freeze mode), with the latter system in charge of our stress response. These changes in our physiology help us perform high-energy activities and deal with tasks that require our continued focus. When we feel in control of the challenges we face, we may not even think of this 'good' stress as being particularly stressful.

In contrast, we experience 'bad' stress when we do not feel in control of our situation – when the pressures and demands we face are overwhelming.[20] It is these chronic forms of stress that are linked to the illnesses and diseases listed above. In particular, stress has been shown to suppress our immune system and create inflammation, diverting all our energy towards dealing with imminent threats and demands.[21] When this becomes a person's default mode of being it is only a matter of time until they get sick.

The impact that SES has on a person's level of chronic stress starts early. By the age of five, the lower a child's SES, the higher their basal glucocorticoid levels and/or the more reactive their glucocorticoid stress response – two key components of chronic stress.[22] This stress has marked impacts on the development and functioning of the brain's frontal cortex, which in turn leads to poorer working memory, emotional regulation, impulse control and executive decision making. Moreover, these development impacts last into adulthood. This is one way in which poverty literally 'gets under the skin'.

A lifetime of stress adds up – chronic stress kills. The SES-health gradient shows that those on the bottom of the SES ladder are more than three times as likely to die prematurely as those at the top. For instance, in the US, the life expectancy gap between affluent and poor people is 12.2 years. As the political theorist Michael Reisch puts it, 'Poverty is a thief ... Poverty not only diminishes a person's life chances, it steals years from one's life.'[23]

The difference in life expectancy between those with a high and low SES is huge. It is the equivalent to the difference in average life expectancy between the richest and poorest nations in the world. As the neurobiologist Robert Sapolski notes: 'Humans committed themselves to a unique trajectory when we invented socioeconomic status. In terms of its caustic, scarring impact on minds and bodies, nothing in the history of animals being crappy to one another about status differences comes within light-years of our invention of poverty.'[24]

And yet we do not tend to view health in this way. We think of illness and disease as the realm of hospitals, doctors and the treatment of individuals, not the result of toxic and stressful environments. When it comes to lifestyle-related diseases such as obesity, adult-onset diabetes and heart disease, we tend to put the blame on individuals for getting sick. It is the responsibility of individuals to be 'healthy' – to eat five fruits and vegetables a day, exercise three to five times a week, drink less and stop smoking. Alternatively, for other diseases, we tend to regard individuals as victims and focus on new medical advances that have the hope of rescuing them. Through a combination of medical treatment and a fighting spirit, unlucky individuals can 'beat' their disease and get better.

As we saw in the previous section, this focus on individuals may well work in the short term. Of course, healthcare is a good thing. But our myopic focus on curing people's broken bodies ignores the wider social conditions that make people ill in the first place. As the cognitive scientist Matthew Walker notes, many modern societies don't have a functioning healthcare system. Instead, they have what is more appropriately called 'sick-care' – a system that focuses on the treatment of individuals to the detriment of preventing illness and disease in the long term.[25] To care for people's health we need to switch from controlling individuals to understanding the wider social conditions that create healthy society.

Disability versus difference

Not all health conditions are the product of our socioeconomic status. For many people, disabilities and ageing are perhaps the most obvious examples of health conditions that in an ideal world we would cure through medical advances. We may quickly imagine what it would be like to lose a limb or one of our primary senses, and it can seem intolerable. Or we may think about the fact that one day we will no longer able to do many of the things we now enjoy. Disabilities and ageing seem to be regrettable features of being fragile embodied creatures, made out of flesh and blood, that slowly decay over time.

This, however, is different from how many people who 'suffer' from disabilities see things. After adapting to their disability, the things that make life hard may not be their physical or mental limitations, but the societal conditions that make their limitations so salient. Researchers refer to this as the 'social model' of disability.[26] According to this model, it is largely social factors that create problems for many people with disabilities. 'Normal' people have constructed society to suit people with similar physical and cognitive abilities. These same conditions can hamper people with different abilities.

For example, we tend to build steps to get into buildings instead of ramps. But if we built ramps instead of steps then wheelchair users would have no problem with access to buildings. According to the social model of disability, it is not the minds and bodies of disabled people that are the problem − it is the social contexts they are situated in. We don't need to see people as 'broken' and heroically endeavour to 'fix' them. We just need to design things better.

New technologies can make it easier to accommodate people with different abilities. For example, in the US, television had the capacity to caption broadcasts for a long time. But networks chose not to make such technology available, which made it difficult, if not impossible, for deaf viewers to follow programmes. Now that all televisions have a decoder chip built into them, deaf viewers can watch and understand any television show.[27]

This is a kind of half-hearted progress. We still fail to acknowledge the different kinds of abilities that people have and the social contexts that can either accommodate or obstruct them. Many 'disability' communities go one step further: they celebrate their differences, showing how we can all benefit from greater physical and mental diversity.[28] For instance, the 'neurodiversity' movement aims to show that we can learn from people with different mental abilities – they provide alternative ways of seeing the world and each other.

As an example, Katherine May, who writes about her life as someone with autism, describes conversation between 'neurotypical' people as colourless and dry:

> Instead of discussing their driving passions, my companions prefer to gossip about near-strangers, or to compete for airtime at the expense of listening and perhaps learning something useful ... They seem able to assimilate news stories that I find too tragic to digest, and to flip them glibly into humour, finding glee in the kind of interpersonal politics that make the air feel thick to me. To me, their company seems superficial, blunt, emotionless.[29]

May's point is not that all people without autism are as she describes. She understands that all individuals have hidden depths behind their overt displays of emotion and the things they say. Nonetheless, people have different mental and physical abilities that dispose them towards seeing things differently.

By paying more attention to the social contexts of people with mental and physical disabilities, not only can we better understand how to accommodate their differences, but we can also benefit from them. Research shows that diversity in the workplace, for instance, tends to lead to greater productivity and better decision making. The wider the range of skills and opinions, the fewer potential blind spots. Greater diversity also increases the potential for creativity.[30]

We are, however, a long way from this ideal. As many people who are labelled with having a disability will testify to, we live in an *ableist* society.[31] People typically view being deaf as a disability, for example. Deafness is the partial or full loss of the ability to hear. But does this loss really matter – is it a loss that significantly reduces quality of life? Many communities of deaf people claim that, within the right social context, it does not. They reject the label of disability, instead referring to themselves as a linguistic minority. When their linguistic abilities (namely, sign language) are accommodated, they do not experience being deaf as a significant disadvantage.[32]

The language of 'loss' in that last paragraph is perhaps telling. We often talk of disabled people having lost an important ability, such as the ability to hear. In evaluating the significance of their condition, we might imagine what it would be like if we were suddenly not able to hear. We do not, however, imagine what it would be like to communicate with people in other ways, or what it would be like to feel music through the vibrations in our feet. In fact, we fail to imagine much at all beyond the experience of not-hearing, which to us seems so terrible. It is no surprise, therefore, that we fail to acknowledge the rich lives that deaf people lead, despite their lack of hearing – lives that include the abilities they've gained from their condition.

We should take seriously the testimonies of people with different abilities. For instance, when deaf individuals turn down the opportunity to 'correct' their hearing with a cochlear implant because they are happy as they are, we should take their word for it.[33] By listening openly to what they have to say, we might come to realise that they understand something we don't.

Of course, there are some physical and mental differences that really do matter, and we would be right to label as a disability. For example, prospective parents can now detect chromosomal and genetic features associated with autosomal recessive disorders, such as Huntington's disease.[34] Eradicating this condition, which causes tremendous difficulties, may well be an appropriate way of reducing the amount of suffering in the world. We need to recognise, however, that, in doing so, we are skating on thin ice. Screening for Huntington's disease may be a good idea, but what about other chromosomal and genetic disorders, such as Down syndrome and cystic fibrosis? To parents of children with Down syndrome or cystic fibrosis, eradicating these conditions may seem akin to ethnic cleansing. To others, it may look like progress.

What we can say is that the quest for human improvement, based on marked differences between 'better' and 'worse' kinds of humans, has a horrifying history. We need only think about the history of eugenics to see how readily humans categorise some people as 'fit' and others as 'unfit' – both mistakenly and with tragic consequences. In fact the founder of eugenics, Francis Galton, separated people into 'paupers' and 'non-paupers', claiming, with good intentions, that we could reduce poverty by sterilising the poor.[35] We now see this practice as horribly misguided. We know that poverty is a social condition created by a lack of resources and opportunities available to those who are poor, not by their genetic make-up.

When considering future forms of eugenics – something that is becoming increasingly possible with new gene editing technologies – we should err on the side of caution. The same goes for other medical procedures that aim to eradicate so-called 'disabilities'. We too readily overestimate the disadvantages of mental and physical differences and try to 'fix' or 'cure' them. Instead of trying to control people's bodies and minds, we would do better to understand the wider social conditions that significantly reduce their quality of life.

'Insane' conditions

The last issue I will consider in this section is mental health. We are currently living in a mental health crisis. In the UK and the US, one in six people is likely to have a mental illness within their lifetime, with anxiety disorders, depression and addictions all on the rise.[36]

Like physical illness and disease, and physical and mental disability, we tend to treat mental health on an individual level. We see people with depression or anxiety disorders, for example, as stuck in unhelpful patterns of thought, feeling and behaviour. Of course, we may also see their worries and concerns as natural responses to situations of loss, trauma or humiliation. And that they, like many other people in modern society, face problems that are multiple, severe and appear irresolvable. But we still tend to view people's mental health as something that can be fixed by a combination of drugs and therapy.

This way of thinking about mental health is encouraged by the practice of psychiatric diagnosis and treatment.[37] Mental disorders are diagnosed solely on the basis of psychological and behavioural symptoms. For example, to be diagnosed with depression, someone needs to display a minimum of five out of eight symptoms, with at least one of those symptoms being either a depressed mood or loss of interest or pleasure. Of course, good clinical practice always seeks to understand a patient's specific circumstances, but when it comes to the criteria for diagnosing depression, social context doesn't come into it.

The same goes for psychiatric treatment. Mental disorders are often put down to changes in someone's 'neurochemistry'. Depression, for instance, is said to be a result of a 'chemical imbalance' in the brain rather than people being unable to cope with their situation.[38] This is similar to how wheelchair users are told their problem is their lack of legs, not the fact that there aren't enough ramps. The fact that people with mental disorders have hard lives and lack the support they need often goes unrecognised. Instead, they are simply told that something has gone wrong with their brain.

The consequences of focusing on the individual are similar to how we treat people with physical illnesses and diseases. Recall that, when it comes to lifestyle-related diseases such as obesity, we tend to put the blame on individuals for getting sick – they should have had a better diet or done more exercise. Similarly, we often blame or shame people with mental disorders.[39] We might think that someone's mental condition is an attempt 'to get attention', 'control others', or they could 'stop being lazy' and are 'being selfish'. After all, many people have hard lives and lack the support that's needed. People with mental disorders should simply 'pull themselves together' and 'get over it'.

Alternatively, when we see mental disorders as a 'real' neurological condition, much like a non-lifestyle-related disease, we tend to make victims of individuals and focus on psychiatric treatments that can rescue them from their maladies. Through a combination of drugs and therapy, unfortunate individuals can fix their broken brains. This may remove the moral stigma attached to mental disorders, but it also removes people's sense of agency and normalcy. A person's psychological condition is no longer a natural response to their situation, but instead a result of their underlying brain pathology.

Instead of focusing on the individual – and either blaming them or conferring victimhood on them – we should pay more attention to someone's social context and the wider social conditions that cause mental disorders. We know, for instance, that mental illness is more common among women and people who suffer socioeconomic disadvantage and other forms of adversity and hardship.[40] Psychological distress is a natural response to not being able to cope with the constant bombardment of 'insane demands'.[41]

But are psychological distress and mental illness the same thing? Mental disorders are significantly different from feelings of helplessness. Chronic depression, for instance, is not the same as being consistently sad or lonely. Mental illness is an extreme and debilitating form of suffering. We call people 'mad' or 'crazy' because their psychological condition can appear to be an abnormal and unintelligible response to their situation.[42] It makes sense to feel anxious in response to situations of loss, trauma or humiliation, for example. But feeling anxious about life in general, including the most minor of things, seems absurd. Does it not make sense, therefore, to assume that something must have gone wrong at the level of a person's neurobiology?

As unintelligible as mental disorders might seem, I think we would be wrong to assume that this can be explained entirely by changes in the brain. This fails to account for the role that culture and social contexts play in defining what is normal and what makes sense in the first place. We all face situations of adversity and hardship in life and very quickly learn what kinds of responses are acceptable and unacceptable and what kinds of help are available. We know, for example, that it is acceptable to grieve over the loss of a loved one, and that our friends and family will support us throughout our grief. The reality of grief as a profound form of suffering is recognised in our society. In contrast, the suffering experienced by people who claim to have a 'shopping addiction' is not well recognised. Without diagnosing themselves with a mental disorder, people who claim to be addicted to shopping may not receive the help they need.

My point is that even if such mental disorders seem 'crazy' – psychological conditions that can only be explained by an underlying brain pathology – they may in fact be responses to a person's social context that are recognised by society as legitimate and worthy of medical support. These responses may still seem unintelligible from the outside. But they may also be the forms of thought, feeling and behaviour that are recognised in our culture as sure signs that someone cannot cope and is in dire need of help. I am not saying that such mental disorders are any less real or any less genuine than other psychological conditions. My point is that what we consider to be 'normal' or 'crazy' is determined by our social context.

Psychological distress and mental illness are not, then, the same thing. Depression is not the same as being very sad. Mental disorders differ from feelings of helpless and other forms of suffering because they are strange. But this does not mean their unintelligibility can only be explained at the level of the individual – that something has gone wrong in someone's brain, making them 'mad' or 'crazy'. What we consider normal or abnormal is a social affair.[43] Instead of seeing someone as having a broken brain and trying to fix it, we should see their situation as broken and better understand the resources and circumstances they need to cope with the challenges they face.

Of course, we should provide people with psychiatric drugs and therapies if that helps them to cope better with their situation. But – much like criminal behaviour and physical illness and disease we must acknowledge that this is not a long-term solution. In addition to mental health treatment, we can pay more attention to the wider social conditions that cause mental illness. Research shows that to improve mental health, we need poverty relief and employment and education opportunities. People also need to belong to a community, have a sense of purpose and forge meaningful relationships. In fact, some researchers claim that the opposite condition of depression or addiction is *connection*.[44]

We can learn from mental disorders about the societal changes we need to make to help people cope with the challenges they face. We should focus less on manipulating people's brain chemistry and more on understanding the helplessness of their situations. Without this understanding, we may continue to live in a mental health crisis for the foreseeable future.

Poverty: understanding 'the stupid' and 'the lazy'

In the previous two sections – looking at the underlying social conditions behind crime and health – poverty has been a common theme. In this section, we will look at poverty itself. Although poverty is a social condition, we often look at being poor as an individual problem. We might think that poor people are less talented, motivated or competent. If only they were more determined, they could work their way out of poverty. This is, of course, a fantasy. Blaming and shaming poor people as 'stupid' or 'lazy' and providing them with incentives to work harder may work for some people in the short term. But it ignores the wider social conditions that keep too many people in poverty.

The story of meritocracy

To hold individuals as personally responsible and deserving of their wealth is the idea of meritocracy. It is similar to the story of retributive justice discussed above, which holds that offenders are personally responsible for their actions and that they deserve to be punished as a result. Meritocracy is the complementary story. It does not involve punishing people for doing bad things, but rewarding them for doing things that are deemed worthwhile by others. It is a system of distribution that allocates resources on the basis of individual merit.

Meritocracy might not seem so bad in comparison to its historical predecessors. Aristocracy, for instance, is a system of distribution that allocates resources on the basis of birthright. Alternatively, plutocracy allocates resources on the basis of wealth. Meritocracy is almost certainly an improvement.[45] And the basic idea seems sound: if everyone has an equal amount of opportunities to attain resources through their labour then people will get what they deserve.

The American Dream is perhaps the most well-known version of this you-get-out-what-you-put-in story. It rests on the idea that anyone can 'make it' in society, no matter what background you come from. Throughout much of the 20th century this dream motivated a large proportion of the US population to be productive workers within the industrial capitalist system.[46] Of course, it obscures the fact that underpaid women, and African Americans and other minority groups, also helped the US become an economically prosperous nation. But even if the American Dream is built on lies, slavery and oppression, it is an inspirational narrative that, to some extent, worked and continues to do so. For people who live in deprived conditions, it is a story of hope.

Unfortunately, this story is still more of a dream than a reality. The statistics on social mobility in the US, for instance, are shocking.[47] If you are born into the bottom fifth of households in the overall income distribution, you have a 36 per cent chance of staying there and only a 10 per cent chance of making it to the top fifth. Things are worse for Black Americans born in the bottom fifth: with a 51 per cent chance of staying at the bottom and only a 3 per cent chance of making it to the top. The picture is similar for those with unmarried parents: a 50 per cent chance of staying in the bottom fifth and 5 per cent chance of being in the top fifth. Even worse for high school dropouts: 54 per cent chance of being in the bottom, and 1 per cent of being at the top.

These statistics tell a very different story from the American Dream. In reality, the ideals of meritocracy quickly fall apart. If a person is born into the bottom fifth of the income distribution in the US, the best route out of poverty is either to be born a White American, or to have well-educated married parents, or be fortunate enough to have the opportunity to go to college.[48] Despite the rhetoric of equal opportunity, social mobility is simply not realistic for poor people in the US. They do not have the control over their fates that the American Dream instills.

Why is this the case? After all, modern societies like the US are characterised by universal education and market economies that provide people with educational and employment opportunities. The problem is there are a few key dynamics that, over time, subtly skew things in favour of the rich and make life much harder for the poor. If we want to reduce poverty, we need to better understand these wider social dynamics, instead of simply focusing on how to make poor people work harder and be more productive.

The first dynamic is that the game of meritocracy is rigged from the start. People are born with different advantages and disadvantages. The most obvious advantage is financial. Between 1979 and 2013 in the US, the top fifth of households received a $4 trillion increase in pre-taxed income. The remaining four fifths received a total of $3 trillion.[49] People who are born into the top tend to stay at the top partly because they inherit wealth from their parents.

In addition to financial capital, people inherit cultural and social capital.[50] Educational values and opportunities, wrapped up in people's class status, are passed down from generation to generation. For instance, upper-middle-class parents invest more in their children's education – they read to their children at a young age, pay for private tutoring and have higher educational aspirations. People also inherit connections and work opportunities. Upper-middle-class individuals have a greater amount of 'weak ties' – the kinds of connections you can draw on for bagging prized internships or paid employment.

In contrast, people who are born into deprived conditions face a number of disadvantages. As we saw in the previous section on health inequalities, poorer individuals grow up in more toxic environments, with greater levels of crime. They also have less access to good schools, nutritious food and other public goods such as green spaces. Growing up in a harder environment also means growing up with 'harder' parents. Studies in the US show that parenting in poor neighbourhoods tends to be 'authoritarian' in nature – kids are taught how to be narrowly successful, obedient and conformist.[51] We have also seen how the stress of childhood poverty has marked impacts on the development and functioning of the brain's frontal cortex, which in turn leads to poorer working memory, emotional regulation, impulse control and executive decision making. Research shows that socioeconomic status in childhood predicts a range of important life factors, including life expectancy, educational attainment, chances of incarceration and income.[52]

It gets worse. The second dynamic is that initial advantages and disadvantages increase over time, rather than getting ironed out. An obvious example of this is genetically inherited advantages. Suppose, for example, that some people are born with greater capacities for grit and determination. These are exactly the kinds of skills that meritocracy is founded on. The idea of meritocracy is that people have earned their attained resources through their labour. But nobody has earned their genetic predispositions towards the skills and capacities that help them outcompete those less fortunate.[53]

The initial cards we are dealt with in life – genetic or otherwise – set us up for further advantages. Malcolm Gladwell, in his book *Outliers*, documents a nice example of how this process works.[54] Gladwell notes there are more players in the Canadian National Hockey League born in January, February and March than any other months. Why? Because, in Canada, where children start playing hockey at a very young age, the eligibility cutoff for age-class hockey programmes is 1 January. At the ages of 6 and 7, being 10 or 11 months older gives one a distinct advantage over one's competitors.

The key point is that these initial advantages – caused by luck – increase, rather than iron out, over time. Since the older players tend to do better, they end up getting more playing time. As they progress through the ranks they are selected for better teams and more elite programmes, receive better coaching and play more games against better competition. What begins as a small advantage, a mere matter of luck, snowballs and leads to an ever-widening gap of success.

This is how minor differences in propensities for different mental and physical skills lead to the idea that people are simply good or bad at those skills. Factors such as feedback, practice, encouragement and self-belief tend to be ignored, obscured by the magical notion of talent.[55]

The third and final social dynamic that makes it hard for individuals to make their way out of poverty is that deprivation is full of *risk*. In the previous section on health inequalities, and in Chapter One, we saw that the poorer people are the less control they have over their lives. With less material and financial security, it is more likely that, if one thing in our lives goes wrong, everything else will fall apart. Conversely, the more resources and opportunities we have, the more we can buffer ourselves against these negative knock-on effects.

The continuous lack of control caused by poverty is stressful on a daily basis. Scraping to come up with routine living expenses – food, shelter, transportation – can cause chronic insomnia and anxiety. This increases the chances of suffering from debilitating, life-threatening ills, from diabetes to high blood pressure and heart disease. It is also increases the likelihood of taking up drinking, smoking and other addictive behaviours which escalate these health risks. Planning for the future, making the right choices and adopting healthy lifestyles within chronically stressful conditions is hard when you only have 48 hours of food left. Research shows that poverty comes with a 'massive cognitive load': the stress of living in poverty is akin to losing 13 IQ points.[56]

It is hard to hold down a stable job when you are sick, let alone being chronically stressed, sleep deprived and living in a toxic and unsafe environment. Poverty is a cruel and unforgiving trap that it is extremely hard to crawl out of.

A realistic dream

Despite these three wider social dynamics that keep people in poverty, we persist in believing in the ideals of meritocracy and the American Dream. We encourage poor individuals to have higher aspirations without paying attention to the barriers they are up against. Not only is this story of individual responsibility unrealistic, it also places an undue burden on the self-worth of people who live in poverty.

For instance, the sociologist Michele Lamont, in her book *The Dignity of Working Men*, shows that having a stable job is one of the primary factors that give worth to individuals in the modern-day US.[57] With all the opportunities to be a 'self-made man' at your disposal, failure to make it, instead of being viewed as the result of bad luck, is seen as a symptom of bad moral character. The stigma and shame associated with unemployment and not being able to work is part of the 'crisis of meaning' associated with the devastating opioid epidemic that has spread across working–class America.[58]

The shame and social anxieties associated with class status are not confined to the US and the American Dream. For instance, one study compared people's experiences of poverty across a range of different countries and circumstances – from people living in urban social housing in Norway to rural mud huts in India. It found the social implications of poverty to be strikingly similar. As the authors note, 'Despite respondents generally believing they've done their best against all odds, they mostly considered they've both failed themselves by being poor and that others saw them as failures. This internalisation of shame was further reinforced in the family, the workplace, and in their dealings with officialdom.'[59]

Poverty has become a personal affair – we think about poor people differently from how we think about rich people. For instance, the psychological field of 'social cognition' shows that we tend to think of poor people as more 'warm' and less 'competent' than rich people.[60] We put down the success of the rich to their individual skills and efforts. In contrast, poor people must be either lazy or stupid, or both. When these stereotypes are confronted – when rich and poor people have to witness the unwarranted suffering of another poor person – it is the rich who feel most distress and, as a result, are *less* likely to try and help.[61]

Poverty – and our attitudes towards it – is a predominantly social affair, not a personal one. We can help people make their way out of poverty through social reforms such the predistribution and redistribution of resources. Examples of predistribution include having a minimum and maximum wage and workplace democracies to avoid rises in inequality. Examples of redistribution include income, consumption, asset and inheritance taxes, and investing in public services and welfare. As the epidemiologists Richard Wilkinson and Kate Pickett show in their influential book *The Spirit Level*, countries with equal patterns of distribution tend to have higher rates of social mobility, as well as lower rates of a number of health and social problems.[62]

Focusing less on controlling individuals and more on understanding the underlying social conditions of poverty does not mean getting rid of all inequalities. Societies need some kind of system for efficiently sorting people into jobs.[63] Meritocracy can be viewed simply as a sorting mechanism: those who are most skilled or who put in the most effort are those who are most suited to the job. We can continue to reward people for great technological innovations, or for being the best authors.

People who win this game deserve these rewards in an institutional sense – much the same way in which lottery winners deserve their winnings. However, the idea of meritocracy goes one step further – that people deserve these rewards in some kind of moral way; that they have earned them. There is no truth to this. Most people work hard in life. It is not the case that the top 1 per cent are those who have put the most blood, sweat and tears into their labour.

We need to disassociate the idea that people should be rewarded for their efforts and outcomes from the idea that those same people have a greater amount of moral worth and entitlement. As the philosopher Kwame Anthony Appiah notes:

> We should not mix an efficient sorting procedure with ideas about people's intrinsic worth. People who have repeatedly been labelled a dunce are no less able to find meaningful work, given the right training and opportunities. Failing to do so means we will miss out on thousands of Mozarts and Einsteins, which we no doubt already have.[64]

A curious and compassionate society is one that does not try to control individuals through unrealistic dreams and incentives. These methods, as well as the moral judgements of blame and shame attached to them, may work in the short term, but are not a long-term solution. We should instead pay attention to the societal barriers that keep people in poverty, and better understand the wider social conditions that can lift as many people out of it as possible.

Democratic disagreement: understanding 'the ignorant', 'the selfish' and 'the naive'

In each section of this chapter we have looked at how we can better understand the underlying social causes of a political issue (crime, health, poverty) rather than focusing solely on how we can control the behaviour of individuals. Many of the systemic changes we need to make require political action. This, however, is far from straightforward. Within democratic societies, disagreement over policies, values and ideologies is part of the political process.

In this section we will look at how we often approach democratic disagreement from the mindset of certainty and control. We can and should, however, do things differently. In addition to persuading others to change their beliefs and opinions, we can learn from them. We can pay more attention to their values and social context and gain a deeper understanding of why people believe and say the things they do. This is different from attitudes of tolerance and respect and building bridges. We should approach democratic disagreement with curiosity and compassion if we want to understand the wider social conditions that different members of society need.

'We' are right and 'they' are wrong

It doesn't take long to see that attempting to understand the perspectives of others is not the top priority when it comes to democratic disagreements in modern society. Political dialogue is typically infused with emotion and hostility. After all, the stakes are high. The difference between public policies can be a matter of life or death, such as the implementation of public smoking bans (which have been shown to save lives) and austerity measures (which have been shown to do the opposite).[65] As we saw in Chapter One, we are dependent on the political institutions and structures that we are a part of. We are not merely a social species; we are a political one.

The political very quickly gets personal. For instance, research shows that we attribute changes of personal identity on the basis of people's moral and political values more than any other personal attribute, such as their memories, life narratives or capacities for agency.[66] Someone can lose all their memories or dramatically change their personal narrative and we would still consider them, essentially, the same person. But if, after a lifetime of being a liberal, they suddenly voted conservative and started to espouse right-wing values, we tend to think that a substantial change in their identity must have taken place. This suggests that who we are is largely a matter of the moral and political communities we belong to. If this is true, when people disagree with our moral and political values, our personal identity is literally under threat.

It is no surprise, therefore, that we are so good at detecting whether or not people are likely to hold the same political views as us. Within moments of meeting someone, we instantly judge whether or not they are 'like us' – whether they are part of our tribe, whether they are safe to trust and cooperate with.[67] Just think of the difference between a middle-aged, short-haired man in a suit and a young, casually dressed man with a beard and long hair. Which one do you think is more liberal or conservative? Without knowing anything else about these fictional characters, we can guess their moral and political affiliations. We carefully construct personal images and project them out into the world to make sure we can spend time with, and rely on, likeminded others.

Our group identities, however, have a dark side. We often blindly follow the views of the political party or tribe we belong to rather than weighing up the evidence related to the views in question.[68] When we do care about evidence, we suffer from a confirmation bias.[69] We look for evidence that confirms the view of our political tribe and discount evidence against it. And we look for evidence that refutes the opposing view and discount evidence in support of it.

This last point is important. We do not just hold that our moral and political views are objectively right. We also seek to discredit and demonise those who believe otherwise. We are right and they are wrong. This is the territory of in-group / out-group dynamics – 'us' versus 'them'.[70] People tend to treat members of their own tribe ('us') as intelligent individuals with rich inner lives. Which makes sense: most of the people we know and form intimate relationships with will share our moral and political values (they are one of us). The problem, however, is that we don't tend to treat members of the other tribe ('them') in the same way. We tend to view people outside our moral community as more stupid and homogeneous in nature ('they're all the same'). Without unique identities and with limited reasoning faculties no wonder it is so hard to get members of the other side to change their minds.

The upshot is that instead of weighing up evidence in favour of a political view, we tend to adopt it if people 'like us' say it's true. Conversely, we tend to reject views that are held by members of the other side. In fact, when we are presented with evidence against the view of our political tribe, we may not just discount the evidence, but also end up holding the view more strongly. This is what researchers call the 'backfire effect'.[71] We have probably all experienced this when trying to convince other people that they are wrong.

We should not be surprised by these biases and dynamics. In a complex and uncertain world, we do not have the time, energy and resources to investigate the evidence related to each political issue we are exposed to. This is a problem at the heart of democracy – we must all vote on issues that we are inevitably uninformed about, simply because the issues are so nuanced and complicated.[72] We overcome this problem largely by appealing to *secondary* sources of evidence. What sources of evidence can we know and trust? Who are the experts and the authorities on a particular subject?

We look towards our political tribe – including the media outlets affiliated with it – to find out what is true. For example, I believe that climate change is real and humans are responsible. Although I'm familiar with some of the primary evidence in favour of this view, I would be fooling myself to think that I've based my opinions on a thorough review of all the available evidence. Moreover, it would be foolish to suggest such a thing. This is the job of other people – namely, the world's climate scientists – who are in a much better position to do so. I trust the International Panel on Climate Change as a secondary source of evidence. We may not like to admit it, but this is (rightly) how we form most of our political views.

The result of this process is that we know less than we might think. We are not the experts we need to be to evaluate complex social issues. Instead, we hold most of our political views on the basis of simple narratives that are handed down to us by trusted authorities. As the sociologist Arlie Hochschild shows in her studies of liberals and conservatives in the US, people primarily deal in stories that have emotion at the core of them rather than dealing in facts.[73]

We might think that we are right and the other side is wrong. But 'they' also think the same think about 'us'. They might think we are naive or privileged, and we might think they are selfish or prejudiced. The fact that both sides equally view the other as demons or monsters gives us reason to pause. Of course, it is possible that we are entirely right and they are entirely wrong. But it is much more likely that at least some of our own views are wrong, or not the complete picture. The ongoing stability of political polarisation is enough to suggest that we have something to learn from the views of the other side.

Putting values into context

People's political views are not random. They are partly the result of personality differences and social contexts. By paying attention to why people have the moral and political values they do, we can gain a deeper understanding of the wider social conditions they need. We can learn from the left and the right, and work towards a more sophisticated, 'ambidextrous politics'.

Consider, first, the personality differences between liberals and conservatives. Research shows that liberals tend to be more 'approach motivated' and open to new experiences, whereas conservatives tend to be more 'avoidance motivated' and sensitive to threats. Liberals also tend to more conscientiousness, whereas conservatives tend to be more agreeable.[74] These differences clearly reflect the different kinds of political views favoured by each party. Liberals tend to focus on how to change society for the better, emphasising the gains to be had over the potential losses. In contrast, conservatives tend to focus on how to keep things as they are, with an emphasis on stability and security.

These findings fit the different kinds of values that liberal and conservatives tend to endorse. The psychologist Jonathan Haidt, in his book *The Righteous Mind*, argues that there are five foundational moral values, which everyone cares about.[75] The values are care, fairness, loyalty, authority and purity. Where liberals and conservatives differ, according to Haidt, is over the priority they give to each of the values in their moral and political views. Conservatives tend to care about all five values equally, whereas liberals prioritise the values of care and fairness, downplaying the importance of loyalty, authority and purity.

What should we make of these differences in personality and values? Haidt and other political theorists have shown that the different sets of values endorsed by liberals and conservatives reflect different ways of structuring society.[76]

Let us consider the more conservative set of values first. Conservatives tend to give more weight to 'groupish' values – loyalty, authority and purity. These values all help maintain groups built on mutual relationships of trust and support. This is important when members of the group depend on each other for their wellbeing and survival. It is the shared norms and practices, the ties of loyalty and communal traditions, that bind a community together.

Perhaps the most obvious example of this is religion.[77] Local churches have traditionally provided a place for communities to come together and carry out shared practices, rituals and celebrations – norms that combine values of authority and purity. They also promote values of loyalty – members of local church congregations are encouraged to look out for each other, to 'love thy neighbour'. This groupish mentality can be summed up by the phrase 'charity begins at home' – that you should look after your own family, friends and community before caring for others. This makes sense when your own wellbeing is largely dependent on the wellbeing of the group.

Who individuals see as their community, or 'people', however, is a moveable feast. The Mafia is a good example of how familial terms such as 'uncle' can be used to extend our bonds of loyalty to a wider circle of individuals. Similarly, solidarity movements often refer to their members as 'brothers' and 'sisters'. Nationalism takes this process of identification a step further, with the ideas of national identity and belonging. The political theorist Yoram Hazony, in his book *The Virtue of Nationalism*, claims that it is on collective traditions and bonds of loyalty that nations are built.[78] We should not underestimate the importance of these binding moral values in helping groups of people, small and large, to trust and cooperate with each other.

The more liberal set of values supports a very different kind of social structure. Liberals tends to give more weight to the values of care and fairness. These values all help maintain the rights of individuals – that they have an adequate amount of resources and opportunities and equal social and economic freedoms. This is most important for minority and other vulnerable groups that suffer from forms of oppression, marginalisation and stigmatisation. According to the liberal mindset, we cannot rest content loving our neighbours or keeping charity within the confines of our home. We should care equally for those in need, wherever they live and whatever our relationship to them.

An obvious example of this in practice is the welfare state. The political theorist Patrick Deneen, in his book *Why Liberalism Failed*, shows that over the past 250 years modern societies have witnessed the steady erosion of social capital in the form of local community, religion and the wider family. In the 20th century, many of these structures were replaced by the welfare state.[79] Individuals are no longer dependent on their local community for their wellbeing and survival. It is now the state that provides them with economic opportunities and social support. The difference between these two structures is not just their size, but also the kinds of relationships they are made up of. Whereas communities are built on mutual relationships of trust and support, the welfare state is more impartial.[80] The point of the welfare state is that it doesn't matter who you are and where you belong – all members of society deserve the same rights and level of support.

Liberals often employ this sense of impartiality beyond the welfare state. In contrast to nationalism, the more liberal set of values fits nicely with cosmopolitanism ideals – expanding of our moral circle of concern to all human beings.[81] We may not be able to have mutual relationships of trust and support with everyone in the world, but we can aim to create political systems and interdependent structures of trade that benefit as many people as possible.

Learning from the other side

The different social structures supported by conservative and liberal sets of values can be summed up as follows: conservative values are primarily about *social order*; liberal values are primarily about *social change*. Both processes are suited to different kinds of wider social conditions.

Social order is required within conditions of *scarcity* and *group dependence*. Conservative values help maintain close-knit communities, through shared norms and practices, to avoid potential threats. Out of scarcity and group dependence comes meaning and community.

In contrast, social change is required within conditions of *opportunity* and *group interdependence*. Liberal values help create wider circles of concern, through impartial systems of individual rights and social support, to improve people's welfare, in particular that of those who are most in need. Out of opportunity and group interdependence comes progress and freedom.

These differences nicely map onto the personality differences between liberals and conservatives outlined above. Recall that conservatives tend to be more agreeable and sensitive to threats – they care about the people they encounter in their daily lives and they stick to what they know. In contrast, liberals tend to be more conscientious and open to new experiences – they care about people in the abstract and are interested in new ways of doing things.

On a personal level, we can see the limitations of being fixed in one mindset. Sometimes it might be good for the person with the more conservative personality type to loosen up a bit and try something new. And sometimes the person with the more liberal personality type should respect the way things are generally done – things are probably that way for a reason. But we rarely apply the same principles to the social level. When engaged in democratic debate, we typically assume that one side is right and the other side is wrong. We mostly fail to see the value in the views that we disagree with.

This situation is not helped by the fact that political parties and politicians are trying their best to get elected and mainstream media outlets are increasingly polarised in nature. In addition, social media encourages easy stories and blurts of opinion over complex and subtle arguments. The result is that we fail to realise that both sides have a part to play. We may be encouraged to think that we are always right and they are terrifyingly wrong. But in reality, different sets of moral and political values may serve as counterweights to each other.

We need a balance between social order and social change. Sometimes we may need shared norms and practices that help us cope with localised threats. And sometimes we may need impartial systems of rights and support that help us improve people's welfare. The tricky part is figuring out when the more conservative or liberal approach is more appropriate, or when we need to adopt a more nuanced combination of the two. We can only do this by paying more attention to the political views we disagree with and gaining a deeper understanding of their merits. Instead of opposing political tribes talking past each other, we need to work out ways of learning from the other side.

There is a parallel here with our close relationships and friendships. In much the same way that we make commitments to people we care about, we can make commitments to people we are in a democratic relationship with. At the heart of this commitment is the assumption that whatever disagreements we have, we cannot simply put them down to the moral character of those we disagree with. We are all, to some extent, ignorant of the issues at hand. To call members of the other side 'ignorant' may be true, but also hypocritical. Other simplified narratives about the moral character of individuals also miss the point: conservatives are not inherently 'selfish', nor are liberals woefully 'naive'.

Instead, we must take the time to learn from people who are not like us, seeing whatever good we can in their 'abhorrent' views. This does not mean we have to agree with them. With curiosity and compassion, we can learn within disagreement. This is what civil dialogue is all about – staying in the room, even when disagreement is uncomfortable.[82] The democratic commitments we make can help us better understand the wider social conditions that people need.

The need for understanding is perhaps greater than ever. The major problems of today are global in nature, such as the threats of climate change, nuclear war and technological unemployment.

These global problems require global solutions.[83] However, partly in reaction to the impersonal process of globalisation, we are also witnessing the rise of nationalism, protectionism and populism. If we are to solve many of the problems that threaten humanity today we need to move beyond this global/local binary. We need to figure out how to solve them without either stretching too far the bonds that communities and nations are built upon, or shrinking too much our circle of concern that includes those who are most in need. This is no easy task. We can begin by spending less time trying to control the thoughts and opinions of others and more time listening.

Limits of morality

In this chapter we have looked at the societal issues of crime, health, poverty and democratic disagreement. We often try to solve these and other societal problems by controlling individuals – punishing offenders or curing people who are ill, for example. And these solutions are often wrapped up in forms of moralisation: judging offenders as 'bad' or those with mental illness as 'mad'. I have shown that instead of simply trying to control individuals we can better understand the wider social conditions that make people who they are. Controlling individuals may solve our problems in the short term, but, in the long term we need to change the underlying social conditions that will continue to cause them.

This myopic focus on simple narratives of individual responsibility may be an inherent limitation of trying to change society on the basis of common-sense morality. Our intuitive moral judgements are primarily about consistency – people behaving in stable, predictable ways, despite potential changes in their personality or social context. We need people to act consistently in order to cooperate with them – barring any serious excuses, we need to rely on others to act in line with our expectations.[84] This is where moral judgements and stories of individual responsibility come in. If people fail to consistently act in line with our normative expectations then we moralise their behaviour – we call them 'bad', 'evil', 'mad', 'crazy' and so on. These judgements hold people to account. They motivate individuals to live up to moral norms and rules, even if people sometimes have good reason to do otherwise (they might be tired or busy, for example). This is why moral character traits such as integrity, bravery and honesty are often about being consistent in the face of temptations or challenges.

The problem with trying to change society on the basis of common-sense morality is that it takes people's wider social conditions as a given. Moral judgements are about making individuals act consistently within a given social context – to have integrity in the face of temptations or be brave in the face of challenges. They do not look beyond the behaviour of individuals and question whether things have to be this way in the first place – whether we could remove some of the temptations or challenges that people face. The strategy of understanding the wider social changes that I have been arguing in favour of in this chapter requires going beyond the limited remit of our intuitive moral judgements and practices.

Instead of blaming individuals or casting them as victims, we can pay more attention to their social contexts and better understand what caused them to be the way they are. What were the wider social conditions that made someone desperate enough to harm others? Or what were the social contexts that made someone unable to cope with their situation? Whereas morality deals with rights and wrongs, understanding others deals with the complexities of people's lives – the circumstances they face and the resources they have to respond to them. The mindset we need is not judgement and certainty, but curiosity and compassion.

The societal issues we have looked at in this chapter can give us a window into the wider social conditions we all face. From 'the bad' we can understand what makes people desperate. From 'the sick', we can understand what makes people unhealthy. From 'the disabled', we can understand what people need to function well. From 'the mad', we can understand what people need to cope with the challenges they face. From 'the poor', we can understand what makes people insecure. From 'the other side', we can understand what makes people want change or stability. Our social contexts are far from perfect – to a certain extent, we all feel desperate, unhealthy and insecure.

Changing the wider social conditions that make people feel these ways is not easy. It may be often be quicker and more straightforward to try and punish all the 'bad' people or fix all the 'broken' people. In contrast, making the kinds of wider social changes I am advocating is a two-step process. First, it requires mobilisation – creating a collective powerful enough to create the required changes within a democratic context. Second, once that collective has been formed, the group needs to act against other powerful interests that would prefer to keep things as they are. As we saw in the section on democratic disagreement, this second step is also far from straightforward – sometimes, the benefits of wider social change can outweigh the potential threats of doing things differently; at other times, such changes can be met with greater resistance.

In response to these challenges, it is tempting to give up – to instead focus on controlling individual members of society. In fact, the difficulty of making wider social changes can lead to us giving up before we've even started. The political theorist Cass Sunstein gives the following anecdote to illustrate this process:

> Say your doctor tells you that you must undergo a year of grueling treatment for a serious illness. You might question the diagnosis and insist on getting a second opinion. But if the doctor says you can cure the problem just by taking a pill, you might just take the pill without asking further questions.[85]

Sunstein's point is that we often judge the seriousness of a problem on the basis of how realistic or desirable we find the potential solution. Psychologists refer to this bias as 'solution aversion' – a form of motivated reasoning that affects the kinds of societal issues we think are most important.[86] For instance, Jennifer Zamzow's research shows that people in the US who support gun control tend to judge violent burglary as less of a problem if they're told tighter laws are required to solve it.[87] This may be one of the reasons why people so often talk past each other in political debates. We may disagree over the causes of crime, health, poverty and so on because these facts may be too difficult to face.

We can, however, take solace in history and see that our social contexts are not set in stone. With hope and trust, we can continue to work towards the kinds of wider social changes we need. This is, ultimately, how we create a better society.

EIGHT

Changing the world

In Chapter Seven we saw how we try to create a better society by controlling individuals. We blame and punish 'bad' people. We try and fix 'broken' people. We don't help 'lazy' people. And we demonise 'ignorant' people. These strategies of control may work in the short term, but they do not remove the underlying causes of crime, ill-health, poverty and democratic disagreement – the wider social conditions that make people 'bad', 'broken', 'lazy' or 'ignorant' in the first place. To solve these problems in the long run, we need to switch our focus from control to understanding – from the moral character of individuals to the social contexts that make them who they are.

In this chapter we will see how we also try and create a better world through strategies of control – not just by controlling individuals, but also by controlling entire nations and the natural environment. We think that we can stop climate change with renewable energies and other technological fixes. And we think that we can end global poverty through a combination of aid and economic growth. These methods of control are often a good means of progress in the short term, but are less effective as long-term solutions, and may even make things worse – in the case of climate change, potentially much worse.

There is, however, an alternative. We can switch our focus away from control towards understanding. We can better understand the underlying *systemic* causes of climate change and global poverty and work to remove them. This may be more difficult to achieve in the short term – and, to many, appears overly idealistic – but it is a more effective long-term solution, and avoids the risks associated with trying to control both the natural environment and large groups of people.

Climate change: understanding 'nature'

All of the societal issues we looked at in the previous chapter were about how we treat individuals. We often moralise people in an attempt to control them, judging them as 'bad', 'mad', 'lazy', 'ignorant' and so on. We saw the limits of these common-sense moral judgements when it comes to changing society. These simple narratives of moral responsibility *dehumanise* individuals – they reduce people to character traits that fail to account for the complexity of their whole selves and the social contexts they live in.

However, it is important to realise that these strategies of control still recognise individuals as people. We still view 'bad' people as subjects who we stand in relationship to, rather than as objects that we can use, manipulate and control in whatever way we see fit. In the next section, we will see how we don't treat distant others in the same way. We often view people who are living in extreme poverty around the world and other powerless individuals more like objects under our control than subjects deserving of our respect. Subjects are to be understood. Objects are to be used.

We can see this dynamic of objectification most clearly when it comes to the natural world. We typically treat anything that is non-human – other animals, plants and natural environments – like objects, not subjects. With the possible exception of our pets, we tend to think that non-human animals have a significantly lower moral status than humans. In fact, to all extent and purposes, we treat non-human animals as morally *insignificant*. So much so that we have no problem with killing 74 billion farmed animals every year.[1]

This stands in stark contrast to more traditional cultures that are still dependent on non-human animals for transport and agriculture. For example, traditional Mongolian herdsmen only take a horse away from the herd to work for a week at a time because the herdsmen acknowledge and respect that the horses have their own society. Indigenous cultures, whose short- and long-term survival still depends on the sustainability of their natural surroundings, take this one step further. Many of these cultures personify parts of their environment that they depend on – rivers, prey, predators and so on. Through their personification of these subjects, they can endeavour to have harmonious relationships with them. Unlike people in modern societies, indigenous peoples tend to treat their natural environment as made of up subjects they stand in relationship to, not as objects they are separate from.[2]

We are beginning to see why these differences matter. We are beginning to see the limits of our control and exploitation of the natural environment in the form of potentially catastrophic climate change.

In this section, we will look at how our attempts to try and solve the problem of climate change through further controlling the natural environment may be less effective in the long term, and may potentially make things much worse. Instead, I will show that we need to understand the wider systemic conditions that cause climate change and work towards changing these systems on a planetary scale.

Fixing the climate

Since the Industrial Revolution, the Earth's global temperature has increased by 1°C. This global warming can largely be put down to human activity: higher concentrations of carbon dioxide (CO_2) in the Earth's atmosphere created largely by the burning of fossil fuels. Although 1°C increase doesn't seem that significant, the Earth's climate and natural ecosystems are finely balanced. We can already see the impact than a 1°C increase is having on more extreme weather, rising sea levels and species extinction rates. Further increases in the Earth's global temperature are likely to result in increasingly catastrophic consequences. For example, a total increase of 1.5°C would result in the death of 70–90 per cent of the world's coral reefs; with 2°C of global warming, almost all the core reefs will be lost. The consequences of 3–5°C of global warming, due to climate feedback effects, are close to unimaginable.[3]

Clearly, urgent action is required to prevent further climate change. In 2016, global leaders at the United Nations Framework Convention on Climate Change signed the Paris Agreement, declaring that, to limit global warming to 1.5°C, human-caused global emissions of CO_2 need to fall by 45 per cent from 2010 levels by 2030 and reach 'net zero' by 2050. In practice, this requires rapid and far-reaching transitions in land, energy, industry, buildings, transport and cities. For example, in 2017, the French government announced a plan to ban all petrol and diesel vehicles in France by 2040, to no longer use coal to produce electricity after 2022 and invest US$4 billion into boosting the nation's energy efficiency.

The main solution offered by researchers and policy makers is to switch from fossil fuels to renewable energy sources, and to incentivise this switch through the use of a global carbon tax.[4] The more expensive it is to emit CO_2 into the atmosphere, the more incentive there is to rely on renewable energy sources such as wind, solar and hydropower. Beyond renewable energy, other solutions include ways of reducing non-carbon greenhouse gases. For example, switching to more plant-based diets is one way of reducing the total amount of methane emissions caused by industrial livestock farming.[5]

More recently, as the required reductions in global greenhouse gas emissions are looking increasingly unlikely, researchers and policy makers have turned their attention to geo-engineering solutions.[6] If we can't reduce CO_2 emissions, we might be able to create technologies that remove CO_2 from the air. Other potential solutions involve offsetting the warming effects of greenhouse gases by artificially cooling the Earth's atmosphere – what is known as 'solar radiation management'.

The idea that we can control or 'manage' the Earth's climate is a tempting one. After all, it is through our scientific knowledge that we have come to learn about the problem of climate change. And it is our own actions since the Industrial Revolution that have caused it. It makes sense that we can use our scientific knowledge to find ways of acting differently and solving the problem.

Of course, things are, unfortunately, not so straightforward. Perhaps most obviously, the proposed changes required to reduce carbon emissions are in tension with powerful interests. Carbon taxes have been met with resistance wherever they have been proposed.[7] The Earth's atmosphere has, so far, been an available resource to use (and misuse) free of charge. The introduction of a carbon tax changes that. Businesses that have previously dumped their waste into airways and waterways free of charge will be forced to bear the opportunity costs of their actions by paying taxes or purchasing emissions rights. Not surprisingly, these businesses have resisted such changes, calling on an array of lobbyists, think tanks and friendly politicians to defend their interests.

In addition, public support for policies that aim to mitigate climate change comes up against several psychological barriers.[8] On an individual level, climate change forces us to drastically rethink our current carbon-intensive lifestyles, from how often we fly to how much meat we consume.[9] Making significant changes in these parts of our lives doesn't just go against our ingrained habits. It also goes against the behaviours of those around us, who, as we saw in Chapter Three, we look towards to find out what's possible. Moreover, climate change requires us to go beyond individual lifestyle changes and focus on how to make the necessary policy changes required to mitigate it. This collective effort is more challenging – the actions of any one individual make little difference to the overall desired outcome.[10] The result is that people feel powerless to do anything about climate change, even if they see it as the emergency that it is.

This is supported by psychological research that shows people have a tendency to see human systems as more inviolable than natural ones.[11] As David Wallace-Wells notes in his book *The Uninhabitable Earth*:

> renovating capitalism so that it doesn't reward fossil fuel extraction can seem unlikelier than suspending sulfur in the air to dye the sky red and cool the planet off by a degree or two. It's why creating global factories to suck carbon out of the atmosphere might appear to be easier than simply ending fossil-fuel subsidies.[12]

In the face of unlikely systemic change, technological fixes can seem like our only hope to control the natural environment and prevent a global climate breakdown.

Understanding the climate – it's complicated

Powerful interests and psychological barriers are not the only major problems with the main solutions proposed to mitigate climate change. A major difficulty with these kinds of solutions – for example, reducing global greenhouse gas emissions by switching from fossil fuels to renewable energy sources – is that they aim to mitigate climate change by controlling the natural environment. Of course, this may be necessary in the timescales we have left to deal with the problem. As mentioned above and in Chapter Seven, desperate times call for immediate, urgent solutions. But climate change also presents us with an opportunity to better understand the natural environment. In the remainder of this section, we will look at the wider systemic conditions that created climate change in the first place, and how we could mitigate these underlying causes.

It is too simplistic to blame climate change on higher levels of CO_2 in the atmosphere caused by the burning of fossil fuels since the Industrial Revolution. For instance, greenhouse gases have also been released due to significant changes in land use.[13] A century ago, only 15 per cent of Earth's surface was used to grow crops and raise livestock. Today, more than 77 per cent of land and 87 per cent of the ocean has been modified by human activity. The Earth is estimated to have lost about half its shallow water corals in the past 30 years and 20 per cent of the Amazon rainforest has disappeared in just 50 years. Although 25 per cent of carbon emissions are caused by heat and power generation, changes in land use contribute almost as much. The world is warming not only because of the burning of fossil fuels, but also because carbon sinks – environments that sequester CO_2 from the atmosphere such as soils, forest and wetlands – are being rapidly destroyed.

Switching to renewable energy sources, therefore, is only part of the solution. But paying attention to the degradation of natural ecosystems reveals a more fundamental problem. What makes natural ecosystems so important is their complexity and interrelatedness with other ecosystems.[14] We are beginning to understand, through complexity science – like our modelling of the Earth's climate – that almost everything we try and control is more complicated than we initially think. This is because everything exists in connection with everything else. For instance, we know that climate change is partly caused by the degradation of healthy mangroves, rainforests, fish in the deep seas, sea grass and kelp forests. But we cannot precisely quantify the importance of each of these factors. The overall impact of any one given factor on the Earth's climate depends on how all of the different factors interact, which is messy, complex and hard to predict. These interconnected, complex systems are the reason why we face the very real threat of runaway climate change.

This complexity is not unique to the Earth's climate system. We are also beginning to understand just how complex things are on a micro scale: the multitudes of bacteria and parasites that make up healthy immune systems, and the bacteria and fungi that make up healthy soil. Both of these contexts show that trying to control complex systems can only get us so far. For instance, industrial farming revolutionised food production in the 1950s, only to find out that it has been slowly depleting the soil. Now, according to estimates from the UN, we have just 50–60 harvests left before industrial farming methods become impossible.[15] Similarly, with our immune system, germ theory led the way to practices of hygiene that saved many people from dying in surgery, childbirth or via communicable bacterial diseases. Now, according to our current understanding of the gut biome, we know that low bacteria environments are responsible for a number of modern autoimmune diseases, allergies and intolerances.[16]

The question is, where do we go from here? We now understand the limits of control when it comes to the industrial farming, sterilised environments and the Earth's climate. But how can we continue to grow food, be healthy and use the Earth's natural resources within this complexity?

One obvious implication is to conserve the intact, natural complex systems that we still have. When it comes to mitigating climate change, the best technologies we have available may in fact be healthy soils, forests and wetlands. Not only do we need to stop destroying these natural ecosystems at an alarming rate, we should do whatever we can to promote their regeneration. For instance, the renowned ecologist E.O. Wilson, in his book *Half-Earth*, proposes that half of the Earth's land should be designated a human-free natural reserve to preserve biodiversity.[17] Conserving these natural ecosystems may also help stabilize the Earth's climate.

To many, the idea of conservation on such a mass scale may seem like a nice dream, but one that ignores the realities of human needs and deprivation, along with an ever-increasing global population. Instead of leaving half the world untouched, would it not be better to efficiently manage the regeneration of the Earth's natural ecosystems? For example, could we not plant new fast-growth forests or embark on similar carbon sequestration projects?

Again, these kinds of activities, much like other technological fixes, may be useful responses to the urgent situation we face. But it is important to recognise that they are not ideal and could even make things worse in the long term. This is because they go against the logic of complex natural ecosystems. Ecosystems are non-linear in nature. They rely on homeostatic feedback mechanisms – such as relationships of symbiosis, positive and negative feedback loops, autocatalytic loops and trophic cascades – all working in parallel to maintain a balanced system.[18] The result is that we cannot straightforwardly change one part of an ecosystem without it having an effect on every other part.

For example, we know that trees are useful for sequestering carbon. But we don't know the extent to which already intact forests are much more efficient forms of carbon sequestration than planting new fast-growth forests. We are increasingly discovering how crucial different parts of natural ecosystems are to the functioning of whole ecosystems.[19] For instance: in the 1990s, we discovered the crucial role that mycorrhizae fungi play in carbon sequestration; in the 2000s, we discovered the role that boreal forests play in forming low-altitude clouds that cool the planet; in the 2010s, we discovered the importance of megafauna, such as whales, in transporting nutrients around the globe, which in turn supports natural environments that sequester vast amounts of CO_2 from the atmosphere.

Understanding this more complex picture is the opposite to strategies of control. Methods of control tend to focus on fixing one problem at a time, in isolation of other relevant factors. When it comes to complex systems, these linear methods are likely to create more problems in the long term. For example, insecticides may reduce insect damage to crops in the short term, but have been shown to create further problems, such as fungal damage, as a result of killing species that used to keep the ecosystem in balance. Of course, we can then use fungicides to solve that problem, but they have been shown to reduce soil integrity and water retention, which requires another solution, and so on.[20] Each technical fix may come with its own benefits in the short term, but accrue further problems in the future – all while failing to solve the underlying issue at hand.

The underlying cause of climate change is that we have manipulated complex natural systems to the extent that they are now out of our control. In response, we can continue to try and control parts of these ecosystems, which may well produce short-term wins. Or we can seek to re-establish them, in all their complexity, maintaining the stability of the Earth's climate in the long run.

Working with nature, not against it

So far, I have shown that by switching our focus from controlling the Earth's climate to understanding it in all its complexity, we can work towards re-establishing the natural ecosystems that help maintain it. We can, however, learn more from the natural world. By paying attention to the underlying causes of climate change and environmental degradation, we can understand the kinds of relationships we need to forge with the natural environment and each other.

Humans are unique in our ability to control and dominate our environment. In contrast, other species typically don't have the energy and resources to outcompete one another. Who knows, maybe they would happily control and dominate their environments if they could? But instead, they must opt for paths of least resistance – accommodating and adapting to the ends of other nearby species, often forming relationships of mutual dependence.[21] It is through this process that natural ecosystems reach transitory states of equilibrium. Each species must learn, over countless iterations of life, how to construct a way of living that either directly or indirectly benefits every other part of the ecosystem.

The history of human civilization is one in which we have gained increased amounts of control over our environment from new forms of energy and resources.[22] Whereas other species must rely on food as their primary energy source, humans have learned how to harness energy from a wide range of sources. For half a million years, we have used fire to transform materials; for five thousand years, we have used animals to plough fields and carry loads; for several hundred years we have burned coal, oil and gas to power industrial technology. The more energy we have had at our disposal, the greater the scale on which we have imposed order on each other and the natural world.

I have questioned whether we can continue to control things in this way now that they've started to get complicated. The free ride that we have had from our natural environment so far may be starting to catch up with us. But beyond regenerating many of the natural ecosystems we have destroyed, what can we learn from nature about how to create to a better world?

First, we can learn that the local and the global are connected. We cannot control one part of an ecosystem without having an impact on all the other parts. We can't chop down one rainforest without having an impact on the wider planetary ecosystem. This understanding has the potential to unify different political perspectives on the kinds of environmental policies we need.[23] On the one hand, there are those who advocate local, 'bottom-up' changes – where people take sufficient care of their own environment out of a sense of beauty, home and responsibility. On the other hand, there are those who advocate global, 'top-down' changes – emphasising that mitigating climate change requires a global focus and global action.

From a complex ecosystems point of view we can understand the value of both perspectives. From a local, bottom-up perspective, people taking sufficient care of their environment will also have a positive impact on the wider planet. From a global, top-down perspective, policies can ensure that local communities can take care of their own environment without creating externalities that prevent other local communities from doing the same. Moreover, in democracies, top-down solutions cannot be implemented and sustained without sufficient bottom-up support. People need to understand how the local and the global are connected so that effective environmental policies receive sustained support.

Second, by understanding the underlying causes of climate change, we can learn how to form mutually beneficial relationships with each other and the natural world. These lessons can be found within all living things. For instance, we tend to think that non-human animals and plants are less intelligent than humans – they do not have sophisticated forms of language or culture. But from a complex systems perspective, the opposite might be the case. Non-human animals and plants are incredibly adept at dealing with the problems they face within their own biological niches.[24] They work with the limited resources they have to cooperate with members of their own and other species. For example, some trees have been shown to bank 10 per cent of the rainwater in the soil, which they only use to water the forest around them when it's dry. The idea of 'biomimicry' is that these principles – of limits, buffers and cooperation – can inform structures of local and global governance.[25] Principles from complex natural systems can provide the basis for a rich and refined human civilization.

Paying attention to climate change can help us understand that our modern ideals of human civilisation and global progress were mistaken. Throughout the Industrial Revolution and beyond, modern people assumed that nature was separate from humans – inert, predictable and under our control. But we now know that nature has never been like that. Things are more complex – we are as much a part of nature as everything else. Instead of trying to dominate the natural environment, we can learn how to form mutually beneficial relationships with it through attitudes of care. When we care about someone, we see what they need and find opportunities to help them, without thinking about what's in it for us. We can treat the natural environment in a similar way. Through caring for nature, we can work out forms of cooperation that leave everyone better off.

Of course, we may be able to continue down our path of control and manipulation, and power and dominance, instead. Perhaps we can replace the biosphere with techno-engineered systems designed to serve exclusively human interests. This is entirely possible. The problem with this process, however, is it's risky. It also fails to appreciate what we can do with the resources we already have available to us, rather than always trying to get more and more. The issue of climate change shows that there is much to be gained from understanding and working within the complex systems we are a part of and, perhaps more importantly, much to be lost from going to war with them.

Global poverty: understanding 'the insignificant'

The control and objectification of nature – treating the natural environment as a resource that we can easily use and manipulate in whatever way we see fit – fails to account for its full value and complexity. Instead of going to war with nature, we would do better to respect it and understand it.

In this section, we will see how we control and objectify distant others in a similar way – to the extent that we often see other human beings as morally 'insignificant'. This dynamic of control and objectification is a well-known feature of slavery, oppression, war and genocide. In times of war, for example, soldiers are 'sacrificed' for the greater good and citizen fatalities are seen as 'collateral damage'. They cease to be seen as people with rich inner lives, and instead become separate objects – things that can be easily used and manipulated by others. We will see that our control and domination over the world's poorest nations creates a similar dynamic. Through strategies of control, we end up reducing the global poor to numbers and statistics, rather than seeing them as subjects who we care about and stand in relation to.

The story of doing good

We live in a globally connected world. It is almost impossible to ignore the existence of global poverty in the modern day. The news is full of bad things happening to poor people around the world: famines and epidemics in Africa; sweatshops in Asia; natural disasters, civil wars and dictatorships all over. It is easy to feel powerless in the face of distant suffering. What can we possibly do to help? When solutions are offered – such as natural disaster relief, global aid or military force against authoritarian regimes – they tend to receive popular support. And when no solutions seem possible, we must normalise the suffering – distant others on the news become regrettable numbers and statistics.

In response to this situation, we might think that a more compassionate society is one that simply *did more* – gave more aid or intervened in more civil wars. This is the spirit of popular events such as Live Aid, where Bob Geldof and other rock stars implored the general public to just 'give us your fucking money'. It's the spirit of worldwide charities that aim to relieve the suffering of those who are most in need. And it's the spirit of tech entrepreneurs and wealthy philanthropists such as Bill Gates, who believe they can save the world one problem at a time, from eradicating malaria to promoting female education.

Of course, these are all well-intentioned solutions and often save many lives. My point is not to diminish their importance – if we can help people in these ways then we should. We should not, however, rest content with acts of charity. To do so would be to ignore the bigger picture of global poverty – its underlying systemic causes which, no matter how many altruistic actions we take as a society, will keep millions, if not billions,[26] of people in poverty for the foreseeable future.

We are beginning to see this bigger – more complex and messy – picture when it comes to global aid. Over the past couple of decades, aid from rich to poor countries has been criticised on a number of accounts.[27] First, it often fails to take into account the needs of people on the ground. Aid may provide anti-malarial nets, for example, which are then either sold or fashioned into something more useful. Second, aid can do damage through providing only short-term benefits. Charities may build a water pump, for example, which changes the practices and priorities of a local community, only for the water pump to cease working and not be properly maintained in the long term. Third, and perhaps most importantly, aid given to poor nations without the right political institutions can end up creating further corruption and oppression.

We no longer believe that aid and charity are the answer to all the world's problems. In response, the 'effective altruism' movement promotes projects and interventions that have shown to be cost-effective – proven ways of saving the most lives (and quality-adjusted life-years) for the least amount of money.[28] According to these principles, if you really care about alleviating global poverty, the best thing you can do as an individual is to earn as much money as you can and give it away to the most cost-effective charities and non-governmental organisations.[29] Almost everyone, within rich nations at least, has the potential to save lives.

This response, however, only scratches at the surface of the problem. Aid and charity – no matter how cost-effective – aim to relieve the symptoms of global poverty, ignoring its underlying causes. There is, of course, a place for this. As noted in the previous chapter, desperate situations sometimes call for immediate, urgent responses. Sometimes putting a plaster on the problem is useful. However, if we want to cure the problem in the long term, we need to better understand the wider systemic conditions that create global poverty.

Fortunately, this is something that most developmental economists do. Economists tend to acknowledge that ending global poverty is a complex and messy process, and something that cannot be easily controlled through a combination of effective aid and charity. Instead, they focus on understanding the wider social conditions that can reduce extreme poverty in the long term, such as the public institutions and infrastructure required for poor nations to achieve stable economic growth.[30]

This is exactly the kind of shift in focus – away from control and towards understanding – that I believe we need to create a better world. In fact, with this wider social focus, developmental economists now recognise that foreign aid has an important long-term role to play. Foreign aid and nation states are well placed to build the infrastructure required to established new market economies – the road, or the mobile phone tower, to the region where there is no economic activity, as well as the schools and the hospitals.

This more complex, indirect approach has largely been successful. We are slowly solving the problem of global poverty. In fact, the dramatic picture we began this section with – of poor, starving children in Africa – is an outdated one. According to World Bank statistics, the world is now more equal than ever.[31] We no longer live in a world that can be neatly divided into rich and poor, 'developed' and 'developing' nations. Only 12.5 per cent of the world's population is in extreme poverty; the majority of people live somewhere in the middle. Further research shows that we systematically tend to think that people in the 'developing' world are poorer, shorter-lived and less educated than they actually are.[32]

Over the past 50 years we have witnessed substantial economic growth throughout the world. This growth has not just happened in China and India, but also across Asia, Latin America and Africa. In 1980, over 2 billion people lived in extreme poverty (defined as living on less than $1.90 a day). Today, this figure has dropped to under 1 billion.[33] According to many development economists, the end of extreme poverty is in sight – one of the UN Sustainable Development Goals is to eradicate extreme poverty for all people everywhere by 2030.[34]

The story of economic development

Unfortunately, however, this story of economic development is incomplete. Although the switch in focus – away from control and towards understanding – is a good one, it may not have gone far enough. Developmental economists may now focus on the wider social conditions required to get people out of poverty, but they often pay little attention to the wider global economic system. Even if stable economic growth in poor nations is gradually putting an end to extreme poverty, there are also global systemic conditions that keep people poor for longer than is necessary. We can begin to understand these systemic conditions by looking at the history of economic prosperity and development.

This history of development is entwined with the history of colonialism – the process in which European empires forcefully took control over nations across the globe from the 15th century to the aftermath of the Second World War.[35] This process of domination, under the rhetoric of modernisation and opening trade opportunities, was bloody and brutal on an unprecedented scale.

For instance, after European nations colonised Latin America in 1492, the indigenous population fell from between 50–100 million to about 3.5 million by the mid-1600s.[36] The indigenous population died from foreign diseases, from slavery, from being slaughtered or starved to death after being kicked off their land. This is the same process that created the African-American slave trade, which saw up to 15 million slaves shipped across the Atlantic from Africa between 1619 and 1865.[37] It also witnessed mass famine in India. The British Empire and its reorganisation of the Indian agricultural system caused up to 30 million Indians to die of famine during the last few decades of the 19th century.[38] The lives of millions of people from the indigenous populations of colonial nations were sacrificed for the 'greater good' of the empire.

These atrocities were carried out under the guise of economic development. It was, however, a process that benefited Europeans at the cost of colonial nations. For instance, according to economist Angus Maddison, before the British invasion, India made up 27 per cent of the world economy. By the end of colonial rule, this figure had fallen to 3 per cent.[39] Similarly, China's share of the world economy fell from 32 per cent to 7 per cent.[40] This was not simply the result of the Industrial Revolution 'taking off' in European nations before it did in other parts of the world. In addition, European empires used the natural and human resources of colonial nations in Asia, Africa and the Caribbean to develop their economies, while holding back progress in what we now call the global South.[41]

We like to think that these global systemic injustices ended with the collapse of European colonialism in the wake of the Second World War. This, however, is not what happened. As the historian Noel Maurer points out in his book *The Empire Trap*, a combination of a) authoritarian political regimes across the global South supported by Western nations, b) stifling Third World Debts, and c) 'structural adjustment programs' implemented by the World Bank and the International Monetary Fund (IMF), all helped the global power structures created by colonialism to continue to this day.[42] As the historian Kehinde Andrews notes: 'It is the height of delusion to think that the impact of slavery ended with emancipation, or that empire was absolved by the charade of independence being bestowed on the former colonies.'[43]

The result is that poor nations continue to help develop rich nations, rather than the other way around. Although rich countries give out about US$1.3 trillion in aid to poor countries each year, according to one study, US$3.3 trillion flows from poor countries to rich countries in a number of forms, such as the profits of multinational companies, tax havens and debt repayments.[44]

If we want to reduce global poverty as soon as possible, we need to understand these systemic injustices and remove them. We cannot continue to control the global economy to our liking – to do our best at reducing poverty on a national scale while maintaining business as usual on an international level. In the long term, poor countries need a global economic system that is fair and just.

There are a number of systemic changes that could be made.[45] Institutions such as the IMF and the World Bank could be democratised, giving equal power to developed and developing nations. The World Trade Organization could shut down tax havens and other illicit financial flows out of developing countries. And rich nations could rapidly reduce the debts of countries in the global South.

Each of these changes involves rich, powerful nations relinquishing the control they have over the economies of poor nations – economies and resources they have historically been free to dominate and manipulate for their own gain. This is something that is unlikely to happen without considerable political pressure.

We might wonder whether such unlikely and potentially unrealistic changes are worth fighting for. After all, according to the UN Sustainable Development Goals, we are on target to completely eradicate extreme poverty by 2030. Maybe we don't need long-term solutions to the problem of global poverty? Maybe this is an example where the strategy of control, and business as usual, gets us the result we want? Contrary to this optimism, I believe systemic changes are necessary for two reasons.

First, having a fair and just global economic system may be intrinsically worthwhile. Without addressing the global systemic injustices that exist today as remnants of our colonial past, we may be less capable of making fair and just progress in the future. As the American civil rights activist Malcolm X noted, 'if you stick a knife in my back nine inches and pull it out six inches, that's not progress. If you pull it all the way out, that's not progress. The progress comes from healing the wound that the blow made.'[46] At the moment, rich nations 'won't even admit the knife is there'.

This is similar to the logic behind the colonial reparations movement, which calls for Western nations not only to apologise for the atrocities they caused, but also to financially compensate former colonial nations.[47] We don't have to endorse the idea of reparations, however, to understand that we should create a fairer global economic system. In rich nations, we like to tell ourselves that we are the good guys – the ones that abolished slavery, won the Second World War and treat women equally. We don't like to acknowledge the very real possibility that we might in fact be the bad guys, and that we need to change the systemic injustices at the heart of the status quo.

The second important reason to create a more just global economic system is that ending global poverty may take much longer than we think. Unfortunately, the optimism of the UN Sustainability Goals may not be warranted. According to one study, on our current trajectory of economic growth, completely eradicating extreme poverty will take 100 years, not just over a decade.[48]

Moreover, so far we have just been talking about extreme poverty. The notion of extreme poverty – currently defined as living on less than US$1.90 a day – is a controversial one. Many theorists regard this baseline to be inadequately low.[49] It is not enough to achieve basic nutrition or sustain normal human activity. There are many different views over what the definition of poverty should be, ranging from $3.20/day to $8/day. If set at $7.40/day – the amount required to achieve normal human life expectancy – the time it would take to completely eradicate extreme poverty would be much longer. According to the same study mentioned above, ending global poverty would take over 200 years.

If there are systemic changes we can make to speed up this process then we should do everything in our power to make them. The standard developmental narrative is that we are doing everything we can to end global poverty – that people living in extreme poverty around the world today are a regrettable chapter in a slowly-but-surely story of economic progress. This is simply not true. People who die from malnutrition, preventable illnesses or infant mortalities – or those who suffer from a lack of education, a life of hard labour or human rights abuses – are not reducible to numbers and statistics. They are not objects that can be justifiably sacrificed as part of a larger global trend. We must recognise that they currently suffer because the game has been rigged in favour of the global rich. Citizens of poor nations are subjects who we stand in relation to, and who we can help by changing the rules of the game.

In this section, we have seen that a curious and compassionate world is not necessarily one in which people simply *do more* about global poverty – one in which we all give more money to charity or foreign aid. By switching our focus from control to understanding, we can pay more attention to the underlying systemic causes of global poverty. We can understand the conditions required for the stable economic growth of poor nations, and the systemic barriers that keep millions, if not billions, of people in poverty for longer than they should be.

Global progress

In the previous two sections, we have seen how the problems of climate change and global poverty can be solved with a better understanding of their wider systemic causes. In this section, we will see how both these issues point towards the problems of trying to achieve global progress through the strategy of control. I will show that, instead of trying to control global progress through the means of human development and economic growth, we need to better understand ways of changing the world that benefit all living beings. Instead of trying to be as productive as we can, we need to be productive within sufficient limits, so that as many living things can benefit from that productivity as possible.

The story of global progress

The problems of climate change and global poverty can both be viewed as problems about property rights, ownership, productivity and control.

Climate change is the result of burning fossil fuels since the Industrial Revolution and degrading the natural ecosystems that keep the Earth's climate in balance. We tend to view parts of the natural environment as objects and resources that we can use, manipulate and destroy for the 'greater good' of human civilization. The threat of catastrophic climate change reflects the potential limits of this practice. The planet's natural ecosystems may be too complex to control.

Global poverty is partly the result of global systemic injustices that exist as remnants of European colonialism. Throughout the colonial period, citizens of colonial nations were viewed as objects and resources that could be used, manipulated and sacrificed for the 'greater good' of the empire. Although significant global progress has been made since the end of colonialism, millions of people in the global South are kept in poverty as a result of systemic conditions that are still justified as being for the 'greater good' of the global economy.

With both these issues, we may agree that our strategies of control are harmful and limited. But we may still think they are worth it *overall*. After all, the world is a cruel and dangerous place, and humans are fragile beings. We cannot hope to solve all of the world's problems. Perhaps we are doing the best we can within these harsh conditions? Our situation may be analogous to military strategists who must admit that 'sacrifices' or 'collateral damage' are necessary in times of war. The means aren't perfect, and may sometimes be horrific. But they are justified in terms of the ends. Perhaps it is through the means of control that we achieve global progress in the long term?

In support of this view is the history of human civilization. Since the origins of agriculture, humans have made considerable progress and have done so through the (often brutal and bloody) means of control.[50] As Steven Pinker notes in his influential books *The Better Angels of Our Nature* and *Enlightenment Now*, life used to be much worse.[51] Over the past 200 years, we have abolished slavery, ended colonialism and introduced universal human rights. Through human development and economic prosperity, individuals have slowly and steadily gained more economic and political freedoms. We have progressed from more oppressive political structures such as aristocracy to more liberal structures such as democracy. In fact, as we saw in Chapter Three, it is our modern-day security and freedoms that create opportunities for people to care about others who are less fortunate, as well as care for the natural environment.[52]

I do not doubt any of these claims. I am also in no position to debate whether the means that brought about these ends were justifiable or not. What I am interested here is whether we can do things *better*.

First of all, it is important to realise that despite these leaps of progress global justice remains a distant goal. As mentioned in Chapter Seven, the problem with progress is that it is often an unfinished process. We can, and should, ask ourselves what terrible things we are doing today that people in the future will look back on in the same way as we now look back at slavery? We no longer think that the ownership and control of other humans is a necessary part of human development. We also no longer think that the ownership and control of other nations, in the form of colonialism, is necessary. We do, however, think it is necessary to control the movement of individuals across national borders.[53] And, as the philosopher Leif Wenar notes in his book *Blood Oil*, we still think it is necessary for undemocratically elected regimes to control a nation's resources – we implicitly support these authoritarian regimes through buying their oil.[54]

Of course, we may continue to make progress and soon see these issues as a thing of the past. With continued human development and economic prosperity, people may become free to move across borders, and all national resources may come under citizen control. From the history of human development, we can see that economic prosperity provides nations and individuals with a greater amount of power and control over their own affairs.[55] We can imagine a future where this continued story of human progress provides every individual with enough resources and opportunities to have control over their own lives.

The global risks of control

The problem with this story is that it is risky on two counts. The first major risk has to do with physics. This continued process of human development requires a tremendous amount of energy. We saw this in our discussion of climate change. We are currently living well beyond our planetary limits.[56] Humans require 1.7 planets to offset our use of natural resources each year. This is likely to rise to three planets by 2050 as the population grows to around ten billion and industrial development continues across the world. Of course, humans are also clever. We can develop new technologies to produce energy and resources more efficiently. But these technologies also require more energy – especially once we take into account the cascade of new problems that are likely to be caused by their introduction (and the technologies created to solve them, and the new problems that they will cause, and so on).

So far, the story of human development rests on humans finding ways of extracting more energy and resources from the natural environment, not less. It remains to be seen whether we can continue to develop while simultaneously reversing this trend. Just because it has never been done before doesn't mean it's not possible. It does, however, mean that our attempts to do so are risky.

The potential risks involved are of a special kind. The potential of runaway climate change, for instance, risks almost everything – the collapse of the Earth's natural ecosystems that all of human civilization relies on. The economist Nassim Nicholas Taleb, in his book *Skin in the Game*, notes that dealing with these risks requires different principles. In particular, the 'precautionary principle' states that, 'if an action or policy has a suspected risk of causing severe harm to the public domain (affecting general health or the environment globally), the action should not be taken in the absence of scientific near-certainty about its safety'.[57] When it comes to the impact of continued human development on the Earth's natural ecosystems, we are nowhere near scientific certainty over its safety.

The second major risk is less to do with physics and more to do with humans. History shows that human development and economic prosperity are the result of increasingly effective means of controlling natural and human resources. Let us suppose that we can overcome the challenges of physics and create technologies that allow us to keep up this trajectory. We may lose some of the natural ecosystems that we know and love, much like how we have lost animal and plant species as a result of past human development. But through ever-greater control over the natural environment, we can avoid environmental collapse. Let us also suppose that we can avoid other existential risks created by the control of our natural and human environments, such as the risk of antibiotic resistance caused the industrial farming of animals or the risk of nuclear war caused by digital technologies and cyber terrorism.

What is the problem here? Although this process may avoid catastrophic outcomes, the means by which they were avoided are likely to continue. In this chapter, we have seen that the strategy of control reduces natural and human subjects to objects that can be readily used and manipulated. Another way of putting this point is that natural and human resources are viewed in terms of their *instrumental value* – they become a means to an end, not something that is valuable in and of itself. It is this mindset that makes us able to sacrifice soldiers in a war or destroy a rainforest to produce cheap palm oil.

We might think that, at our current stage of human progress, the ends justify the means. People around the world are starving, and millions of people die each year of preventable diseases.[58] These are, of course, grave issues – forms of mass suffering that we need to do our best to alleviate. We must also realise, however, that this kind of instrumental reasoning is a potentially *slippery slope*. If we can destroy the natural world for the purpose of having longer and healthier lives, what other forms of destruction are justifiable? When do we stop trying to control people as objects and resources under the guise of human development? At what point does the strategy of control end?

I think the most likely answer to this question is that it doesn't. As long as we can see the worth of controlling someone or something to our liking then we will continue to do so. The important question, however, is whether continued human development and economic prosperity is likely to either, a) provide every individual with enough resources to have control over their own lives, or b) provide a minority of individuals with enough resources to control the majority?

The answer to this question is complex, but there are two main factors at play. The first is the *amount* of resources created by the process of human development. The history of human civilization has shown that individuals have gained increasing large amounts of resources and control over their own lives. The Industrial Revolution, for instance, saw the spread of democracy, the middle class and the welfare state – revolutions in human freedoms and wellbeing.

The second factor, however, is the *distribution* of these resources. The vast majority of the resources created by human development have gone to the wealthiest 1 per cent of the world's population. Never before in history have so few people accrued so much wealth and power.[59] There is no logical reason, from the perspective of control, why this small minority would not reduce less powerful individuals to objects and resources to be used in whatever ways are instrumentally valuable. Through this process, the majority of individuals may be deprived of the control they have over their own lives.

If this sounds over the top, like some kind of sci-fi dystopia, we do not need to look far to see this process already in action. In the US, a combination of globalisation and automation has increased unemployment among the working class.[60] This increase in unemployment and pervasive sense of insignificance has led to the political isolation of the working class and may be an important factor in the spread of the US opioid epidemic.[61]

In Europe, economic inequality has risen since the mid-1980s, alongside neoliberal political agendas. Research shows that these increases in inequality are linked with a decline in people's loyalty and trust in democracy. For instance, according to one study, people in European nations are now more likely to agree with the statement that, 'wealthy people have a very strong hold on political power. People of average or poorer income have some degree of influence but only on issues that matter less for wealthy people.'[62]

This gap between the poor and the super-rich is likely to increase with technological unemployment caused by advances in artificial intelligence (AI). We may witness a 'hollowing out' of the middle class as more and more skilled jobs are performed by intelligent machines, not humans. Without substantial political changes, advances in technology and AI are likely to cause an even greater concentration of wealth within the top 1 per cent and 0.1 per cent.[63]

From one perspective, this distribution of wealth and power is not a problem – so long as everyone gains from the prosperity created by these changes, it doesn't matter that a minority of people gain a lot more. But, from the perspective of control, where people are judged (and controlled) by their instrumental value, these differences matter. From this perspective, the powerful not only can exert control over those who are least powerful, but they also *should* if doing so creates better outcomes in the long run. The strategy of control is a different value system to the strategy of understanding. It is one where the ends continue to justify the means. But – and this is the important point – the ends are determined by those who have all the control.

We can continue this line of thought with all sorts of fanciful scenarios. With new biological and cognitive enhancements, maybe the top 0.1 per cent will become an altogether different kind of human, with reason to control the other 99.9 per cent?[64] Or with big data and surveillance technologies, maybe powerful interests will be able to control the decisions of every individual?[65] Or perhaps AI will see the instrumental value of controlling all humans for the 'greater good'?[66]

My point is not to imagine what the future will be like, but to illustrate that, according to the strategy of control and the logic of instrumental reasoning, humans are only valuable insofar as they are *useful*. A world ruled by this kind of moral reasoning is an inherently risky one. It is one where slavery or war or genocide or poverty can be justified for economic reasons. It is one where we can kill 74 billion animals a year for cheap and tasty food. And it is one where we can seriously contemplate the destruction of almost the entire natural environment for the development of the human race. It is naive to think that the values we have now – where each individual still has intrinsic worth – will continue in a future where we are guided by instrumental reasoning and no longer depend on each other for our survival and wellbeing. The risk is that, under such conditions, the majority of humans will witness what it is like to be the objects and resources that we currently exploit for the 'greater good'.

A different story

The opposite to the strategy of control is one of understanding. Instead of assuming that we know what is most worthwhile, and then applying instrumental reasoning to maximise it, we can gain a deeper understanding of what's valuable. We can endeavour to make progress and change the world while respecting the intrinsic value of the natural and human environments that we are a part of and depend upon.

What might this look like in practice? First of all, it's important to see that there are parallels here with what we learned in Chapter Six about how to improve our own lives within insecurity. As insecure human beings, our lives depend on the existence – and death and suffering – of countless other living things. The less concerned we are with controlling everything in our lives to our liking, the more we realise this fact, and the more we acknowledge the insecurity of others and ourselves. A simple way of putting this point is, the less we try and control our lives, the more *connected* we feel to the things that they depend upon.

In Chapter Six, we saw that there are two natural responses to this sense of connection: gratitude and grief. We can feel gratitude for all the living things that our survival and wellbeing depend on. And we can feel grief for all the harms that we inevitably cause them throughout our lives. Most importantly, both gratitude and grief can compel us to *give* something back in return for all the gifts we have received.

The same principles – of connection, gratitude and grief and giving – can be applied on a much larger scale, albeit in a more complex form. The systemic changes we need to create a better world are those that rest on principles of *cooperation, sufficiency, redistribution*.

We already live in vast, complex systems of cooperation. The natural resources we depend on are sustained by complex natural ecosystems, where different species coexist in non-linear, mutually beneficial relationships. The human resources we depend on are also sustained by complex human ecosystems, such as the interconnected relationships that make up market economies. The principle of cooperation is simple: the more living things cooperate with each other, the more everyone's lives can improve. By creating the conditions for equal forms of cooperation, we can avoid the risks associated with strategies of control and instrumental reasoning. Cooperation requires conditions of sufficiency and redistribution.

Sufficiency is about acknowledging the worth of our existing resources and the ways in which we can draw on them to look after the things we care about. It is the practical import of gratitude and contentment. In the context of changing the world, the principle of sufficiency is to work with what we already have, rather than controlling parts of our natural and human environments to accumulate more resources. This is how species within complex ecosystems work, where no one species has the energy or resources to outcompete other species – instead, each species must work with what they have. The most important part of this process is that, for it to work in the long term, there must be slack in the system. This is achieved through each species creating an *excess* amount of resources, despite having to work within the limits imposed by the ecosystem as a whole. This excess acts as a buffer to ensure that the ecosystem can survive unpredictable shocks, such as drought.

Sufficiency is about limits *and* excess. This excess is what creates room for slack within those limits. We often see the opposite to this process with the history of human development and economic prosperity. For example, the historian Ellen Meiksins Wood shows how the enclosure movement in England removed these excesses and with them a sense of sufficiency.[67] The enclosures began in 1235, where wealthy elites fenced off commons and systematically forced peasants off the land which they relied on for their livelihood – forests, game, fodder, waters, fish and other necessary resources. After enclosure, peasants had to compete with each other for leases to farm on the newly privatised land, which were allocated on the basis of productivity. Of course, this new process increased productivity and the new landowners took all the excess created from this activity. The end result was a greater amount of wealth produced in total, but with all the excess wealth in the hands of a few.

When the excesses are removed from a system, there are no longer any buffers against unpredictable, yet inevitable, shocks. Sufficiency is replaced by scarcity. This was seen throughout the period of colonisation, as the British wealthy elite applied the same process of enclosure throughout the British Empire. The result was famine in regions of the world that were still exporting large amounts of food. The same process continued in the wake of colonialism. The Nobel Prize-winning economist Amartya Sen has shown that famines in poor nations – such as the 1974 famine in Bangladesh and the Ethiopian famine of 1984 – are not necessarily the result of low amounts of food production.[68] These famines are often caused by drought and other natural disasters, which, if it hadn't been for food being exported elsewhere, would not have been so disastrous. Trying to increase productivity without sufficiency – excess and limits – is too risky.

The second condition required for systems of cooperation to work is redistribution. This principle comes into play when there is a greater amount of excess than required to buffer from unpredictable shocks. Instead of keeping this excess to gain further control over the natural or human environment, we can distribute it to those that need it most. This is similar to the trees that bank 10 per cent of the rainwater in the soil for when it's dry. They do not store the rainwater for themselves, but for the forest around them.

Redistribution ensures that everyone has the chance to contribute towards the greater good. Interestingly, economic inequalities are often justified on completely the opposite grounds – that inequality helps productivity and is therefore required for the greater good. We now know that this isn't strictly true. Although some forms of economic inequality can make people more productive, too much inequality can in fact decrease productivity. Research shows that *entrenched* inequalities – where economic inequality creates unequal access to education, labour markets and finance – tend to have a negative impact on productivity.[69] This is because entrenched inequalities prevent people from contributing towards the greater good. Without distribution, people do not have sufficient resources to contribute to society. With distribution, a greater number of people can contribute to the economy, which in turn creates more productivity, diversity and flexibility within the wider system.

The welfare state is an obvious example of the principles of sufficiency and redistribution in practice. After the Second World War, the welfare state was created in the UK to ensure that everyone had sufficient resources to contribute to society, economically or otherwise. In fact, after its introduction, the UK witnessed high rates of growth and productivity, despite a top rate of income tax of 98 per cent.[70] This changed in the 1980s, with neoliberal policies that abandoned the principles of sufficiency and redistribution in favour of unlimited productivity.

By switching our focus from control to understanding, we can bring back the same principles upon which the welfare state was created. In fact, I believe we can and should go much further. In 1930, the economist John Maynard Keynes famously predicted that the economy would rapidly become so productive that people would have to work for no more than 15 hours a week to satisfy all their material needs.[71] Although productivity has increased much more than Keynes predicted, the abundance that he foresaw has not come to pass. The mechanism required for this to happen is much greater sufficiency and mass redistribution.

For instance, drawing on statistics from the *World Inequality Report*, the anthropologist Jason Hickel notes that since 1980 the incomes of the richest 1 per cent have grown by 100 times more than those of the poorest 60 per cent. Redistributing a third of the income of the richest 1 per cent to the poorest 4.2 billion people could end global poverty in a stroke. It would also still leave the 1 per cent with a sufficient income: of US$175,000 per year.[72]

Sufficiency and redistribution create the conditions for cooperation to take place within stable limits. The result may not be the most productive world possible, but instead one where everyone plays a part and benefits from the whole.

Hope for a better world

In the previous chapter, we saw the necessity of looking beyond morality to solve our biggest societal issues such as crime, health and poverty. Our judgements of people's moral characters are about individuals acting consistently within their given social contexts. But to create a better society in the long term, we need to change people's social contexts, and not just control individuals.

In this chapter we have seen a similar thing about creating a better world. We need to look beyond business as usual to solve our biggest global issues such as poverty and climate change. Our standard methods of control, such as continued rates of economic growth and technological advancement, are ways of solving global problems within our current systems of power and governance. But to create a better world in the long term, we need to change these wider systemic conditions, and not just control natural and human environments.

Of course, it may be even harder to change these global systems and power structures than it is to change things on a societal level. As mentioned towards the end of the Chapter Seven, change on this level requires mobilisation and collective action, and going up against powerful interests that want to keep things as they are. We must also overcome 'solution aversion', where easier, short-term solutions can seem more important. Again, in response to these challenges, with hope and trust, we can continue to work towards the kinds of wider global changes that will, ultimately, create a better world.

One difference between the global focus of this chapter and the societal focus of the previous one is that the issues of climate change and global poverty may eventually force us into making the kinds of systemic changes we have been discussing. Climate change and mass technological unemployment may end up creating conditions in which we are no longer in control. Instead of trying to solve these problems while maintaining the status quo, we may be forced to change things on a systemic level. Business as usual may reach a dead end.

This scenario should not bring us hope. If things do get this serious, we also risk witnessing the collapse of civilization before being able to make the systemic changes we require. We should, instead, view the global risks we face today as a wake-up call, and use our current level of control and understanding to make the systemic changes we need before it's too late.

CONCLUSION

The happiness opportunity

A happy ending?

At the beginning of this book, I said that I couldn't guarantee you will be happier by the end of it (and that there was a good chance you'd be the opposite). Despite having the word 'happiness' on the cover, it's just not that kind of book. What I did promise, however, was that you would have a better understanding of what it means to be happy without being blind to what really matters. I hope I have come true on that promise.

The problem with the way we think about happiness in modern society is that we think it comes from control. We think that happiness comes from achieving the list of things in our heads – having a meaningful job, a loving relationship, a beautiful home, a healthy body, a calm mind and so on. These things may all be perfectly worthwhile. But no matter how important each of them seems, what we have in our head will not come close to being an exhaustive list of the things in life that matter most. Our lives are simply too messy and complex for that.

We cannot control everything in our lives to our liking and expect to receive a lasting sense of satisfaction and meaning in return. We will still be insecure. We will still be vulnerable to things falling apart or not going to plan. The idea of receiving happiness through the means of control is a fantasy.

We have seen that there is another way – one that switches our focus from control to understanding. This does not mean that we abandon the items on our list, or try and escape the list in our heads altogether. It means we can aim to achieve the things we care about while remaining open to what we don't know. We can both question the items on our list and pay more attention to what might be missing. Of course, we may well continue to think that, 'if only we had ___ then we'd be happy'. But we can recognise that this is an illusion – that, whatever we fill in the blank with, achieving it will not make us happy. This can help us see the world differently. We can be more curious about the items on our list. We can explore how to improve our lives both with and without them. And over time, we can begin to understand and commit to what really matters.

We can apply the same process on a social and global level. When it comes to our most pressing political issues – such as climate change, crime and health – we often have a list of things in our heads that we think will make everything better. We think we can solve climate change by switching to renewable energy sources, reduce crime rates through policies of retribution or rehabilitation or create a healthier society with advances in medical treatment. All of these things are likely to help. But none of them focuses on the underlying causes of the problems, and they therefore lack the ability to make us all better off in the long term.

Like our individual lives, our political issues are too messy and complex to solve by focusing only on the things we can readily control. We need to understand the wider social conditions that result in criminal behaviour and make people ill. And we need to understand the global systemic causes of climate change. With a better understanding of these issues, we can begin to make real social change.

This is how happiness and politics are connected. In modern societies, both currently fall under the same logic of control. And both can benefit from being thought about differently: with less control and more understanding.

Control versus understanding

Control and understanding have been the two main characters of this book. But both of these protagonists have had their own motley crew of support roles.

The strategy of control is about going to war with reality, with the ultimate aim of achieving *security* and *stability*. We get there through the means of control, with a mindset of *certainty* and *predictability*. Other notable characters include habit, order, manipulation, power and separation.

The strategy of understanding is about striving for peace with reality, with the ultimate aim of living well within *insecurity*. We get there through the means of *curiosity*, *compassion* and *care*, with a mindset of *uncertainty* and *possibility*. Honourable mentions go to attention, creativity, flexibility, trust and connection.

What I don't want to do is give the impression that one side is good and the other side is evil. Our psychological capacities for control and understanding work together – we need to both to live good and meaningful lives. If, at times, I have come across as calling the control-crew the 'bad guys' and the understanding-crew the 'good guys' this is because, as a culture, we have swung way too far in the direction of control. The idea that happiness comes from control is the predominant one in society. We think that, if only we get everything in our lives just right – the perfect job, relationship, home and so on – then we'd be happy. And it is through our attempts to readily control all our social issues that we end up with simple narratives, temporary solutions and technological fixes rather than removing their underlying causes. I am not saying that we should relinquish all control over our personal and collective lives. But we could do with trying to control things a lot less than we are currently doing.

Still, the idea of having less control over our lives is a scary one. Without any control, we will inevitably suffer. We might reasonably ask, therefore, how much we should switch our focus from control to understanding? Can we be curious and compassionate all the time? And even if we can learn from our suffering, when do we stop trying to better understand the world and change it instead?

We can search for evidence to help us answer these questions. Psychology and cognitive science offer pointers that we can seek to apply in our lives as individuals. For instance, these disciplines are beginning to show how harmful it can be to get 'stuck' in habitual patterns of thoughts, feelings and behaviours, and how beneficial it can be instead to remain open to different ways of seeing the world.[1] Addiction and depressive and anxiety disorders may be instances of an overly rigid mind. Practices of mindfulness and other cognitive therapies may be good examples of how to relate to this mental solidity. Moreover, we don't need to suffer from a mental illness to apply these insights to our own personal circumstances.

On a societal level, we also have plenty of evidence that shows the harms of control and the benefits of understanding. For instance, in Chapter Seven, we looked at the problems with controlling criminal behaviour through punishment and incarceration. Incarceration rates in the US are not only expensive to maintain, but also fail to deter criminal behaviour and cripple the socioeconomic situation of families and communities with members in prison. High incarceration rates are a clear example of the limits of control and the need for more understanding. Alternative policies such as focusing on prevention and rehabilitation have been shown to be more effective in the long term.[2]

Throughout this book, we have looked at a wide range of this kind of research. Ultimately, however, we do not yet have enough of it to know how much we can switch our focus from control to understanding. And we are unlikely to have this kind of evidence anytime soon. Our individual and collective lives are too uncertain and complex to be able to come up with a definitive balance or perfect ratio of understanding and control. The right balance is likely to differ for each society, each person, and for every situation we are in.

Instead of trying to find the perfect balance between understanding and control, we should treat this gradual switch from control to understanding as a *process*. We can begin by recognising that in most parts of our lives, we have probably veered too far towards control and could benefit from going in the opposite direction. We can then continue from there. Every time we think we are certain about something – that we should do X, that we need Y, or that Z must happen for everything to be okay – we have the opportunity to see things differently. We can see whether we benefit from paying more attention to what we don't know – embracing uncertainty and being curious and compassionate towards our lives. We may not find this beneficial. But we can only find out by trying.

As we saw in Chapter Five, this process of embracing uncertainty may be the only way in which we can find out what we most care about and are truly capable of. This ongoing process of appreciation, exploration and commitment may not be an easy one, but it is how we can begin to discover what really matters.

The more we commit to this process, the more we realise that a focus on understanding can be valuable *in itself*. Whereas the strategy of control is about being *useful*, the strategy of understanding is about discovering what is *true*. There is something beautiful about opening ourselves up to the bigger picture. Not only do we get the benefits of seeing the world in non-habitual ways – of beauty, gratitude and flexibility – we also get to see reality more clearly. We get to live with our eyes open. This may not be a life in which we are happy all the time, but it will be a full life. It will include all the good bits and all the bad bits, and each bit will have a part to play.

This way of approaching life is not only more oriented towards truth; it is also more *connected*. Our psychological capacities for connection and understanding feed off each other. When we spend time with our loved ones, for instance, we pay them a different kind of attention from how we treat strangers. Instead of making quick, glancing judgements, we make sure to listen to what our loved ones have to say. We want to understand who they are and how they feel. Through this deeper understanding, we can care for them better. This form of open, generous attention defines our intimate relationships. It is what makes us see our loved ones not merely as objects that exist to gratify our own needs, but as subjects who we stand in relation to and who have rich inner lives of their own.

The switch in focus from control to understanding is about giving this kind of attention to our lives in general. According to the strategy of control, the world is populated by predictable objects which we can use and manipulate for our own gain. In contrast, according to the strategy of understanding, the world is full of meaningful subjects (including ourselves) who we can connect with and understand better. The world of understanding is a much more beautiful and connected one than the cold, instrumental world of control.

The need for understanding

In modern society, we may need understanding and connection more than ever. Many of the individual and social problems that define our time have disconnection and a lack of understanding at the heart of them.

On an individual level, we are encouraged to be the 'best possible version of ourselves' or find our 'true, authentic selves', rather than connect with, and better understand, the messy, complex, multiple and diverse humans that we are. It is no surprise that perfectionism and burn-out are on the rise, as are mental disorders such as depression, generalised anxiety and addiction.

On a societal level, we are witnessing increasingly vast inequalities between the top 1 per cent and the rest, as well as between the upper-middle and working classes. This disconnect has no doubt contributed to the rise of populism and extremism. On a global level, our lack of connection and understanding with the natural world has created the very real threat of catastrophic climate change.

Out attempts to control these problems may make things better in the short term, but can also make them much worse in the long term. In this book, we have seen that the problem with control is that it comes with significant opportunity costs. The things we can most easily control are often the things that have the least impact – they often help with the symptoms of problems, but not their underlying causes. We can see this clearly with addiction. It may be more readily under someone's control to temporarily relieve their cravings than deal with the deeper problems they are trying to escape from. But we all know that this strategy only makes things worse in the long run.

There is, however, a positive side to opportunity costs. They are costly because the opportunities to do things differently are out there – we just aren't taking them. This is why the strategy of understanding can be so effective in the long term. It is how the happiness problem can become the happiness opportunity.

On a personal level, we may not need all the stuff we have, to achieve as much as we think we do, to be defensive in front of loved ones, to always be reliable and dependable, or funny and smart and so on. We might be able to spend more time doing what we are interested in and enjoy, or be vulnerable in front of others, or kinder to people who are different from us. Taking these opportunities is far from easy, and may come with little guarantee of success. But with understanding, we can see that a different kind of life is possible.

We also have the opportunities to do thing differently on a social level. We can solve our major social problems by focusing on their underlying causes and understanding the wider social conditions that people need to live well. And we can make global progress by understanding what all nations, groups, individuals and species need to cooperate with each other and make everyone better off. We are a long way away from this vision of social and global change. But understanding that a radically different world is possible is the first step towards achieving it.

My hope is that, from switching our focus from control to understanding, not only can we discover where we need to go, but we will also have more of the resources we need to get us there. There is something perversely comforting about the fact that the list of things inside our heads will not make us happy – that we can never have the secure and stable circumstances and the lasting sense of meaning and satisfaction that we so long for. Acknowledging our insecurity, alongside our psychological capacities for understanding, can give us a kind of inner resource to live well without having to achieve all the items on our list.

With this inner strength and flexibility, we can continue to work towards the better kind of life, society and world that we know are possible. We can commit to making the changes that really matter, secure in the knowledge that, even once they have been made, there will still be plenty of work to do.

Notes

Chapter One

1   Arendt, H. (1998) *Love and Saint Augustine*. University of Chicago Press, p 10.
2   Brickman, P., Coates, D. and Janoff-Bulman, R. (1978) Lottery winners and accident victims: Is happiness relative? *Journal of Personality and Social Psychology*, 36(8).
3   Seligman, M. (2011) *Flourish: A Visionary New Understanding of Happiness and Wellbeing* [Reprint]. Free Press.
4   Easterlin, R. (1974) Does economic growth improve the human lot? Some empirical evidence. *Nations and Households in Economic Growth*, 89.
5   Frey, B. (2008) *Happiness: A Revolution in Economics*. MIT Press.
6   Gilbert, D. (2007) *Stumbling on Happiness*. Harper Perennial. Haidt, J. (2007) *The Happiness Hypothesis: Putting Ancient Wisdom to the Test of Modern Science*. Arrow. Nettle, D. (2006) *Happiness: The Science Behind Your Smile*. Oxford University Press.
7   Helliwell, J., Layard, R. and Sachs, J. (eds) (2018) *World Happiness Report 2018*. https://worldhappiness.report/ed/2018
8   Layard, R. (2011) *Happiness: Lessons from a New Science*. Penguin.
    Graham, C. (2009) *Happiness Around the World: The Paradox of Happy Peasants and Miserable Millionaires*. Oxford University Press.
9   www.ons.gov.uk/peoplepopulationandcommunity/wellbeing/articles/understandingwellbeinginequalitieswhohasthepoorestpersonalwellbeing/2018-07-11
10 Diener, E. and Biswas-Diener, R. (2008) *Happiness: Unlocking the Mysteries of Psychological Wealth*. Wiley-Blackwell.
11 Argyle, M. (2001) *The Psychology of Happiness*. Routledge. Dolan, P. (2015) *Happiness by Design: Finding Pleasure and Purpose in Everyday Life*. Penguin.
12 Brickman, P., Coates, D. and Janoff-Bulman, R. (1978) Lottery winners and accident victims: Is happiness relative? *Journal of Personality and Social Psychology*, 36(8).
13 Lyubomirsky, S. (2010) *The How of Happiness: A Practical Guide to Getting That Life You Want*. Piatkus.
14 Naydler, J. (2018) *In the Shadow of the Machine: The Prehistory of the Computer and the Evolution of Consciousness*. Temple Lodge Publishing.
15 Harari, Y. (2014) *Sapiens: A Brief History of Humankind*. Harvill Secker.
16 *The World Health Report 2001: Mental Health: New Understanding, New Hope*. World Health Organization. www.who.int/whr/2001/en/
17 Robert Wood Johnson Foundation & Partnership for Solutions (2004) *Chronic Conditions: Making the Case for Ongoing Care*. Johns Hopkins University.
18 Amato, P. (2010) Interpreting divorce rates, marriage rates and data on the percentages of children with single parents. National Healthy Marriage Resource Center. www.healthymarriageinfo.org/wp-content/uploads/2017/12/Interpreting-Divorce-Rat.pdf

19 Davis, W. (2015) *The Happiness Industry: How the Government and Big Business Sold Us Well-Being*. Verso Books.

20 Frank, R. (2017) *Success and Luck: Good Fortune and the Myth of Meritocracy*. Princeton University Press.

21 Panksepp, J. (2004) *Affective Neuroscience: The Foundations of Human and Animal Emotions*. Oxford University Press.

22 Prinz, J. (2006) *Gut Reactions: A Perceptual Theory of Emotion*. Oxford University Press. Klein, C. (2015) *What the Body Commands: The Imperative Theory of Pain*. MIT Press.

23 Damasio, A. (2018) *The Strange Order of Things*. Random House Inc, p 100.

24 Nussbaum, M. (2003) *Upheavals of Thought: The Intelligence of the Emotions*. Cambridge University Press. Lazarus, R. (1994) *Emotion and Adaptation*. Oxford University Press. Frijda, F. (2017) *Laws of Emotion*. Psychology Press.

25 van der Kolk, B. (2015) *The Body Keeps the Score: Mind, Brain and Body in the Transformation of Trauma*. Penguin, pp. 96-7.

26 Hufendiek, R. (2015) *Embodied Emotions: A Naturalistic Approach to a Normative Phenomenon*. Routledge. Colombetti, G. (2014) *The Feeling Body: Affective Science Meets the Enactive Mind*. MIT Press.

27 Damasio, A. (2006) *Descartes' Error: Emotion, Reason and the Human Brain*. Vintage. LeDoux, J. (1999) *The Emotional Brain: The Mysterious Underpinnings of Emotional Life*. Weidenfeld & Nicolson.

28 Carel, H. (2018) *Illness: The Cry of the Flesh*. Routledge.

29 Robert Wood Johnson Foundation & Partnership for Solutions (2004) *Chronic Conditions: Making the Case for Ongoing Care*, Johns Hopkins University.

30 Brady, M. (2016) *Emotional Insight: The Epistemic Role of Emotional Experience*. Oxford University Press.

31 Williams, B. (1981) *Moral Luck*. Cambridge University Press.

32 Perry, B. and Szalavitz, M. (2010) *Born for Love: Why Empathy is Essential – and Endangered*. HarperCollins.

33 Barrett, L. (2018) *How Emotions are Made: The Secret Life of the Brain*. Pan.

34 Gopnik, A (2009) *The Philosophical Baby: What Children's Minds Tell Us About Truth, Love & the Meaning of Life*. Bodley Head.

35 Greenwood, J. (2015) *Becoming Human: The Ontogenesis, Metaphysics, and Expression of Human Emotionality*. MIT Press.

36 Churchland, P. (2012) *Braintrust: What Neuroscience Tells Us about Morality*. Princeton University Press.

37 van der Kolk, B. (2015) *The Body Keeps the Score: Mind, Brain and Body in the Transformation of Trauma*. Penguin.

38 Freud, S. (2013) *An Outline of Psychoanalysis*. Penguin Classics.

39 Cassidy, J. and Shaver, P. (eds) (2018) *Handbook of Attachment: Theory, Research, and Clinical Applications*. Guilford Press.

40 Holodynski, M. and Friedlmeier, W. (2006) *The Development of Emotions and Emotional Regulation*. Springer.

41 Sternberg, E. (2001) *The Balance Within: The Science Connecting Health and Emotions*. Palgrave.

42 Heller, R. and Levine, A. (2012) *Attached: The New Science of Adult Attachment and how It Can Help You Find – and Keep – Love*. Jeremy P Tarcher.

43 de Botton, A. (2017) *The Course of Love*. Penguin.

44 Finkel, E. (2017) *The All-Or-Nothing Marriage: How the Best Marriages Work*. Dutton Books.

45 Brown, B. (2010) *The Gifts of Imperfection: Let Go of Who You Think You're Supposed to Be and Embrace Who You Are*. Hazelden Firm.

46 Sullivan, A. (1999) *Love Undetectable: Notes of Friendship, Sex, and Survival*. Vintage.

47 Junger, S. (2017) *Tribe: On Homecoming and Belonging*. Fourth Estate.

48 Pinker, S. (2015) *The Village Effect: Why Face-to-Face Contact Matters*. Atlantic Books.

49 Hari, J. (2019) *Lost Connections: Why You're Depressed and How to Find Hope*. Bloomsbury Publishing.

50 Rath, T. (2016) *Vital Friends: The People You Can't Afford to Live Without*. Gallup Press.

51 Fredrickson, F. (2014) *Love 2.0: Finding Happiness and Health in Moments of Connection*. Plume.

52 Lieberman, M. (2014) *Social: Why Our Brains Are Wired to Connect*. Broadway Books.

53 Zadro, L., Williams, K.D. and Richardson, R. (2004). How low can you go? Ostracism by a computer is sufficient to lower self-reported levels of belonging, control, self-esteem, and meaningful existence. *Journal of Experimental Social Psychology*, 40(4).

54 Besser-Jones, L. (2017) *Eudaimonic Ethics: A Contemporary Theory of the Philosophy and Psychology of Living Well*. Routledge.

55 Kasser, T. (2003) *The High Price of Materialism*. MIT Press.

56 Bradford, G. (2015) *Achievement*. Oxford University Press.

57 Harford, T. (2012) *Adapt: Why Success Always Starts with Failure*. Abacus. Harford, T. (2016) *Messy: How to Be Creative and Resilient in a Tidy-Minded World*. Little Brown.

58 Sims, P. (2012) *Little Bets: How Breakthrough Ideas Emerge from Small Discoveries*. Random House Business. Syed, M. (2016) *Black Box Thinking: The Marginal Gains and the Secrets of High Performance: The Surprising Truth About Success*. John Murray. Schulz, K. (2011) *Being Wrong: Adventures in the Margin of Error*. Portobello Books.

59 Gawdat, M. (2019) *Solve for Happy: Engineer Your Path to Joy*. Bluebird.

60 Bargh, J. (2018) *Before You Know it: The Unconscious Reasons We Do What We Do*. Windmill Books. Thaler, R. and Sunstein, C. (2009) *Nudge: Improving Decisions about Health, Wealth and Happiness*. Penguin. Schroeder, T. (2004) *Three Faces of Desire*, Oxford University Press.

61 Seligman, P., Railton, P., Baumeister, R. and Sripanda, C. (2016) *Homo Prospectus*. Oxford University Press.

62 Csikszentmihalyi, M. (2013) *Creativity: The Psychology of Discovery and Innovation*. Harper Perennial.

63 Snow, N. (2009) *Virtue as Social Intelligence*. Routledge.

64 Nettle, D. (2009) *Personality: What Makes You the Way You Are*. Oxford University Press.

65 Little, B. (2016) *Me, Myself, and Us: The Science of Personality and the Art of Well-Being*. PublicAffairs.

66 Kaag, J. (2018) *Hiking with Nietzsche: On Becoming Who You Are*. Farrar, Straus and Giroux.

67 Dwyer-Lindgren, L, Bertozzi-Villa, A., Stubbs, R. (2017) Inequalities in life expectancy among US counties, 1980 to 2014. *JAMA Internal Medicine*, 177(7).

68 Sapolski, R. (2018) *Behave: The Biology of Humans at Our Best and Worst*. Vintage.

69 Sapolski, R. (2018) *Behave: The Biology of Humans at Our Best and Worst*. Vintage.

70 Bregman, R. (2018) *Utopia for Realists: And How We Can Get There*. Bloomsbury.

71 Cooper, C. (2017) Why poverty is like a disease. *Nautilus*, 47. http://nautil.us/issue/47/consciousness/why-poverty-is-like-a-disease.

72 Cooper, C. (2017) Why poverty is like a disease. *Nautilus*, 47. http://nautil.us/issue/47/consciousness/why-poverty-is-like-a-disease.

73 Wolff, J. and de-Shalit, A. (2007) *Disadvantage*, Oxford University Press, USA.

74 Marmot, M. (2016) *Status Syndrome: How Your Place on the Social Gradient Directly Affects Your Health.* Bloomsbury Press.

75 Wilkinson, R. and Pickett, H. (2018) *The Inner Level: How More Equal Societies Reduce Stress, Restore Sanity and Improve Everyone's Wellbeing.* Allen Lane.

76 Frank, R. (2012) *The Darwin Economy: Liberty, Competition, and the Common Good.* Princeton University Press.

77 Reeves, R. (2016) *Dream Hoarders: How the American Upper Middle Class Is Leaving Everyone Else in the Dust, Why that is a Problem, and What to Do about It.* Brookings Institution.

78 Pinker, S. (2018) *Enlightenment Now: The Case for Reason, Science, Humanism, and Progress.* Allen Lane.

79 Harari, Y. (2017) *Homo Deus: A Brief History of Tomorrow.* Vintage.

80 Klein, N. (2015) *This Changes Everything: Capitalism vs the Climate.* Penguin.

81 Jackson, T. (2016) *Prosperity without Growth.* Routledge.

82 Diamond, J. (2011) *Collapse: How Societies Choose to Fail or Survive.* Penguin.

Chapter Two

1 Dickinson, E. *Low at my problem bending.* https://en.wikisource.org/wiki/Low_at_my_problem_bending

2 Ware, B. (2012) *The Top Five Regrets of the Dying: A Life Transformed by the Dearly Departing.* Hay House UK.

3 McMahon, D. (2006) *Happiness: A History.* Atlantic Monthly Press.

4 McMahon, D. (2006) *Happiness: A History.* Atlantic Monthly Press.

5 McMahon, D. (2006) *Happiness: A History.* Atlantic Monthly Press.

6 Layard, R. (2011) *Happiness: Lessons from a New Science.* Penguin.

7 Helliwell, J., Layard, R. and Sachs, J. (eds) (2019) *World Happiness Report 2019.* https://worldhappiness.report/ed/2019

8 Kahneman, D. (2012) *Thinking, Fast and Slow.* Penguin. Dunn, E. and Norton, M. (2014) *Happy Money: The New Happiness of Smarter Spending.* Oneworld Publications.

9 Frey, B. (2008) *Happiness: A Revolution in Economics.* MIT Press. Graham, C. (2009) *Happiness Around the World: The Paradox of Happy Peasants and Miserable Millionaires.* Oxford University Press.

10 Rosling, H., Rosling, O. and Rosling Rönnlund, A. (2018) *Factfulness: Ten Reasons We're Wrong About the World – and Why Things Are Better than You Think.* Spectre.

11 Rosling, H., Rosling, O. and Rosling Rönnlund, A. (2018) *Factfulness: Ten Reasons We're Wrong About the World – and Why Things Are Better than You Think.* Spectre.

12 Twenge, J. (2017) *iGen: Why Today's Super-Connected Kids Are Growing Up Less Rebellious, More Tolerant, Less Happy – and Completely Unprepared for Adulthood – and What that Means for the Rest of Us.* Atria.

13 Twenge, J. (2019) The sad state of happiness in the United States and the role of digital media. In Helliwell, J., Layard, R. and Sachs, J. (eds) *World Happiness Report 2019.*

14 Newport, C. (2018) *Digital Minimalism.* MIT Press.

15 Newport, C. (2018) *Digital Minimalism.* MIT Press.

16 Duhigg, C. (2013) *The Power of Habit: Why We Do What We Do, and How to Change.* Random House Books. Dean, J. (2013) *Making Habits, Breaking Habits: How to Make Changes that Stick.* Oneworld Publications. Clear, J. (2018) *Atomic Habits: An Easy and Proven Way to Build Good Habits and Break Bad Ones.* Random House Business.

17 Mate, G. (2018) *In the Realm of Hungry Ghosts: Close Encounters with Addiction*. Vermilion. Hari, J. (2016) *Chasing the Scream: The First and Last Days of the War on Drugs*. Bloomsbury.

18 Twenge, J. (2019) The sad state of happiness in the United States and the role of digital media. In Helliwell, J., Layard, R. and Sachs, J. (eds) *World Happiness Report 2019*.

19 Helliwell, J., Layard, R. and Sachs, J. (eds) (2019) *World Happiness Report 2019*. https://worldhappiness.report/ed/2019

20 Sussman, S. (2017) *Substance and Behavioral Addictions: Concepts, Causes, and Cures*. Cambridge University Press.

21 Kasser, T. (2003) *The High Price of Materialism*. MIT Press.

22 Lane, R. (2001) *The Loss of Happiness in Market Democracies*. Yale University Press.

23 Graham, C. (2017) *Happiness for All? Unequal Hopes and Lives in Pursuit of the American Dream*. Princeton University Press.

24 Offer, A. (2007) *The Challenge of Affluence: Self-Control and Well-Being in the United States and Britain since 1950*. Oxford University Press.

25 Alexandrova, A. (2017) *A Philosophy for the Science of Wellbeing*. Oxford University Press.

26 Calhoun, C. (2018) *Doing Valuable Time: The Present, the Future, and Meaningful Living*. Oxford University Press.

27 Setiya, K. (2017) *Midlife: A Philosophical Guide*. Princeton University Press.

28 Rauch, J. (2018) *The Happiness Curve: Why Life Gets Better After Midlife*. Green Tree.

29 Rauch, J. (2018) *The Happiness Curve: Why Life Gets Better After Midlife*. Green Tree.

30 Carstensen, L., Turan, B., Scheibe, S., Ram, N., Ersner-Hershfield, H., Samanez-Larkin, G.R., Brooks, K.P. and Nesselroade, J.R. (2011) Emotional experience improves with age: Evidence based on over 10 years of experience sampling. *Psychology and Aging*, 26(1), p 22.

31 de Botton, A. (n.d.) The secret sorrows of over-achievers. www.theschooloflife.com/thebookoflife/the-secret-sorrows-of-over-achievers

32 Rachlin, H. (2004) *The Science of Self-Control*. Harvard University Press.

33 Storr, W. (2018) *Selfie: How the West Became Self-Obsessed*. Picador.

34 Hameresh, D. (2019) *Spending Time: The More Valuable Resource*. Oxford University Press.

35 Naish, J. (2009) *Enough: Breaking Free from the World of Excess*. Hodder.

36 Shafran, R. (2018) *Overcoming Perfectionism*. Robinson.

37 Twenge, J. (2014) *Generation Me: Why Today's Young Americans Are more Confident, Assertive, Entitled – and more Miserable than ever Before*. Atria Books.

38 Heller, R. and Levine, A. (2012) *Attached: The New Science of Adult Attachment and how It Can Help You Find – and Keep – Love*. Jeremy P. Tarcher.

39 Dolan, P. (2019) *Happy ever After: Escaping the Myth of the Perfect Life*. Allen Lane.

40 Gottman, J. (2018) *The Seven Principles for Making Marriage Work*. Orion Spring. Fredrickson, F. (2014) *Love 2.0: Finding Happiness and Health in Moments of Connection*. Plume.

41 Graziano, M. (2018) *The Spaces Between Us: A Story of Neuroscience, Evolution, and Human Nature*. Oxford University Press.

42 Jollimore, T. (2011) *Love's Vision*. Princeton University Press.

43 Furedi, F. (2018) *How Fear Works: Culture of Fear in the Twenty-First Century*. Bloomsbury.

44 Haidt, J. and Lukianoff, G. (2018) *The Coddling of the American Mind: How Good Intentions and Bad Ideas Are Setting Up a Generation for Failure*. Allen Lane.

45 Taleb, N. (2013) *Antifragile: Things that Gain from Disorder*. Penguin.

46 Spaulding, S. (2018) *How We Understand Others: Philosophy and Social Cognition.* Routledge.

47 Banaji, M. (2016) *Blindspot: Hidden Biases of Good People.* Bantam.

48 Alfano, M. (2015) *Character as Moral Fiction.* Cambridge University Press.

49 Wilson, T. (2011) *Redirect: The Surprising New Science of Psychological Change.* Penguin.

50 Ericsson, A. and Pool, R. (2017) *Peak: How All of Us Can Achieve Extraordinary Things.* Vintage. Flynn, J. (2009) *What is Intelligence? Beyond the Flynn Effect.* Cambridge University Press. Newport, C. (2016) *Deep Work: Rules for Focused Success in a Distracted World.* Piatkus.

51 Prinz, J. (2013) *Beyond Human Nature: How Culture and Experience Shape Our Lives.* Penguin.

52 Heyes, C. (2018) *Cognitive Gadgets: The Cultural Evolution of Thinking.* Harvard University Press.

53 Brown, B. (2010) *The Gifts of Imperfection: Let Go of Who You Think You're Supposed to Be and Embrace Who You Are.* Hazelden Firm.

54 Fine, C. (2011) *Delusions of Gender: The Real Science behind Sex Differences.* Icon Books.

55 Manne, K. (2019) *Down Girl: The Logic of Misogyny.* Penguin.

56 Thomason, K. (2018) *Naked: The Dark Side of Shame and Moral Life.* Oxford University Press.

57 Moran, C. (2015) *How to Build a Girl.* Harper Perennial, pp. 261-2.

58 Bejan, T. (2017) *Mere Civility: Disagreement and the Limits of Toleration.* Harvard University Press.

59 Berreby, J. (2008) *Us and Them: The Science of Identity.* University of Chicago Press.

60 Sapolski, R (2018) *Behave: The Biology of Humans at Our Best and Worst.* Vintage.

61 Sperber, D. and Mercier, H. (2018) *The Enigma of Reason: A New Theory of Human Understanding.* Penguin.

62 Greene, J. (2015) *Moral Tribes: Emotion, Reason and the Gap between Us and Them.* Atlantic Books.

63 Nussbaum, M.C. (2018) *The Monarchy of Fear: A Philosopher Looks at Our Political Crisis.* Oxford University Press, p 4.

Chapter Three

1 Clark, A. (2019) *Surfing Uncertainty: Prediction, Action, and the Embodied Mind.* Oxford University Press.

2 Gopnik, A. (2009) *The Philosophical Baby: What Children's Minds Tell Us about Truth, Love and the Meaning of Life.* Bodley Head.

3 Barrett, L. (2018) *How Emotions Are Made: The Secret Life of the Brain.* Pan.

4 Winnicott, D. (1990) *Winnicott on the Child.* Perseus Publishing.

5 Chabris, C. and Simons, D. (2010) *The Invisible Gorilla: And Other Ways Our Intuition Deceives Us.* Harper Collins.

6 Horowitz, A. (2013) *On Looking: About Everything there Is to See.* Simon & Schuster.

7 Clark, A. (2019) *Surfing Uncertainty: Prediction, Action, and the Embodied Mind.* Oxford University Press. Seligman, P., Railton, P., Baumeister, R. and Sripanda, C. (2016) *Homo Prospectus.* Oxford University Press. Barrett, L. (2018) *How Emotions Are Made: The Secret Life of the Brain.* Pan.

8 Clark, A. (2019) *Surfing Uncertainty: Prediction, Action, and the Embodied Mind.* Oxford University Press.

9 Sperber, D. and Mercier, H. (2018) *The Enigma of Reason: A New Theory of Human Understanding.* Penguin.

Notes

10 Barrett, L. (2018) *How Emotions are Made: The Secret Life of the Brain*. Pan.

11 Siegel, S. (2017) *The Rationality of Perception*. Oxford University Press.

12 Doris, J. (2010) *Lack of Character: Personality and Moral Behaviour*. Cambridge University Press.

13 Miller, C. (2018) *The Character Gap: How Good Are We?* Oxford University Press.

14 Merchant, J. (2016) *Cure: A Journey into the Science of Mind over Body*. Canongate Books.

15 Merchant, J. (2016) *Cure: A Journey into the Science of Mind over Body*. Canongate Books.

16 Rankin, L. (2013) *Mind Over Medicine: Scientific Proof that You Can Heal Yourself*. Hay House.

17 Dweck, C. (2017) *Mindset: Changing the Way You Think to Fulfil Your Potential*. Robinson.

18 Baumeister, R. and Tierney, J. (2012) *Willpower: Why Self-Control is the Secret to Success*. Penguin.

19 Clark, A. (2019) *Surfing Uncertainty: Prediction, Action, and the Embodied Mind*. Oxford University Press.

20 Lotto, B. (2017) *Deviate: The Science of Seeing Differently*. Weidenfeld & Nicolson.

21 Dawkins, R. (2006) *The Blind Watchmaker*. Penguin.

22 Cochrane, T. (2019) *The Emotional Mind: A Control Theory of Affective States*. Cambridge University Press.

23 Tappolet, C. (2016) *Emotions, Values, and Agency*. Oxford University Press.

24 LeDoux, J. (1999) *The Emotional Brain: The Mysterious Underpinnings of Emotional Life*. Weidenfeld & Nicolson. Damasio, A. (2006) *Descartes' Error: Emotion, Reason and the Human Brain*. Vintage.

25 Greenwood, J. (2015) *Becoming Human: The Ontogenesis, Metaphysics, and Expression of Human Emotionality*. MIT Press. Holodynski, M. and Friedlmeier, W. (2006) *The Development of Emotions and Emotional Regulation*. Springer.

26 Frijda, F. (2017) *Laws of Emotion*. Psychology Press.

27 Damasio, A. (2018) *The Strange Order of Things*. Random House Inc.

28 Jasanoff, A. (2018) *The Biological Mind: How Brain, Body, and the Environment Collaborate to Make Us Who We Are*. Basic Books.

29 Nussbaum, M. (2003) *Upheavals of Thought: The Intelligence of the Emotions*. Cambridge University Press.

30 Prinz, J. (2009) *The Emotional Construction of Morals*. Oxford University Press.

31 Prinz, J. (2006) *Gut Reactions: A Perceptual Theory of Emotion*. Oxford University Press.

32 Goldie, P. (2002) *The Emotions: A Philosophical Introduction*. Clarendon Press. Roberts, R. (1999) *Emotion: An Essay in Aid of Moral Psychology*. Cambridge University Press.

33 Haybron, D. (2010) *The Pursuit of Unhappiness: The Elusive Psychology of Well-Being*. Oxford University Press.

34 Haybron, D. (2013) *Happiness: A Very Short Introduction*. Oxford University Press.

35 Haybron, D. (2010) *The Pursuit of Unhappiness: The Elusive Psychology of Well-Being*. Oxford University Press.

36 Nettle, D. (2009) *Personality: What Makes You the Way You Are*. Oxford University Press.

37 Little, B. (2016) *Me, Myself, and Us: The Science of Personality and the Art of Well-Being*. PublicAffairs.

38 Baumeister, R., & Tierney, J. (2012) *Willpower: Why Self-Control is the Secret to Success*. Penguin.

39 Nettle, D. (2009) *Personality: What Makes You the Way You Are*. Oxford University Press.

40 Jasanoff, A. (2018) *The Biological Mind: How Brain, Body, and the Environment Collaborate to Make Us Who We Are*. Basic Books.

41 Gopnik, A. (2009) *The Philosophical Baby: What Children's Minds Tell Us About Truth, Love and the Meaning of Life*. Bodley Head.

42 Heyes, C. (2018) *Cognitive Gadgets: The Cultural Evolution of Thinking*. Harvard University Press.

43 Greenwood, J. (2015) *Becoming Human: The Ontogenesis, Metaphysics, and Expression of Human Emotionality*. MIT Press.

44 Gopnik, A (2009) *The Philosophical Baby: What Children's Minds Tell Us About Truth, Love & the Meaning of Life*. Bodley Head.

45 Cochrane, T. (2019) *The Emotional Mind: A Control Theory of Affective States*. Cambridge University Press.

46 Cochrane, T. (2019) *The Emotional Mind: A Control Theory of Affective States*. Cambridge University Press.

47 Churchland, P. (2012) Braintrust: *What Neuroscience Tells Us about Morality*. Princeton University Press.

48 Fredrickson, F. (2014) *Love 2.0: Finding Happiness and Health in Moments of Connection*. Plume.

49 Cochrane, T. (2019) *The Emotional Mind: A Control Theory of Affective States*. Cambridge University Press.

50 Gelfand, M. (2018) *Rule Makers, Rule Breakers: How Tight and Loose Cultures Wire Our World*. Robinson.

51 Christakis, N. and Fowler, J. (2011) *Connected: The Surprising Power of Social Networks and How They Shape Our Lives*. HarperPress.

52 Layard, R. (2011) *Happiness: Lessons from a New Science*. Penguin.

53 Kahneman, D. (2012) *Thinking, Fast and Slow*. Penguin.

54 Dunn, E. and Norton, M. (2014) *Happy Money: The New Happiness of Smarter Spending*. Oneworld Publications.

55 Lichtenberg, J. (2013) *Distant Strangers: Ethics, Psychology, and Global Poverty*. Cambridge University Press.

56 Bicchieri, C. (2016) *Norms in the Wild*. Oxford University Press.

57 Sheldon, K. (2004) *Optimal Human Being: An Integrated Multi-Level Perspective*. Psychology Press.

58 Alfano, M. (2015) *Character as Moral Fiction*. Cambridge University Press. Dweck, C. (2017) *Mindset: Changing the Way You Think to Fulfil Your Potential*. Robinson.

59 Shaw, J. (2017) *The Memory Illusion: Remembering, Forgetting, and the Science of False Memory*. Random House Books.

60 Doris, J. (2017) *Talking to Our Selves: Reflection, Ignorance, and Agency*. Oxford University Press.

61 McAdams, D. (2016) *The Art and Science of Personality Development*. Guilford Press.

62 Nisbett, R. (2005) *The Geography of Thought: How Asians and Westerners Think Differently – And Why*. Nicholas Brealey Publishing.

63 Prinz, J. (2009) *The Emotional Construction of Morals*. Oxford University Press.

64 Tiberius, V. (2010) *The Reflective Life: Living Wisely Within Our Limits*. Oxford University Press.

65 Welzel, C. (2014) *Freedom Rising: Human Empowerment and the Quest for Emancipation*. Cambridge University Press.

66 Welzel, C. (2014) *Freedom Rising: Human Empowerment and the Quest for Emancipation*. Cambridge University Press.

67 Welzel, C. (2014) *Freedom Rising: Human Empowerment and the Quest for Emancipation*. Cambridge University Press, p. xxiii

68 Prinz, J. (2013) *Beyond Human Nature: How Culture and Experience Shape Our Lives*. Penguin.

69 Flanagan, O. (2019) *The Geography of Morals: Varieties of Moral Possibility*. Oxford University Press.

70 Sapolski, R (2018) *Behave: The Biology of Humans at Our Best and Worst*. Vintage.

71 Gelfand, M. (2018) *Rule Makers, Rule Breakers: How Tight and Loose Cultures Wire Our World*. Robinson.

72 Nisbett, R. (1996) *Culture of Honour: The Psychology of Violence in the South*. Westview Press.

73 David, S. (2017) *Emotional Agility: Get Unstuck, Embrace Change and Thrive in Work and Life*. Penguin Life.

74 Haidt, J. (2007) *The Happiness Hypothesis: Putting Ancient Wisdom to the Test of Modern Science*. Arrow.

75 Milgram, S. (1974) *Obedience to Authority: An Experimental View*. HarperCollins.

76 Doris, J. (2010) *Lack of Character: Personality and Moral Behaviour*. Cambridge University Press.

77 Arendt, H. (2006) *Eichmann in Jerusalem*. Penguin Classics.

78 Snow, N. (2009) *Virtue as Social Intelligence*. Routledge.

Chapter Four

1 Nussbaum, M., Moyers, B. and Flowers, B. (1989) Martha Nussbaum, classicist and philosopher, in *A World of Ideas: Conversations with Thoughtful Men and Women About American Life Today and the Ideas Shaping Our Future*. Doubleday.

2 McGilchrist, I. (2012) *The Master and His Emissary: The Divided Brain and the Making of the Modern World*. Yale University Press.

3 Seneca (2005) *On the Shortness of Life*. Translated by John W. Basore. Penguin Books, p. 13.

4 Langer, E. (2010) *Counterclockwise: A Proven Way to Think Yourself Younger and Healthier*. Hodder Paperbacks.

5 Clark, A. (2019) *Surfing Uncertainty: Prediction, Action, and the Embodied Mind*. Oxford University Press.

6 McGilchrist, I. (2012) *The Master and His Emissary: The Divided Brain and the Making of the Western World*. Yale University Press.

7 Schecter, E. (2018) *Self-Consciousness and Split Brains: The Mind's I*. Oxford University Press.

8 Gigerenzer, G. (2008) *Gut Feelings: Short Cuts to Better Decision Making*. Penguin. Ariely, D. (2009) *Predictable Irrational: The Hidden Forces that Shape Our Decisions*. Harper.

9 Pannebaker, J. (2013) *The Secret Life of Pronouns: What Our Words Say About Us*. Bloomsbury Press.

10 Prinz, J. (2006) *Gut Reactions: A Perceptual Theory of Emotion*. Oxford University Press. Lazarus, R. (1994) *Emotion and Adaptation*. Oxford University Press.

11 Hufendiek, R. (2015) *Embodied Emotions: A Naturalistic Approach to a Normative Phenomenon*. Routledge. Colombetti, G. (2014) *The Feeling Body: Affective Science Meets the Enactive Mind*. MIT Press.

12 Gopnik, A. (2009) *The Philosophical Baby: What Children's Minds Tell Us About Truth, Love and the Meaning of Life*. Bodley Head.

13 Murdoch, I. (2001) *Sovereignty of the Good*. Routledge, p. 82

14 Smith, A. (1987) History of astronomy. In Heilbroner, R. (ed.) *The Essential Adam Smith*. W.W. Norton & Company, p. 25

15 Smith, A. (1987) History of astronomy. In Heilbroner, R. (ed.) *The Essential Adam Smith*. W.W. Norton & Company, p. 26.

16 James, W. (1983) *Varieties of Religious Experience: A Study in Human Nature*. Penguin Classics. Maslow, A. (2018) *Religions, Values, and Peak Experience*. Print on Demand.

17 Cottingham, J. (2005) *The Spiritual Dimension: Religion, Philosophy and Human Value*. Cambridge University Press. Schneider, K. (2017) *The Spirituality of Awe: Challenges to the Robotic Revolution*. Waterside Productions.

18 de Botton, A. (2012) *Religion for Atheists*. Penguin. Asma, S. (2018) *Why We Need Religion: An Agnostic Celebration of Spiritual Emotions*. Oxford University Press.

19 Samuelson, S. (2018) *Seven Ways of Looking at Pointless Suffering: What Philosophy Can Tell Us about the Hardest Mystery of All*. University of Chicago Press. Brady, M. (2018) *Suffering and Virtue*. Oxford University Press.

20 Attributed to Paul Éluard (1895–1952), French poet and one of the leading figures in the Surrealist movement. The quotation has also been attributed to W.B. Yeats, but not to any poem in particular.

21 Evans, J. (2018) *The Art of Losing Control: A Philosopher's Search for Ecstatic Experience*. Canongate Books.

22 Tuama, P. (2015) *In the Shelter: Finding a Home in the World*. Hodder & Stoughton.

23 Sheldrake, R. (2017) *Science and Spiritual Practices: Reconnecting through Direct Experience*. Coronet.

24 Jenkinson, S. (2015) *Die Wise: A Manifesto for Sanity and Soul*. North Atlantic Books. Jenkinson, S. (2018) *Coming of Age: The Case for Elderhood in a Time of Trouble*. North Atlantic Books.

25 Haidt, J. (2007) *The Happiness Hypothesis: Putting Ancient Wisdom to the Test of Modern Science*. Arrow.

26 Ackerman, D. (2000) *Deep Play*. Vintage.

27 Tomasello, M. (2019) *Becoming Human: A Theory of Ontogeny*. Harvard University Press.

28 Harari, Y. (2014) *Sapiens: A Brief History of Humankind*. Harvill Secker.

29 Hirshfield, J. (2017) in *Ten Windows: How Great Poems Transform the World*. Random House, p.12.

30 Lightman, A. (2006) *A Sense of the Mysterious: Science and the Human Spirit*. Vintage.

31 Csikszentmihalyi, M. (2008) *Flow: The Psychology of Optimal Experience*. Harper Perennial.

32 Segal, L. (2017) *Radical Happiness: Moments of Collective Joy*. Verso.

33 Sheldrake, R. (2017) *Science and Spiritual Practices: Reconnecting through Direct Experience*. Coronet.

34 Sachs, O. (2015) *Gratitude*. Picador.

35 Kant, E. (2009) *The Critique of Judgement*. Oxford University Press.

36 Slingerland, E. (2015) *Trying Not to Try: The Ancient Art of Effortlessness and the Surprising Power of Spontaneity*. Canongate Books.

37 Brown, B. (2017) *Braving the Wilderness: The Quest for True Belonging and the Courage to Stand Alone*. Vermilion.

38 Wright, R. (2018) *Why Buddhism is True: The Science and Philosophy of Meditation and Enlightenment*. Simon & Schuster. Harris, S. (2015) *Waking Up: Searching for Spirituality without Religion*. Black Swan.

39 Dweck, C. (2017) *Mindset: Changing the Way You Think to Fulfil Your Potential*. Robinson.

40 Puett, M. and Gross-Loh, C. (2017) *The Path: A New Way to Think About Everything.* Viking.

41 Puett, M. and Gross-Loh, C. (2017) *The Path: A New Way to Think About Everything.* Viking.

42 Boss, P. (2000) *Ambiguous Loss: Learning to Live with Unresolved Grief.* Harvard University Press.

43 Kalanithi, P. (2017) *When Breath Becomes Air.* Vintage.

44 Chodron, P. (2007) *When Things Fall Apart.* Element Books.

45 Bastian, B. (2018) *The Other Side of Happiness: Embracing a more Fearless Approach to Living.* Allen Lane.

46 McAdams, D. (2016) *The Art and Science of Personality Development.* Guilford Press.

47 Bradford, G. (2015) *Achievement.* Oxford University Press.

48 Taylor, S. (2017) *The Leap: The Psychology of Spiritual Awakening.* Hay House.

49 Frankl, V. (2014) *Man's Search for Meaning.* Rider.

50 Hanh, T.N. (2015) *No Mud, No Lotus: The Art of Transforming Suffering.* Parallax Press.

51 Kramer, B. and Wurzer, C. (2017) *We Know how this Ends: Living while Dying.* University of Minnesota Press.

52 Gould, P. (2013) *Why I Die: Lessons from the Death Zone.* Abacus.

53 Solnit, R. (2010) *A Paradise Built in Hell: The Extraordinary Communities that Arise in Disaster.* Penguin Books, p xvii.

54 Soojung-Kim Pang, A. (2018) *Rest.* Penguin Life. Taylor, S. (2017) *The Leap: The Psychology of Spiritual Awakening.* Hay House.

55 de Botton, A. (2012) *Religion for Atheists.* Penguin.

56 Asma, S. (2018) *Why We Need Religion: An Agnostic Celebration of Spiritual Emotions.* Oxford University Press.

57 Carstensen, L. (2011) *A Long Bright Future.* Public Affairs.

58 Sheldrake, R. (2017) *Science and Spiritual Practices: Reconnecting through Direct Experience.* Coronet.

59 Evans, J. (2018) *The Art of Losing Control: A Philosopher's Search for Ecstatic Experience.* Canongate Books.

60 Maslow, A. (2018) *Religions, Values, and Peak Experience.* Print on demand.

61 Newberg, A. and Waldman, M. (2017) *How Enlightenment Changes Your Brain: The New Science of Transformation.* Avery Publishing Group.

62 Pollan, M. (2018) *How to Change Your Mind: The New Science of Psychedelics.* Allen Lane. Richards, W. (2018) *Sacred Knowledge: Psychedelics and Religious Experience.* Columbia University Press.

63 Evans, J. (2018) *The Art of Losing Control: A Philosopher's Search for Ecstatic Experience.* Canongate Books.

64 Wallace, R.J. (2013) *The View from Here: On Affirmation, Attachment, and the Limits of Regret.* Oxford University Press.

65 Kramer, B. and Wurzer, C. (2017) *We Know how this Ends: Living while Dying.* University of Minnesota Press.

Chapter Five

1 Lamott, A. (2018) *Almost Everything: Notes on Hope.* Riverhead Books, p. 63.

2 Horowitz, A. (2013) *On Looking: About Everything there Is to See.* Simon & Schuster.

3 Wilczek, F. (2016) *A Beautiful Question: Finding Nature's Deep Design.* Penguin.

4 Wright, R. (2018) *Why Buddhism Is True: The Science and Philosophy of Meditation and Enlightenment.* Simon & Schuster. Harris, S. (2015) *Waking Up: Searching for Spirituality without Religion.* Black Swan.

5 Iyer, P. (2014) *The Art of Stillness: Adventures in Going Nowhere.* Simon & Schuster, p. 4.

6 Batchelor, S. (2017) *After Buddhism: Rethinking Dharma for a Secular Age.* Yale University Press.

7 Nehamas, A. (2019) *Only a Promise of Happiness: The Place of Beauty in a World of Art.* Princeton University Press.

8 Gibran, K. (2013) On beauty, in *The Prophet.* Vintage Classics.

9 Lyubomirsky, S. (2010) *The How of Happiness: A Practical Guide to Getting that Life You Want.* Piatkus.

10 Tiberius, V. (2010) *The Reflective Life: Living Wisely within Our Limits.* Oxford University Press.

11 Verhaeghe, P. (2014) *What about Me? The Struggle for Identity in a Market-Based Society.* Scribe. Monbiot, G. (2017) *How Did We Get into this Mess? Politics, Equality, Nature.* Verso.

12 Calhoun, C. (2018) *Doing Valuable Time: The Present, the Future, and Meaningful Living.* Oxford University Press.

13 Kashdan, T. (2009) *Curious? Discover the Missing Ingredient to a Fulfilling Life.* William Morrow & Co.

14 Mate, G. (2018) *In the Realm of Hungry Ghosts: Close Encounters with Addiction.* Vermilion.

15 Haidt, J. (2007) *The Happiness Hypothesis: Putting Ancient Wisdom to the Test of Modern Science.* Arrow.

16 Sussman, S. (2017) *Substance and Behavioral Addictions: Concepts, Causes, and Cures.* Cambridge University Press.

17 Banaji, M. (2016) *Blindspot: Hidden Biases of Good People.* Bantam.

18 Sheldon, K. (2004) *Optimal Human Being: An Integrated Multi-Level Perspective.* Psychology Press.

19 Kahneman, D. (2012) *Thinking, Fast and Slow.* Penguin. Baumeister, R. (1992) *Meanings in Life.* Guilford Press.

20 Lyubomirsky, S. (2010) *The How of Happiness: A Practical Guide to Getting that Life You Want.* Piatkus.

21 Kazez, J. (2017) *The Philosophical Parent: Asking Hard Questions about Having and Raising Children.* Oxford University Press.

22 Metz, T. (2016) *Meaning in Life.* Oxford University Press.

23 Nettle, D. (2009) *Personality: What Makes You the Way You Are.* Oxford University Press.

24 Little, B. (2016) *Me, Myself, and Us: The Science of Personality and the Art of Well-Being.* PublicAffairs.

25 Whyte, D. (2015) Self-knowledge. In *Consolations: The Solace, Nourishment, and the Underlying Meaning of Everyday Words.* Many Rivers Press.

26 Milner, M. (1986) *A Life of One's Own.* Virago, p. 62.

27 Bastian, B. (2018) *The Other Side of Happiness: Embracing a more Fearless Approach to Living.* Allen Lane.

28 Peterson, J. (2019) *12 Rules for Life: An Antidote to Chaos.* Penguin.

29 Newberg, A. and Waldman, M. (2017) *How Enlightenment Changes Your Brain: The New Science of Transformation.* Avery Publishing Group.

30 Peterson, J. (2019) *12 Rules for Life: An Antidote to Chaos.* Penguin.

Notes

31 Ehrenreich, B. (2010) *Bright Sided: How Positive Thinking Is Undermining America.* Picador.

32 Barrett, L. (2018) *How Emotions Are Made: The Secret Life of the Brain.* Pan.

33 Paul, L.A. (2016) *Transformative Experience.* Oxford University Press.

34 Harford, T. (2012) *Adapt: Why Success Always Starts with Failure.* Abacus. Harford, T. (2016) *Messy: How to Be Creative and Resilient in a Tidy-Minded World.* Little Brown.

35 Sims, P. (2012) *Little Bets: How Breakthrough Ideas Emerge from Small Discoveries.* Random House Business. Syed, M. (2016) *Black Box Thinking: The Marginal Gains and the Secrets of High Performance: The Surprising Truth About Success.* John Murray. Schulz, K. (2011) *Being Wrong: Adventures in the Margin of Error.* Portobello Books.

36 Dweck, C. (2017) *Mindset: Changing the Way You Think to Fulfil Your Potential.* Robinson.

37 Gladwell, M. (2009) *Outliers: The Story of Success.* Penguin.

38 Ericsson, A. and Pool, R. (2017) *Peak: How All of Us Can Achieve Extraordinary Things.* Vintage. Newport, C. (2016) *Deep Work: Rules for Focused Success in a Distracted World.* Piatkus.

39 Freeburg, E. (2013) *The Age of Edison: Electric Light and the Invention of Modern America.* Penguin.

40 Prinz, J. (2013) *Beyond Human Nature: How Culture and Experience Shape Our Lives.* Penguin.

41 Aristotle (2009) *Nicomachean Ethics.* Oxford University Press.

42 Snow, N. (2009) *Virtue as Social Intelligence.* Routledge.

43 Puett, M. and Gross-Loh, C. (2017) *The Path: A New Way to Think About Everything.* Viking.

44 Churchland, P. (2014) *Touching a Nerve: Our Brains, Our Selves.* W.W. Norton & Co.

45 Einstein, A. (1995 [1954]) *Ideas and Opinions.* Crown Publications.

46 Buyandelgeriyn, M. (2007) Dealing with uncertainty: Shamans, marginal capitalism, and remaking of history of postsocialist Mongolia. *American Ethnologist*, 34.

47 Buyandelgeriyn, M. (2007) Dealing with uncertainty: Shamans, marginal capitalism, and remaking of history of postsocialist Mongolia. *American Ethnologist*, 34.

48 Gopnik, A. (2009) *The Philosophical Baby: What Children's Minds Tell Us about Truth, Love and the Meaning of Life.* Bodley Head.

49 Emerson, R. (2000) Self-Reliance. In *The Essential Writings of Ralph Waldo Emerson.* Modern Library, p. 133.

50 Soojung-Kim Pang, A. (2018) *Rest.* Penguin Life. Newport, C. (2016) *Deep Work: Rules for Focused Success in a Distracted World.* Piatkus.

51 Calhoun, C. (2018) *Doing Valuable Time: The Present, the Future, and Meaningful Living.* Oxford University Press.

52 Williams, B. (1981) *Moral Luck.* Cambridge University Press. Wolf, S. (2012) *Meaning in Life and Why It Matters.* Princeton University Press.

53 Frankfurt, H. (2019) *The Reasons of Love.* Princeton University Press.

54 Calhoun, C. (2018) *Doing Valuable Time: The Present, the Future, and Meaningful Living.* Oxford University Press.

55 Russell, B. (2013 [1930]) *The Conquest of Happiness.* Liveright Publishing Corporation.

56 Schoch, R. (2007) *The Secrets of Happiness: Three Thousand Years of Searching for the Good Life.* Profile Books.

57 Honore, C. (2005) *In Praise of Slowness: Challenging the Cult of Speed.* HarperCollins.

58 Millburn, J. and Nicodemus, R. (2011) *Minimalism: Live a Meaningful Life.* Asymmetrical Press.

59 Tiberius, V. (2010) *The Reflective Life: Living Wisely within Our Limits*. Oxford University Press.

60 Solnit, R. (2016) *Hope in the Dark: Untold Histories, Wild Possibilities*. Canongate Canons.

61 Martin, A. (2013) *How We Hope: A Moral Psychology*. Princeton University Press.

62 Attributed to the poet Emily Dickinson (1830–1886).

63 Sapolski, R (2018) *Behave: The Biology of Humans at Our Best and Worst*. Vintage.

64 King, M. (1991) *A Testament to Hope: The Essential Writings and Speeches of Martin Luther King, Jr.* HarperCollins.

Chapter Six

1 Excerpt from 'Kindness' from *Words Under the Words: Selected Poems* by Naomi Shihab Nye, © 1995. Reprinted with permission of Far Corner Books.

2 Pollan, M. (2018) *How to Change Your Mind: The New Science of Psychedelics*. Allen Lane.

3 Peterson, J. (2019) *12 Rules for Life: An Antidote to Chaos*. Penguin.

4 Pollan, M. (2018) *How to Change Your Mind: The New Science of Psychedelics*. Allen Lane.

5 Taylor, S. (2017) *The Leap: The Psychology of Spiritual Awakening*. Hay House.

6 Pollan, M. (2018) *How to Change Your Mind: The New Science of Psychedelics*. Allen Lane.

7 Pollan, M. (2018) *How to Change Your Mind: The New Science of Psychedelics*. Allen Lane.

8 James, W. (2017) *The Principles of Psychology, Vols. 1-2*. CreateSpace.

9 Solnit, R. (2016) *Hope in the Dark: Untold Histories, Wild Possibilities*. Canongate Canons.

10 Jenkinson, S. (2015) *Die Wise: A Manifesto for Sanity and Soul*. North Atlantic Books.

11 Hanh, T.N. (2018) *How to Love*. Parallax Press.

12 Jollimore, T. (2011) *Love's Vision*. Princeton University Press.

13 Brown, B. (2010) *The Gifts of Imperfection: Let Go of Who You Think You're Supposed to Be and Embrace Who You Are*. Hazelden Firm.

14 Whyte, D. (2015) *Consolations: The Solace, Nourishment and Meaning of Everyday Words*. Many Rivers Press.

15 Brown, B. (2017) *Braving the Wilderness: The Quest for True Belonging and the Courage to Stand Alone*. Vermilion.

16 Maslow, A. (1994) *The Farther Reaches of Human Nature*. Penguin.

17 Fromm, E. (1993) *The Art of Being*. Constable and Company Ltd.

18 Peck, M.S. (1990) *The Road Less Travelled*. Arrow.

19 Metz, T. (2016) *Meaning in Life*. Oxford University Press.

20 Batchelor, S. (2017) *After Buddhism: Rethinking Dharma for a Secular Age*. Yale University Press.

21 Schoch, R. (2007) *The Secrets of Happiness: Three Thousand Years of Searching for the Good Life*. Profile Books.

22 Fukuyama, F. (1995) *Trust: The Social Virtues and the Creation of Prosperity*. The Free Press.

23 Singer, M. (2016) *The Surrender Experiment: My Journey into Life's Perfection*. Yellow Kite.

24 Ricard, M. (2018) *Altruism: The Science and Psychology of Kindness*. Atlantic Books. Neff, K. (2011) *Self-Compassion*. Yellow Kite.

25 Doris, J. (2010) *Lack of Character: Personality and Moral Behaviour*. Cambridge University Press.

26 Prinz, J. (2009) *The Emotional Construction of Morals*. Oxford University Press.

27 Mate, G. (2018) *In the Realm of Hungry Ghosts: Close Encounters with Addiction*. Vermilion.

28 Hanh, T.N. (2018) *How to Love*. Parallax Press.

29 Tutu, D. (2015) *The Book of Forgiving: The Fourfold Path for Healing Ourselves and Our World*. HarperCollins.

30 Nussbaum, M. (2018) *The Monarchy of Fear: A Philosopher Looks at Our Political Crisis*. Oxford University Press. Nussbaum, M. (2016) *Anger and Forgiveness: Resentment, Generosity, and Justice*. Oxford University Press.

31 Chodron, P. (2007) *When Things Fall Apart*. Element Books.

32 Hanh, T.N. (2015) *No Mud, No Lotus: The Art of Transforming Suffering*. Parallax Press.

33 Lamott, A. (2012) *Stitches: A Handbook on Meaning, Hope, and Repair*. Hodder & Stoughton.

34 Weil, S. (2002) *Gravity and Grace*. Routledge.

35 Whyte, D. (2015) *Consolations: The Solace, Nourishment and Meaning of Everyday Words*. Many Rivers Press.

36 Brueggeman, W. (1983) *The Prophetic Imagination*. Fortress Press.

37 Wenar, L. (2017) *Blood Oil: Tyrants, Violence, and the Rules that Run the World*. Oxford University Press.

38 Bloom, P. (2018) *Against Empathy: The Case for Rational Compassion*. Vintage.

39 Singer, P. (2011) *The Expanding Circle: Ethics, Evolution, and Moral Progress*. Princeton University Press.

40 Greene, J. (2015) *Moral Tribes: Emotion, Reason and the Gap Between Us and Them*. Atlantic Books.

41 Macy, J. (2012) *Active Hope: How to Face the Mess We're in without Going Crazy*. New World Library. Eisenstein, C. (2013) *The More Beautiful World Our Hearts Know is Possible*. North Atlantic Books.

42 Jenkinson, S. (2018) *Coming of Age: The Case for Elderhood in a Time of Trouble*. North Atlantic Books.

Chapter Seven

1 Gibran, K. (2015) On Crime and Punishment, *The Prophet*. Wisehouse Classics.

2 Sapolski, R (2018) *Behave: The Biology of Humans at Our Best and Worst*. Vintage.

3 Liebling, A. and Maruna, S. (2005) *The Effects of Imprisonment*. Willan.

4 Wolff, J. (2011) *Ethics and Public Policy: A Philosophical Inquiry*. Routledge.

5 Liebling, A. (2004) *Prisons and Their Moral Performance: A Study of Values, Quality and Prison Life*. Oxford University Press.

6 Leigh, A. (2018) *Randomistas: How Radical Researchers Are Changing Our World*. Yale University Press.

7 Nussbaum, M. (2016) *Anger and Forgiveness: Resentment, Generosity, and Justice*. Oxford University Press.

8 Sapolski, R. (2018) *Behave: The Biology of Humans at Our Best and Worst*. Vintage.

9 Sapolski, R. (2018) *Behave: The Biology of Humans at Our Best and Worst*. Vintage.

10 Thibodeau, P. and Boroditsky, L. (2011) Metaphors we think with: The role of metaphor in reasoning. *PLoS ONE*, 6.

11 Caruso, G. (2017) *Public Health and Safety: The Social Determinants of Health and Criminal Behavior*. ResearchLinks Books.

12 Caruso, G. (2017) *Public Health and Safety: The Social Determinants of Health and Criminal Behavior.* ResearchLinks Books.

13 Nussbaum, M. (2016) *Anger and Forgiveness: Resentment, Generosity, and Justice.* Oxford University Press. Wolff, J. (2011) *Ethics and Public Policy: A Philosophical Inquiry.* Routledge.

14 Waller, B. (2017) *The Injustice of Punishment.* Routledge, p. 164.

15 Marmot, M. (2016) *Status Syndrome: How Your Place on the Social Gradient Directly Affects Your Health.* Bloomsbury Press.

16 Wilkinson, R. and Pickett, H. (2018) *The Inner Level: How More Equal Societies Reduce Stress, Restore Sanity and Improve Everyone's Wellbeing.* Allen Lane.

17 Sapolski, R. (2018) *Behave: The Biology of Humans at Our Best and Worst.* Vintage.

18 Wolff, J. and de-Shalit, A. (2007) *Disadvantage.* Oxford University Press, USA.

19 Storoni, M. (2017) *Stress Proof: The Ultimate Guide to a Stress-Free Life.* Yellow Kite.

20 McGonigal, K. (2015) *The Upside of Stress: Why Stress Is Good for You (and how to Get Good at It).* Vermilion.

21 Bullmore, E. (2019) *The Inflamed Mind: A Radical New Approach to Depression.* Short Books Ltd.

22 Sapolski, R. (2018) *Behave: The Biology of Humans at Our Best and Worst.* Vintage.

23 www.help.senate.gov/imo/media/doc/Reisch.pdf

24 Sapolski, R. (2018) *Behave: The Biology of Humans at Our Best and Worst.* Vintage.

25 Walker, M. (2018) *Why We Sleep: The New Science of Sleep and Dreams.* Penguin.

26 Barnes, E. (2016) *The Minority Body: A Theory of Disability.* Oxford University Press.

27 Davis, L. (1995) *Enforcing Normalcy: Disability, Deafness, and the Body.* Verso.

28 Silberman, S. (2015) *NeuroTribes: The Legacy of Autism and How to Think Smarter About People Who Think Differently.* Allen & Unwin.

29 May, K. (2018) Autism from the inside. Aeon. https://aeon.co/essays/the-autistic-view-of-the-world-is-not-the-neurotypical-cliche

30 Sarpong, J. (2019) *Diversify: An Award-Winning Guide to Why Inclusion Is Better for Everyone.* HQ.

31 Davis, L. (1995) *Enforcing Normalcy: Disability, Deafness, and the Body.* Verso.

32 Davis, L. (1995) *Enforcing Normalcy: Disability, Deafness, and the Body.* Verso.

33 Barnes, E. (2016) *The Minority Body: A Theory of Disability.* Oxford University Press.

34 Wilson, R. (2018) *The Eugenic Mind Project.* MIT Press.

35 Wilson, R. (2018) *The Eugenic Mind Project.* MIT Press.

36 Layard, R. and Clark, D. (2015) *Thrive: The Power of Psychological Therapy.* Penguin.

37 Horwitz, A. and Wakefield, J. (2007) *The Loss of Sadness: How Psychiatry Transformed Normal Sorrow into Depressive Disorder.* Oxford University Press.

38 Prinz, J. (2013) *Beyond Human Nature: How Culture and Experience Shape Our Lives.* Penguin.

39 Rashed, M. (2019) *Madness and the Demand for Recognition: A Philosophical Inquiry into Identity and Mental Health Activism.* Oxford University Press.

40 Rashed, M. (2019) *Madness and the Demand for Recognition: A Philosophical Inquiry into Identity and Mental Health Activism.* Oxford University Press.

41 Haybron, D. (2010) *The Pursuit of Unhappiness: The Elusive Psychology of Well-Being.* Oxford University Press.

42 Prinz, J. (2013) *Beyond Human Nature: How Culture and Experience Shape Our Lives.* Penguin.

43 Prinz, J. (2013) *Beyond Human Nature: How Culture and Experience Shape Our Lives.* Penguin.

44 Hari, J. (2019) *Lost Connections: Why You're Depressed and How to Find Hope.* Bloomsbury Publishing.

Notes

45 Huemer, M. (2012) *The Problem of Political Authority: An Examination of the Right to Coerce and the Duty to Obey.* Palgrave Macmillan.

46 Lamont, M. (2002) *The Dignity of Working Men: Morality and the Boundaries of Race, Class and Immigration.* Harvard University Press.

47 Reeves, R. (2016) *Dream Hoarders: How the American Upper Middle Class Is Leaving Everyone Else in the Dust, Why that is a Problem, and What to Do about It.* Brookings Institution.

48 Reeves, R. (2016) *Dream Hoarders: How the American Upper Middle Class Is Leaving Everyone Else in the Dust, Why that is a Problem, and What to Do about It.* Brookings Institution.

49 Reeves, R. (2016) *Dream Hoarders: How the American Upper Middle Class Is Leaving Everyone Else in the Dust, Why that is a Problem, and What to Do about It.* Brookings Institution.

50 Reeves, R. (2016) *Dream Hoarders: How the American Upper Middle Class Is Leaving Everyone Else in the Dust, Why that is a Problem, and What to Do about It.* Brookings Institution.

51 Sapolski, R. (2018) *Behave: The Biology of Humans at Our Best and Worst.* Vintage.

52 Sapolski, R. (2018) *Behave: The Biology of Humans at Our Best and Worst.* Vintage.

53 Martinez, R. (2017) *Creating Freedom: Power, Control and the Fight for Our Future.* Canongate Books.

54 Gladwell, M. (2009) *Outliers: The Story of Success.* Penguin.

55 Prinz, J. (2013) *Beyond Human Nature: How Culture and Experience Shape Our Lives.* Penguin.

56 Bregman, R. (2018) *Utopia for Realists: And How We Can Get There.* Bloomsbury.

57 Lamont, M. (2002) *The Dignity of Working Men: Morality and the Boundaries of Race, Class and Immigration.* Harvard University Press.

58 Quinones, S. (2016) *Dreamland: The True Tale of America's Opiate Epidemic.* Bloomsbury Press.

59 Wilkinson, R. and Pickett, H. (2018) *The Inner Level: How More Equal Societies Reduce Stress, Restore Sanity and Improve Everyone's Wellbeing.* Allen Lane.

60 Fiske, S. and Taylor, S. (2016) *Social Cognition: From Brains to Culture.* Sage Publishing.

61 Bloom, P. (2018) *Against Empathy: The Case for Rational Compassion.* Vintage.

62 Wilkinson, R. and Pickett, H. (2010) *The Spirit Level: Why Equality is Better for Everyone.* Penguin.

63 Appiah, K.A. (2018) *The Lies That Bind: Rethinking Identity.* Profile Books.

64 Appiah, K.A. (2018) Against Meritocracy. Talk at HowTheLightGetsIn Festival, Institute of Art and Ideas, London, 21 September. https://iai.tv/video/against-meritocracy

65 Sunstein, C. (2018) *The Cost-Benefit Revolution.* MIT Press.

66 Prinz, J. and Nichols, S. (2016) Diachronic identity and the moral self. In *The Routledge Handbook of the Social Mind.* Routledge.

67 Churchland, P. (2012) *Braintrust: What Neuroscience Tells Us about Morality.* Princeton University Press.

68 Greene, J. (2015) *Moral Tribes: Emotion, Reason and the Gap Between Us and Them.* Atlantic Books.

69 Sperber, D. and Mercier, H. (2018) *The Enigma of Reason: A New Theory of Human Understanding.* Penguin.

70 Berreby, D. (2008) *Us and Them: The Science of Identity.* University of Chicago Press.

71 Sperber, D. and Mercier, H. (2018) *The Enigma of Reason: A New Theory of Human Understanding.* Penguin.

72 Brennan, J. (2017) *Against Democracy.* Princeton University Press.

73 Hochschild, A. (2016) *Strangers in Their Own Land: Anger and Mourning on the American Right*. The New Press.

74 Haidt, J. (2013) *The Righteous Mind: Why Good People are Divided by Politics and Religion*. Penguin.

75 Haidt, J. (2013) *The Righteous Mind: Why Good People are Divided by Politics and Religion*. Penguin.

76 Deneen, P. (2018) *Why Liberalism Failed*. Yale University Press. Hazony, Y. (2018) *The Virtue of Nationalism*. Basic Books.

77 Deneen, P. (2018) *Why Liberalism Failed*. Yale University Press.

78 Hazony, Y. (2018) *The Virtue of Nationalism*. Basic Books.

79 Deneen, P. (2018) *Why Liberalism Failed*. Yale University Press. Putnam, R. (2001) *Bowling Alone: The Collapse and Revival of American Community*. Simon & Schuster Ltd.

80 Cottam, H. (2018) *Radical Help: How We Can Remake the Relationships Between Us and Revolutionise the Welfare State*. Virago.

81 Appiah, A. (2007) *Cosmopolitanism: Ethics in a World of Strangers*. Penguin. Keller, S. (2013) *Partiality*. Princeton University Press.

82 Bejan, T. (2017) *Mere Civility: Disagreement and the Limits of Toleration*. Harvard University Press.

83 Harari, Y. (2017) *Homo Deus: A Brief History of Tomorrow*. Vintage.

84 Bicchieri, C. (2002) *The Grammar of Society: The Nature and Dynamics of Social Norms*. Cambridge University Press.

85 Sunstein, C. (2018) *The Cost-Benefit Revolution*. MIT Press.

86 Sunstein, C. (2018) *The Cost-Benefit Revolution*. MIT Press.

87 Zamzow, J. (2018) Why we can't agree on gun control. *Washington Post*, 14 November. www.washingtonpost.com/outlook/2018/11/14/why-we-cant-agree-gun-control

Chapter Eight

1 Huemer, M. (2019) *Dialogues on Ethical Vegetarianism*. Routledge.

2 Naydler, J. (2018) *In the Shadow of the Machine: The Prehistory of the Computer and the Evolution of Consciousness*. Temple Lodge Publishing.

3 IPCC (2018) *Special Report: Global Warming of 1.5°C*. www.ipcc.ch/sr15/

4 Curren, R. and Metzger, E. (2017) *Living Well Now and in the Future: Why Sustainability Matters*. MIT Press.

5 Monbiot, G. (2017) *How Did We Get into this Mess? Politics, Equality, Nature*. Verso.

6 Wallace-Wells, D. (2019) *The Uninhabitable Earth: A Story of the Future*. Allen Lane.

7 Wallace-Wells, D. (2019) *The Uninhabitable Earth: A Story of the Future*. Allen Lane.

8 American Psychological Association (2009) *Psychology and Global Climate Change: Addressing a Multi-faceted Phenomenon and Set of Challenges*. www.apa.org/science/about/publications/climate-change

9 Jackson, T. (2016) *Prosperity Without Growth*. Routledge.

10 Klein, N. (2015) *This Changes Everything: Capitalism vs the Climate*. Penguin.

11 Gardiner, S. (2013) *A Perfect Moral Storm: The Ethical Tragedy of Climate Change*. Oxford University Press.

12 Wallace-Wells, D. (2019) *The Uninhabitable Earth: A Story of the Future*. Allen Lane.

13 Monbiot, G. (2017) *How Did We Get into this Mess? Politics, Equality, Nature*. Verso.

14 Eisenstein, C. (2018) *Climate: A New Story*. North Atlantic Books.

15 Kolbert, E. (2015) *The Sixth Extinction: An Unnatural History*. Bloomsbury.

16 Yong, E. (2017) *I Contain Multitudes: The Microbes within Us and a Grander View of Life*. Vintage.

17 Wilson, E.O (2017) *Half-Earth: Our Planet's Fight for Life*. Liveright.

18 Eisenstein, C. (2018) *Climate: A New Story*. North Atlantic Books.

19 Eisenstein, C. (2018) *Climate: A New Story*. North Atlantic Books.

20 Eisenstein, C. (2018) *Climate: A New Story*. North Atlantic Books.

21 Benyus, J. (2002) *Biomimicry: Innovation Inspired by Nature*. HarperCollins.

22 Naydler, J. (2018) *In the Shadow of the Machine: The Prehistory of the Computer and the Evolution of Consciousness*. Temple Lodge Publishing. Lent, J. (2017) *The Patterning Instinct: A Cultural History of Humanity's Search for Meaning*. Prometheus Books.

23 Centre for the Understanding of Sustainable Prosperity (2019) *Essays on the Morality of Sustainable Prosperity*. www.cusp.ac.uk/publication_type/essays/

24 Godfrey-Smith, P. (2018) *Other Minds: The Octopus and the Evolution of Intelligent Life*. William Collins.

25 Benyus, J. (2002) *Biomimicry: Innovation Inspired by Nature*. HarperCollins.

26 Hickel, J. (2018) *The Divide: A brief Guide to Inequality and Its Solutions*. Windmill Books.

27 Deaton, A. (2015) *The Great Escape: Health, Wealth, and the Origins of Inequality*. Princeton University Press. Easterly, W. (2007) *The White Man's Burden: Why the West's Efforts to Aid the Rest Have Done so Much Ill and so Little Good*. Oxford University Press.

28 Singer, P. (2016) *The Most Good You Can Do: How Effective Altruism Is Changing Ideas about Living Ethically*. Picador.

29 MacAskill, W. (2016) *Doing Good Better: Effective Altruism and a Radical New Way to Make a Difference*. Guardian Faber.

30 Acemoglu, D. and Robinson, J. (2013) *Why Nations Fail: The Origins of Power, Prosperity and Poverty*. Profile Books.

31 Milanovic, B. (2018) *Global Inequality: A New Approach for the Age of Globalization*. Harvard University Press.

32 Rosling, H., Rosling, O. and Rosling Rönnlund, A. (2018) *Factfulness: Ten Reasons We're Wrong about the World – and Why Things Are Better than You Think*. Spectre.

33 Milanovic, B. (2018) *Global Inequality: A New Approach for the Age of Globalization*. Harvard University Press.

34 Rosling, H., Rosling, O. and Rosling Rönnlund, A. (2018) *Factfulness: Ten Reasons We're Wrong about the World – and Why Things Are Better than You Think*. Spectre.

35 Hickel, J. (2018) *The Divide: A Brief Guide to Inequality and Its Solutions*. Windmill Books.

36 Hickel, J. (2018) *The Divide: A Brief Guide to Inequality and Its Solutions*. Windmill Books.

37 Andrews, K. (2018) *Back to Black: Retelling Black Radicalism for the 21st Century*. Zed Books.

38 Davis, M. (2017) *Late Victorian Holocausts: El Niño Famines and the Making of the Third World*. Verso.

39 Maddison, A. (2006) *The World Economy*. OECD Publishing.

40 Maddison, A. (2006) *The World Economy*. OECD Publishing.

41 Hickel, J. (2018) *The Divide: A Brief Guide to Inequality and Its Solutions*. Windmill Books.

42 Maurer, N. (2013) *The Empire Trap: The Rise and Fall of the US Intervention to Protect American Property Overseas, 1893–2013*. Princeton University Press.

43 Andrews, K. (2018) *Back to Black: Retelling Black Radicalism for the 21st Century*. Zed Books.

44 Hickel, J. (2018) *The Divide: A Brief Guide to Inequality and Its Solutions*. Windmill Books.

45 Hickel, J. (2018) *The Divide: A Brief Guide to Inequality and Its Solutions*. Windmill Books.

46 Andrews, K. (2017) The west's wealth is based on slavery. Reparations should be paid. *The Guardian*, 28 August. www.theguardian.com/commentisfree/2017/aug/28/slavery-reparations-west-wealth-equality-world-race

47 Andrews, K. (2017) The west's wealth is based on slavery. Reparations should be paid. *The Guardian*, 28 August. www.theguardian.com/commentisfree/2017/aug/28/slavery-reparations-west-wealth-equality-world-race.

48 Hickel, J. (2018) *The Divide: A Brief Guide to Inequality and Its Solutions*. Windmill Books.

49 Hickel, J. (2018) *The Divide: A Brief Guide to Inequality and Its Solutions*. Windmill Books.

50 Harari, Y. (2015) *Sapiens: A Brief History of Humankind*. Vintage.

51 Pinker, S. (2012) *The Better Angels of Our Nature: A History of Violence and Humanity*. Penguin. Pinker, S. (2018) *Enlightenment Now: The Case for Reason, Science, Humanism, and Progress*. Allen Lane.

52 Welzel, C. (2014) *Freedom Rising: Human Empowerment and the Quest for Emancipation*. Cambridge University Press.

53 Bregman, R. (2018) *Utopia for Realists: And How We Can Get There*. Bloomsbury.

54 Wenar, L. (2017) *Blood Oil: Tyrants, Violence, and the Rules that Run the World*. Oxford University Press.

55 Huemer, M. (2012) *The Problem of Political Authority: An Examination of the Right to Coerce and the Duty to Obey*. Palgrave Macmillan.

56 Kolbert, E. (2015) *The Sixth Extinction: An Unnatural History*. Bloomsbury.

57 Taleb, N. (2018) *Skin in the Game: Hidden Asymmetries in Daily Life*. Allen Lane.

58 Hickel, J. (2018) *The Divide: A Brief Guide to Inequality and Its Solutions*. Windmill Books.

59 Dorling, D. (2015) *Inequality and the 1%*. Verso Books. Stiglitz, J. (2013) *The Price of Inequality*. Penguin.

60 Lamont, M. (2002) *The Dignity of Working Men: Morality and the Boundaries of Race, Class and Immigration*. Harvard University Press.

61 Quinones, S. (2016) *Dreamland: The True Tale of America's Opiate Epidemic*. Bloomsbury Press.

62 Lindberg, S. (2019) Are increasing inequalities threatening democracy in Europe? *Reshaping European Democracy Project*. https://carnegieeurope.eu/2019/02/04/are-increasing-inequalities-threatening-democracy-in-europe-pub-78270

63 Cohen, T. (2013) *Average Is Over: Powering America Beyond the Age of the Great Stagnation*. E P Dutton & Co Inc.

64 Bostrom, N. (2015) *Superintelligence: Paths, Dangers, Strategies*. Oxford University Press.

65 Zuboff, S. (2019) *The Age of Surveillance Capitalism: The Fight for a Human Future at the New Frontier of Power*. Profile Books.

66 Harari, Y. (2017) *Homo Deus: A Brief History of Tomorrow*. Vintage.

67 Wood, E. (2015) *The Origin of Capitalism: A Longer View. Verso.* Wood, E. (2015) *The Pristine Culture of Capitalism. Verso.* Shrubsole, G. (2019) *Who Owns England? How We Lost Our Green and Pleasant Land, and How to Take It Back*. William Collins.

68 Sen, A. (2001) *Development as Freedom*. Oxford University Press.

69 Aiyar, S. and Ebeke, C. (2018) Inequality of opportunity, inequality of income and economic growth. *IMF Working Paper* WP/19/34.

Notes

70 Monbiot, G. (2018) *Out of the Wreckage: A New Politics for an Age in Crisis*. Verso Books. Raworth, K. (2018) *Doughnut Economics: Seven Ways to Think Like a 21st Century Economist*. Random House.

71 Skidelsky, E. and Skidelsky, R. (2013) *How Much is Enough? Money and the Good Life*. Penguin. Milanovic, B. (2019) *Capitalism Alone: The Future of the System that Rules the World*. Harvard University Press.

72 Hickel, J. (2018) *The Divide: A Brief Guide to Inequality and Its Solutions*. Windmill Books.

Conclusion

1 David, S. (2017) *Emotional Agility: Get Unstuck, Embrace Change and Thrive in Work and Life*. Penguin.

2 Nussbaum, M. (2016) *Anger and Forgiveness: Resentment, Generosity, and Justice*. Oxford University Press.

Index